Future of War and Peace in Asia

Future of War and Peace in Asia

S.K. Singh

PRASHANT PUBLISHING HOUSE
DELHI-110094

Published by :
Prashant Publishing House
C-34, 28 Foota Road, Gali-3,
West Karwal Nagar, Delhi-110094
Phone : 011-22963970, Mob. : 9810396373
e-mail.: prashantpublishinghouse@gmail.com

Future of War and Peace in Asia

First Published 2017

ISBN 978-93-80565-8-80

PRINTED IN INDIA
Published by Mr. R.K. Jha M/s Prashant Publishing House and Published at H.S. Offset House Press, Delhi.

Contents

Preface

Asia today is a continent on the rise. India and China are the two most populous nations on the planet with over one-third of the global population. Two of the world's top three economies are in Asia, and the economies of most other Asian nations are growing. Korea, the country of my birth, has become a model for nations in the developing world. With its unprecedented growth, South Korea has transformed itself in just half a century from a poor agricultural backwater to a developed and prosperous high-tech economy with growing global influence. This trend is evidence that the centre of global power and influence is shifting from the Atlantic sphere to the sphere of the Pacific and Indian Oceans. Yet the pursuit of economic growth alone is not sufficient to secure hopes for peace and prosperity in the 21st century. Progress must be guided by a vision for the future that calls forth the nobler qualities of the human character.

In recent years the situation has been further complicated by the tendency in public rhetoric for the term "war" to be used to refer to the deployment of organised force against various national or international activities regarded as anti-social – "the war against the Mafia", for example, or "the war against drug cartels". In these conflicts the actions of two types of armed force are confused. One – let's call them "soldiers" – is directed against other armed forces with the object of defeating them. The other – let's call them "police" – sets out to maintain or re-establish the required degree of law and public order within an existing political entity, typically a state. Victory, which has no necessary moral connotation, is the object of one force; the bringing to justice of offenders against the law, which does have a moral connotation, is the object of the other. Such a distinction is easier to draw in theory than in practice, however.

For over 30 years, East Asia has been free of major wars. But East Asia's stable order is based on a unique and remarkable triangular relationship among the region's three biggest powers, and that relationship is now under pressure from China's growth. Asia's future peace will depend on the ability of the United States, China and Japan – and eventually India – to create a new regional order which reflects the emerging economic and power relativities of the Asian Century. Creating a stable new order will require major sacrifices from all three powers: America will have to concede primacy and learn to treat China and Japan as equals; China will have to forgo its own dreams of primacy and accept Japan as a legitimate major power; and Japan will have to accept the costs and complexities of strategic independence.

As for India yes Prime Minister Modi has an ambitious economic agenda but the fact is India cannot rise under threat of possible destabilization by non state actors based in Pakistan who prosper in the shadow of an unstable Afghanistan. And Pakistan cannot become a peaceful state without normal relations with India and without a stable Afghanistan that is at peace with Pakistan. Peace has thus become indivisible in South Asia and also a strategic imperative

Globalization and rise of China and India and opening up of Central Asia offer new economic opportunities to the people of the region and the outside world through possible projects like gas pipelines, transit trade and much talked about New Silk Road –the American version and the Chinese version. What will be the consequences of economic, political, and cultural globalization not only for India and Pakistan but also for smaller states of South Asia specially in their search for stability, development and democracy? All the matter is just compiled and edited in nature. Taken from the various sources which are in public domain.

This book is an insightful analysis of inter- and intra-state conflicts and tensions in the countries of Asia even as the centre of gravity of economic, political and technological power is shifting from the Trans-Atlantic zone to Asia.

—*Editor*

1

Future War in Asia

World War III (WWIII or WW3) and Third World War are names given to a hypothetical third worldwide military conflict subsequent to World War I and World War II. The term has been in use since the end of World War II. Some have applied it loosely to refer to limited or smaller conflicts such as the Cold War or the War on Terror, while others have operated under the assumption that such a conflict would surpass both prior World Wars in both the level of its widespread scope and of its overall destructive impact.

Because of the development and use of nuclear weapons near the end of World War II and their subsequent acquisition and deployment by many countries, the potential risk of a nuclear devastation of Earth's civilization and life is a common theme in speculations of a Third World War. Another major concern is that biological warfare could cause a very large number of casualties, either intentionally or inadvertently by an accidental release of a biological agent, the unexpected mutation of an agent, or its adaptation to other species after use. High-scale apocalyptic events like these, caused by advanced technology used for destruction, could potentially make Earth's surface uninhabitable, what prompts many to believe that after the war, humans would live either in underground facilities or in colonies in space (such as on the Moon or Mars or in a space vehicle).

Prior to the advent of the Second World War, the First World War (1914–1918) was believed to have been the "war to end all wars," as it was popularly believed that never again could there possibly be a global conflict of such magnitude. During the inter-war period between the two World Wars, WW I was typically referred to simply as "The Great War" and was almost never referred to as the First World War. Unfortunately, in 1939 the outbreak of World War II disproved the hope that mankind might have already "outgrown" the need for such widespread global wars.

With the advent of the Cold War in 1947 and with the spread of nuclear weapons technology to the Soviet Union, the possibility of a third global conflict became more plausible. During the Cold War years the possibility of a Third World War was anticipated and planned for by military and civil authorities in many countries. Scenarios ranged from conventional warfare to limited or total nuclear warfare. At the height of the Cold War, in a scenario referred to as MAD (Mutually Assured Destruction), it had been calculated that an all-out nuclear confrontation would most certainly destroy all or nearly all human life on the planet. The spectre of the potential of the absolute destruction of the human race may have contributed to the ability of both American and Soviet leaders to avoid such a scenario.

The Cold War ended in 1991 when the Soviet Union collapsed, leaving the United States as the sole global superpower. With the end of the Cold War, it was believed that the likelihood of a fully unrestricted nuclear confrontation between two superpowers was significantly diminished.

BACKGROUND

In the early 21st century, territorial tensions were rising between many countries, particularly in the Middle East and other parts of Asia. Also, for most parts of the world, economic collapse was imminent. Islamic conservative countries such as Iran began breaking off diplomatic ties with more Westernized counterparts such as Saudi Arabia and the United Arab Emirates. Syria was undergoing a deadly civil war between the government and democratic forces and asks help from Russia and China, but USA says that if Russia and its allies openly support Syria, the USA will take actions.

During the 2020s, China, Russia and other countries with particular anti-West ideologies found a new militar economic block called Shangai Cooperation Organisation (SCO). Its main purpose was to confront and compete with NATO. In response, NATO friendly states of Southeast Asia launch campaigns to improve its military. In North America, Mexico receives support from SCO in Mexican Drug War and this effort makes Mexico a SCO-friendly state. Meanwhile, Turkey is undergoing border clashes against Syria. All these tensions and disputes between pro-West and anti-West forces leads to a great expansion of SCO, which many anti-West nations joining the block. By the late 2020s, SCO becames extensively hostile against NATO and a global conflict becames imminent.

Althought peace efforts have been made, economic and military strength of SCO have managed to divide the world again in "first" and "second" worlds, this time in a dispute between two coallitions.

HISTORICAL CLOSE CALLS

With the development of the arms race in the 1950s, an apocalyptic war between the United States and the Soviet Union was considered possible, and a number of events have been described as potential triggers for a nuclear conflict.

25 June 1950 – 27 July 1953

The Korean War, a war between two factions trying to control the Korean Peninsula: a communist one supported by China and the USSR, and a capitalist one supported by the UN and the United States. Many people believed that it would escalate into full-scale war between the three superpowers. CBS war correspondent Bill Downs wrote in 1951 that, "To my mind, the answer is: Yes, Korea is the beginning of World War III. The brilliant landings at Inchon and the cooperative efforts of the American armed forces with the United Nations Allies have won us a victory in Korea. But this is only the first battle in a major international struggle which now is engulfing the Far East and the entire world." He repeated this belief on *ABC Evening News* while reporting on the USS *Pueblo* incident in 1968.

15–28 October 1962

The Cuban Missile Crisis: a confrontation on the stationing of Soviet nuclear missiles in Cuba, in response to the failed Bay of Pigs Invasion, is considered as having been the closest to a nuclear exchange, which could have precipitated a Third World War. The crisis peaked on 27 October, when a U-2 was shot down over Cuba and another almost intercepted over Siberia, after Curtis LeMay (US Air Force Chief of Staff) had neglected to enforce Presidential orders to suspend all overflights, and a Soviet submarine nearly launched a nuclear-tipped torpedo in response to depth charges (with the launch being prevented by an officer named Vasili Arkhipov). Despite what many believe to be the closest the world has come to a nuclear conflict, throughout the entire standoff, the Doomsday Clock, which is run by the Bulletin of Atomic Scientists to estimate how close the end of the world, or doomsday, is, with midnight being the apocalypse, stayed at a relatively stable seven minutes to midnight. This has been explained as being due to the brevity of the crisis, since the clock monitored more long term factors such as leadership of countries, conflicts, wars, and political upheavals, as well as societies reactions to said factors. The Bulletin now credits the event for stability in future crises and occasions that could have escalated, mainly due to two major factors. The first, a Washington to Moscow direct telephone line, resulted from the communication trouble between the White House and the Kremlin during the crisis, giving the leaders of the two largest nuclear powers the ability to contact each other in real time, rather than sending written messages that needed to be translated and wired, which had dragged out conversations in which seconds could have potentially prevented a nuclear exchange. The second factor was caused in part to the worldwide reaction to how near the US and USSR came to an exchange during the standoff, as the public began to more closely monitor topics involving nuclear weapons, and therefore rallied support for the cause, is the signing of the 1963 test ban treaty, which has to date been signed by 126 total nations, with the most notable exceptions being France and China, who were both still in the relative beginning stages of their nuclear programs at the time and both sought nuclear capabilities independent of their allies. This treaty prevented the testing of nuclear ordinance that detonated in the atmosphere, limiting testing to below ground and under water, decreasing fallout and effects on the environment, and subsequently caused the Doomsday Clock to decrease by five minutes, to arrive at a total of twelve minutes to midnight. Up until this point, over 1000 nuclear bombs had been detonated, and concerns over both long and short term affects to the planet became increasingly more worrisome to scientists.

6–25 October 1973

The Yom Kippur War, also known as the Ramadan War, or October War, began with Arab victories. Israel successfully counterattacked. Tensions grew between the US (which supported Israel) and the Soviet Union (which sided with the Arab states). American and Soviet naval forces came close to firing upon each other. Admiral Murphy of the US reckoned the chances of the Soviet squadron attempting a first strike against his fleet at 40 percent. The Pentagon moved Defcon status from 4 to 3. The superpowers had been pushed to the brink of war, but tensions eased with the ceasefire brought in under UNSC 339.

9 November 1979

The United States made emergency retaliation preparations after NORAD saw on-screen indications that a full-scale Soviet attack had been launched. No attempt was made to use the "red telephone" hotline to clarify the situation with the USSR and it was not until early-warning radar systems confirmed no such launch had taken place that NORAD realized that a computer system test had caused the display errors. A senator inside the NORAD facility at the time described an atmosphere of absolute panic. A GAO investigation led to the construction of an off-site test facility to prevent similar mistakes.

26 September 1983

A false alarm occurred on the Soviet nuclear early warning system, showing the launch of American Minuteman ICBMs from bases in the United States. A retaliatory attack was prevented by Stanislav Petrov, an officer of the Soviet Air Defence Forces, who realised the system had simply malfunctioned (which was borne out by later investigations).

2–11 November 1983

During Able Archer 83, a ten-day NATO exercise simulating a period of conflict escalation that culminated in a DEFCON 1 nuclear strike, some members of the Soviet Politburo and armed forces treated the events as a ruse of war concealing a genuine first strike. In response, the military prepared for a coordinated counter-attack by readying nuclear forces and placing air units stationed in the Warsaw Pact states of East Germany and Poland under high alert. However, the state of Soviet preparation for retaliation ceased upon completion of the Able Archer exercises.

25 January 1995

The Norwegian rocket incident occurred when the Russian Federation's Olenegorsk early warning station accidentally mistook the radar signature from a Black Brant XII research rocket (being jointly launched by Norwegian and US scientists from Andøya Rocket Range), as appearing to be the radar signature of the launch of a Trident SLBM missile. In response, President Boris Yeltsin was summoned and the *Cheget* nuclear briefcase was activated for the first and only time. However, the high command was soon able to determine that the rocket was not entering Russian airspace, and promptly aborted plans for combat readiness and retaliation. It was retrospectively determined that, while the rocket scientists had informed thirty states including Russia about the test launch, the information had not reached Russian radar technicians.

BACKING INTO WORLD WAR III

Think of two significant trend lines in the world today. One is the increasing ambition and activism of the two great revisionist powers, Russia and China. The other is the declining confidence, capacity, and will of the democratic world, and especially of the

United States, to maintain the dominant position it has held in the international system since 1945. As those two lines move closer, as the declining will and capacity of the United States and its allies to maintain the present world order meet the increasing desire and capacity of the revisionist powers to change it, we will reach the moment at which the existing order collapses and the world descends into a phase of brutal anarchy, as it has three times in the past two centuries. The cost of that descent, in lives and treasure, in lost freedoms and lost hope, will be staggering.

Americans tend to take the fundamental stability of the international order for granted, even while complaining about the burden the United States carries in preserving that stability. History shows that world orders do collapse, however, and when they do it is often unexpected, rapid, and violent.

The late 18th century was the high point of the Enlightenment in Europe, before the continent fell suddenly into the abyss of the Napoleonic Wars. In the first decade of the 20th century, the world's smartest minds predicted an end to great-power conflict as revolutions in communication and transportation knit economies and people closer together. The most devastating war in history came four years later. The apparent calm of the postwar 1920s became the crisis-ridden 1930s and then another world war. Where exactly we are in this classic scenario today, how close the trend lines are to that intersection point is, as always, impossible to know. Are we three years away from a global crisis, or 15? That we are somewhere on that path, however, is unmistakable.

And while it is too soon to know what effect Donald Trump's presidency will have on these trends, early signs suggest that the new administration is more likely to hasten us toward crisis than slow or reverse these trends. The further accommodation of Russia can only embolden Vladimir Putin, and the tough talk with China will likely lead Beijing to test the new administration's resolve militarily. Whether the president is ready for such a confrontation is entirely unclear. For the moment, he seems not to have thought much about the future ramifications of his rhetoric and his actions.

China and Russia are classic revisionist powers. Although both have never enjoyed greater security from foreign powers than they do today — Russia from its traditional enemies to the west, China from its traditional enemy in the east — they are dissatisfied with the current global configuration of power. Both seek to restore the hegemonic dominance they once enjoyed in their respective regions. For China, that means dominance of East Asia, with countries like Japan, South Korea, and the nations of Southeast Asia both acquiescing to Beijing's will and acting in conformity with China's strategic, economic, and political preferences. That includes American influence withdrawn to the eastern Pacific, behind the Hawaiian Islands. For Russia, it means hegemonic influence in Central and Eastern Europe and Central Asia, which Moscow has traditionally regarded as either part of its empire or part of its sphere of influence. Both Beijing and Moscow seek to redress what they regard as an unfair distribution of power, influence, and honor in the U.S.-led postwar global order. As autocracies, both feel threatened by the dominant democratic powers in the international system and by the democracies on their borders. Both regard the United States as the principal obstacle to their ambitions, and therefore both seek to weaken the American-led international security order that stands in the way of their achieving what they regard as their rightful destinies.

Until fairly recently, Russia and China have faced considerable, almost insuperable, obstacles in achieving their objectives. The chief obstacle has been the power and coherence of the international order itself and its principal promoter and defender. The American-led system of political and military alliances, especially in the two critical regions of Europe and East Asia, has presented China and Russia with what Dean Acheson once referred to as "situations of strength" that have required them to pursue their ambitions cautiously and, since the end of the Cold War, to defer serious efforts to disrupt the international system.

The system has checked their ambitions in both positive and negative ways. During the era of American primacy, China and

Russia have participated in and for the most part been beneficiaries of the open international economic system the United States created and helps sustain; so long as that system functions, they have had more to gain by playing in it than by challenging and overturning it. The political and strategic aspects of the order, however, have worked to their detriment. The growth and vibrancy of democratic government in the two decades following the collapse of Soviet communism posed a continual threat to the ability of rulers in Beijing and Moscow to maintain control, and since the end of the Cold War they have regarded every advance of democratic institutions — especially the geographical advance of liberal democracies close to their borders — as an existential threat. That's for good reason: Autocratic powers since the days of Klemens von Metternich have always feared the contagion of liberalism. The mere existence of democracies on their borders, the global free flow of information they cannot control, the dangerous connection between free market capitalism and political freedom — all pose a threat to rulers who depend on keeping restive forces in their own countries in check. The continual challenge to the legitimacy of their rule posed by the U.S.-supported democratic order has therefore naturally made them hostile both to that order and to the United States. But, until recently, a preponderance of domestic and international forces has dissuaded them from confronting the order directly. Chinese rulers have had to worry about what an unsuccessful confrontation with the United States might do to their legitimacy at home. Even Putin has pushed only against open doors, as in Syria, where the United States responded passively to his probes. He has been more cautious when confronted by even marginal U.S. and European opposition, as in Ukraine.

The greatest check on Chinese and Russian ambitions has been the military and economic power of the United States and its allies in Europe and Asia. China, although increasingly powerful, has had to contemplate facing the combined military and economic strength of the world's superpower and some very formidable regional powers linked by alliance or common strategic interest — including Japan, India, and South Korea, as well as smaller but still potent nations like Vietnam and Australia. Russia has had to face the United States and its NATO allies. When united, these U.S.-led alliances present a daunting challenge to a revisionist power that can call on few allies of its own for assistance. Even were the Chinese to score an early victory in a conflict, such as the military subjection of Taiwan or a naval battle in the South or East China Sea, they would have to contend over time with the combined industrial productive capacities of some of the world's richest and most technologically advanced nations and the likely cutoff of access to foreign markets on which their own economy depends. A weaker Russia, with its depleted population and oil- and gas-dependent economy, would face an even greater challenge.

For decades, the strong global position enjoyed by the United States and its allies has discouraged any serious challenge. So long as the United States was perceived as a dependable ally, Chinese and Russian leaders feared that aggressive moves would backfire and possibly bring their regimes down. This is what the political scientist William Wohlforth once described as the inherent stability of the unipolar order: As dissatisfied regional powers sought to challenge the status quo, their alarmed neighbors turned to the distant American superpower to contain their ambitions. And it worked. The United States stepped up, and Russia and China largely backed down — or were preempted before acting at all.

Faced with these obstacles, the best option for the two revisionist great powers has always been to hope for or, if possible, engineer a weakening of the U.S.-supported world order from within, either by separating the United States from its allies or by raising doubts about the U.S. commitment and thereby encouraging would-be allies and partners to forgo the strategic protection of the liberal world order and seek accommodation with its challengers.

The present system has therefore depended not only on American power but on coherence and unity at the heart of the democratic world. The United States has had to play its part as the principal guarantor of the order, especially in the military and strategic realm, but the order's ideological and economic core — the democracies of Europe and East Asia and the Pacific — has also had to remain relatively healthy and confident.

In recent years, both pillars have been shaken. The democratic order has weakened and fractured at its core. Difficult economic conditions, the recrudescence of nationalism and tribalism, weak and uncertain political leadership and unresponsive mainstream political parties, and a new era of communications that seems to strengthen rather than weaken tribalism have together produced a crisis of confidence not only in the democracies but in what might be called the liberal enlightenment project. That project elevated universal principles of individual rights and common humanity over ethnic, racial, religious, national, or tribal differences. It looked to a growing economic interdependence to create common interests across boundaries and to the establishment of international institutions to smooth differences and facilitate cooperation among nations. Instead, the past decade has seen the rise of tribalism and nationalism, an increasing focus on the Other in all societies, and a loss of confidence in government, in the capitalist system, and in democracy. We are witnessing the opposite of Francis Fukuyama's "end of history." History is returning with a vengeance and with it all the darker aspects of the human soul, including, for many, the perennial human yearning for a strong leader to provide firm guidance in a time of confusion and incoherence.

This crisis of the enlightenment project may have been inevitable, a recurring phenomenon produced by inherent flaws in both capitalism and democracy. In the 1930s, economic crisis and rising nationalism led many to doubt whether either democracy or capitalism was preferable to alternatives such as fascism and communism. And it is no coincidence that the crisis of confidence in liberalism accompanied a simultaneous breakdown of the strategic order. Then, the question was whether the United States as the outside power would step in and save or remake an order that Britain and France were no longer able or willing to sustain. Now, the question is whether the United States is willing to continue upholding the order that it created and which depends entirely on American power or whether Americans are prepared to take the risk — if they even understand the risk — of letting the order collapse into chaos and conflict.

That willingness has been in doubt for some time, well before the election of Trump and even before the election of Barack Obama. Increasingly in the quarter century after the end of the Cold War, Americans have been wondering why they bear such an unusual and outsized responsibility for preserving global order when their own interests are not always clearly served — and when the United States seems to be making all the sacrifices while others benefit. Few remember the reasons why the United States took on this abnormal role after the calamitous two world wars of the 20th century. The millennial generation born after the end of the Cold War can hardly be expected to understand the lasting significance of the political, economic, and security structures established after World War II. Nor are they likely to learn much about it in high school and college textbooks obsessed with noting the evils and follies of American "imperialism." Both the crises of the first half of the 20th century and its solution in 1945 have been forgotten. As a consequence, the American public's patience with the difficulties and costs inherent in playing that global role have worn thin. Whereas previous unsuccessful and costly wars, in Korea in 1950 and Vietnam in the 1960s and 1970s, and previous economic downturns, such as with the energy crisis and crippling "stagflation" of the mid- to late 1970s, did not have the effect of turning Americans against global involvement, the unsuccessful wars in Iraq and Afghanistan and the financial crisis of 2008 have.

Obama pursued an ambivalent approach to global involvement, but his core strategy was retrenchment. In his actions and his statements, he critiqued and repudiated previous American strategy and reinforced a national mood favoring a much less active role in the world and much narrower definition of American interests. The Obama administration responded to the George W. Bush administration's failures in Iraq and Afghanistan not by restoring American power and influence but by further reducing them. Although the administration promised to "rebalance"

American foreign policy to Asia and the Pacific, in practice that meant reducing global commitments and accommodating revisionist powers at the expense of allies' security.

The administration's early attempt to "reset" relations with Russia struck the first blow to America's reputation as a reliable ally. Coming just after the Russian invasion of Georgia, it appeared to reward Moscow's aggression. The reset also came at the expense of U.S. allies in Central Europe, as programs of military cooperation with Poland and the Czech Republic were jettisoned to appease the Kremlin. This attempt at accommodation, moreover, came just as Russian policy toward the West — not to mention Putin's repressive policies toward his own people — was hardening. Far from eliciting better behavior by Russia, the reset emboldened Putin to push harder. Then, in 2014, the West's inadequate response to the Russian invasion of Ukraine and seizure of Crimea, though better than the Bush administration's anemic response to the invasion of Georgia (Europe and the United States at least imposed sanctions after the invasion of Ukraine), still indicated reluctance on the part of the U.S. administration to force Russia back in its declared sphere of interest. Obama, in fact, publicly acknowledged Russia's privileged position in Ukraine even as the United States and Europe sought to protect that country's sovereignty. In Syria, the administration practically invited Russian intervention through Washington's passivity, and certainly did nothing to discourage it, thus reinforcing the growing impression of an America in retreat across the Middle East (an impression initially created by the unnecessary and unwise withdrawal of all U.S. troops from Iraq). Subsequent Russian actions that increased the refugee flow from Syria into Europe also brought no American response, despite the evident damage of those refugee flows to European democratic institutions. The signal sent by the Obama administration was that none of this was really America's problem.

In East Asia, the Obama administration undermined its otherwise commendable efforts to assert America's continuing interest and influence. The so-called "pivot" proved to be mostly rhetoric. Inadequate overall defense spending precluded the necessary increases in America's regional military presence in a meaningful way, and the administration allowed a critical economic component, the Trans-Pacific Partnership, to die in Congress, chiefly a victim of its own party's opposition. The pivot also suffered from the general perception of American retreat and retrenchment, encouraged both by presidential rhetoric and by administration policies, especially in the Middle East. The premature, unnecessary, and strategically costly withdrawal of American troops from Iraq, followed by the accommodating agreement with Iran on its nuclear program, and then by the failure to hold the line on threats to use force against Syria's president, was noticed around the world. Despite the Obama administration's insistence that American strategy should be geared toward Asia, U.S. allies have been left wondering how reliable the U.S. commitment might be when facing the challenge posed by China. The Obama administration erred in imagining that it could retrench globally while reassuring allies in Asia that the United States remained a reliable partner.

Nature abhors a vacuum

The effect on the two great revisionist powers, meanwhile, has been to encourage greater efforts at revision. In recent years, both powers have been more active in challenging the order, and one reason has been the growing perception that the United States is losing both the will and the capacity to sustain it. The psychological and political effect of the wars in Afghanistan and Iraq in the United States, which has been to weaken support for American global engagement across the board, has provided an opening.

It is a myth, prevalent among liberal democracies, that revisionist powers can be pacified by acquiescence to their demands. American retrenchment, by this logic, ought to reduce tensions and competition. Unfortunately, the opposite is more often the case. The more secure revisionist powers feel, the more ambitious they are in seeking to change the system to their advantage because the resistance to change appears to be lessening. Just look at both China and Russia: Never in the past two centuries have they enjoyed greater security from external attack than they do today. Yet both remain dissatisfied and have become increasingly aggressive in pressing what they perceive to be their growing advantage in a system where the United States no longer puts up as much resistance as it used to.

The two great powers have differed, so far, chiefly in their methods. China has until now been the more careful, cautious, and patient of the two, seeking influence primarily through its great economic clout and using its growing military power chiefly as a source of deterrence and regional intimidation. It has not resorted to the outright use of force yet, although its actions in the South China Sea are military in nature, with strategic objectives. And while Beijing has been wary of using military force until now, it would be a mistake to assume it will continue show such restraint in the future — possibly the near future. Revisionist great powers with growing military capabilities invariably make use of those capabilities when they believe the possible gains outweigh the risks and costs. If the Chinese perceive America's commitment to its allies and its position in the region to be weakening, or its capacity to make good on those commitments to be declining, then they will be more inclined to attempt to use the power they are acquiring in order to achieve their objectives. As the trend lines draw closer, this is where the first crisis is likely to take place.

Russia has been far more aggressive. It has invaded two neighboring states — Georgia in 2008 and Ukraine in 2014 — and in both cases hived off significant portions of those two nations' sovereign territory. Given the intensity with which the United States and its allies would have responded to such actions during the four decades of the Cold War, their relative lack of a response must have sent quite a signal to the Kremlin — and to others around the world. Moscow then followed by sending substantial forces into Syria. It has used its dominance of European energy markets as a weapon. It has used cyberwarfare against neighboring states. It has engaged in extensive information warfare on a global scale.

More recently, the Russian government has deployed a weapon that the Chinese either lack or have so far chosen not to deploy — the ability to interfere directly in Western electoral processes, both to influence their outcomes and more generally to discredit the democratic system.

Russia funds right-wing populist parties across Europe, including in France; uses its media outlets to support favored candidates and attack others; has disseminated "fake news" to influence voters, most recently in Italy's referendum; and has hacked private communications in order to embarrass those it wishes to defeat. This past year, Russia for the first time employed this powerful weapon against the United States, heavily interfering in the American electoral process.

Although Russia, by any measure, is the weaker of the two great powers, it has so far had more success than China in accomplishing its objective of dividing and disrupting the West. Its interference in Western democratic political systems, its information warfare, and its role in creating increased refugee flows from Syria into Europe have all contributed to the sapping of Europeans' confidence in their political systems and established political parties.

Its military intervention in Syria, contrasted with American passivity, has exacerbated existing doubts about American staying power in the region. Beijing, until recently, has succeeded mostly in driving American allies closer to the United States out of concern for growing Chinese power — but that could change quickly, especially if the United States continues on its present trajectory.

There are signs that regional powers are already recalculating: East Asian countries are contemplating regional trade agreements that need not include the United States or, in the case of the Philippines, are actively courting China, while a number of nations in Eastern and Central Europe are moving closer to Russia, both strategically and ideologically. We could soon face a situation where both great revisionist powers are acting aggressively, including by military means, posing extreme challenges to American and global security in two regions at once.

The dispensable nation

All this comes as Americans continue to signal their reluctance to uphold the world order they created after World War II. Donald Trump was not the only major political figure in this past election season to call for a much narrower definition of American interests and a lessening of the burdens of American global leadership. President Obama and Bernie Sanders both expressed a version of "America First." The candidate who spoke often of America's "indispensable" global role lost, and even Hillary Clinton felt compelled to jettison her earlier support for the Trans-Pacific Partnership. At the very least, there should be doubts about the American public's willingness to continue supporting the international alliance structure, denying the revisionist powers their desired spheres of influence and regional hegemony, and upholding democratic and free market norms in the international system.

Coming as it does at a time of growing great-power competition, this narrowing definition of American interests will likely hasten a return to the instability and clashes of previous eras. The weakness at the core of the democratic world and the shedding by the United States of global responsibilities have already encouraged a more aggressive revisionism by the dissatisfied powers. That, in turn, has further sapped the democratic world's confidence and willingness to resist. History suggests that this is a downward spiral from which it will be difficult to recover, absent a rather dramatic shift of course by the United States.

That shift may come too late. It was in the 1920s, not the 1930s, that the democratic powers made the most important and ultimately fatal decisions. Americans' disillusionment after World War I led them to reject playing a strategic role in preserving the peace in Europe and Asia, even though America was the only nation powerful enough to play that role. The withdrawal of the United States helped undermine the will of Britain and France and encouraged Germany in Europe and Japan in Asia to take increasingly aggressive actions to achieve regional dominance. Most Americans were convinced that nothing that happened in Europe or Asia could affect their security. It took World War II to convince them that was a mistake. The "return to normalcy" of the 1920 election seemed safe and innocent at the time, but the essentially selfish policies pursued by the world's strongest power in the following decade helped set the stage for the calamities of the 1930s. By the time the crises began to erupt, it was already too late to avoid paying the high price of global conflict.

In such times, it has always been tempting to believe that geopolitical competition can be solved through efforts at cooperation and accommodation. The idea, recently proposed by Niall Ferguson, that the world can be ruled jointly by the United States, Russia, and China is not a new one. Such condominiums have been proposed and attempted in every era when the dominant power or powers in the international system sought to fend off challenges from the dissatisfied revisionist powers. It has rarely worked. Revisionist great powers are not easy to satisfy short of complete capitulation. Their sphere of influence is never quite large enough to satisfy their pride or their expanding need for security. In fact, their very expansion creates insecurity, by frightening neighbors and leading them to band together against the rising power. The satiated power that Otto von Bismarck spoke of is rare. The German leaders who succeeded him were not satisfied even with being the strongest power in Europe. In their efforts to grow still stronger, they produced coalitions against them, making their fear of "encirclement" a self-fulfilling prophecy.

Give 'em an inch, they'll take a mile

This is a common trait of rising powers — their actions produce the very insecurity they claim to want to redress. They harbor grievances against the existing order (both Germany and Japan considered themselves the "have-not" nations), but their grievances cannot be satisfied so long as the existing order remains in place. Marginal concession is not enough, but the powers upholding the existing order will not make more than marginal concessions unless they are compelled to by superior strength. Japan, the aggrieved "have-not" nation of the 1930s, did not satisfy itself by taking Manchuria in 1931. Germany, the aggrieved victim of Versailles, did not satisfy itself by bringing the Germans of the Sudetenland back into the fold. They demanded much more, and they could not persuade the democratic powers to give them what they wanted without resorting to war.

Granting the revisionist powers spheres of influence is not a recipe for peace and tranquility but rather an invitation to inevitable conflict. Russia's historical sphere of influence does not end in Ukraine. It begins in Ukraine. It extends to the Baltic States, to the Balkans, and to the heart of Central Europe. And within Russia's traditional sphere of influence, other nations do not enjoy autonomy or even sovereignty. There was no independent Poland under the Russian Empire nor under the Soviet Union. For China to gain its desired sphere of influence in East Asia will mean that, when it chooses, it can close the region off to the United States — not only militarily but politically and economically, too.

China will, of course, inevitably exercise great sway in its own region, as will Russia. The United States cannot and should not prevent China from being an economic powerhouse. Nor should it wish for the collapse of Russia. The United States should even welcome competition of a certain kind. Great powers compete across multiple planes — economic, ideological, and political, as well as military. Competition in most spheres is necessary and even healthy. Within the liberal order, China can compete economically and successfully with the United States; Russia can thrive in the international economic order upheld by the democratic system, even if it is not itself democratic.

But military and strategic competition is different. The security situation undergirds everything else. It remains true today as it has since World War II that only the United States has the capacity and the unique geographical advantages to provide global security and relative stability. There is no stable balance of power in Europe or Asia without the United States. And while we can talk about "soft power" and "smart power," they have been and always will be of limited value when confronting raw military power. Despite all of the loose talk of American decline, it is in the military realm where U.S. advantages remain clearest. Even in other great powers' backyards, the United States retains the capacity, along with its powerful allies, to deter challenges to the security order. But without a U.S. willingness to maintain the balance in far-flung regions of the world, the system will buckle under the unrestrained military competition of regional powers. Part of that willingness entails defense spending commensurate with America's continuing global role.

For the United States to accept a return to spheres of influence would not calm the international waters. It would merely return the world to the condition it was in at the end of the 19th century, with competing great powers clashing over inevitably intersecting and overlapping spheres. These unsettled, disordered conditions produced the fertile ground for the two destructive world wars of the first half of the 20th century. The collapse of the British-dominated world order on the oceans, the disruption of the uneasy balance of power on the European continent as a powerful unified Germany took shape, and the rise of Japanese power in East Asia all contributed to a highly competitive international environment in which dissatisfied great powers took the opportunity to pursue their ambitions in the absence of any power or group of powers to unite in checking them. The result was an unprecedented global calamity and death on an epic scale. It has been the great accomplishment of the U.S.-led world order in the 70 years since the end of World War II that this kind of competition has been held in check and great power conflicts have been avoided. It will be more than a shame if Americans were to destroy what they created — and not because it was no longer possible to sustain but simply because they chose to stop trying.

COURSE OF THE WAR

2029

On September 1, 2029, North Korea, a SCO member, invades South Korea in an attempt to unify the two Koreas again. The United States declares war on North Korea hours later. And all of NATO declares war on North Korea 2 weeks later. China tried to stay out of the war but eventually declared war on NATO. Now its NATO vs SCO. North Korea launches a blitzkrieg against

South Korea and captures key points quickly. A few days past and war breaks out in the Middle East when Iran declares war on Israel. Saudi Arabia declares war on Iran. Turkey begins the invasion of Syria supported by Iraq. Iran invades Iraq as a gate-way to help Syria. Most arab countries won't help Israel unless Israel gives independence to Palestine and Israel agrees.

2030

War broke out in Southeast Asia when Myanmar invaded Thailand. India invades Myanmar and Myanmar's army was forced to retreat from Thailand.To prevent Myanmar being invaded from 2 directions, Laos and Cambodia invaded Thailand While China invaded India. Pakistan declared war on India while China invaded Taiwan. A huge naval battle occured in the South China Sea. Reinforcements had arrive to help South Korea ,but the Chinese troops overwhelmed South Korean troops. In the Middle East, Iran had invaded the United Arab Emirates as a gate-way to Saudi Arabia. Meanwhile in South America, Venezuela had invaded and conquered Colombia. Brazil had reacted by invading and reconquered Columbia's lost territories and Venezuela surrendered.

2031

Because of Venezuela's defeat, Chile and Argentina invaded Peru, Bolivia, Brazil in a hope to retake Venezuela but it failed and South America is now under NATO aligned control. Iran has successfully invaded southern Saudi Arabia but failed to conquer Iraq. Russia and its allies are invading the northern part of the Middle East to gain access to Iran and to invade Europe from 2 directions. In eastern Europe heavy fighting occurs between NATO vs SCO.

In southeast Asia, India had invaded eastern Myanmar so Myanmar surrendered, but then Thailand was losing fast so Indonesia, Malaysia, and Singaporean troops came in to help. Philippines is helping Taiwan defending itself from Chinese invasion. In Korea a stalemate occurred and a ceasefire is declared. In North America, a naval battle occurred between Russia and

United States but because the US navy is stretched thin and is nearly wiped out by China, Russia wins. China has invaded and conquer Hawaii and is planning to distract American troops to the west coast so Russia can invade Alaska. China is planning to invade South America as a distraction, then prepare for an invasion on California.

2032

Russia had invaded Alaska and was advancing deeper into North America. Egypt had invaded and conquer Libya and Sudan. Iran had been advancing deeper into Saudi Arabia but was soon blocked by Saudi Arabian and Israeli troops and was undergoing heavy fighting against Iraq at its borders. South Korea invaded and successfully conquer North Korea and the countries reunited at last. India is holding strong against China and Pakistan. Southeast Asia is now under NATO aligned control. China conquers Taiwan and had then began invading the Philippines but failed in conquering Indonesia and Australia. NATO forces had breakthrough the line in eastern Europe and is now invading western Russia.

2033

A stalemate occurred in the fight in western Russia. Saudi Arabia is back to its original borders and is preparing the invasion of southern Iran. The Russian advancement in North America is halted and a stalemate is declared. Australia and NATO friendly states in southeast Asia is halting Pakistani-Chinese advance in India and because of that USA has retaken Hawaii. Korean and NATO forces land full-scale invasion of Manchuria. Russian forces were advancing slowly in the Middle East. The SCO economy was running down and riots were becoming more common and harder to control.

2034

Iraq and Saudi Arabia invaded Iran and is making progresses fast. SCO troops in India are retreating because of massive reinforcements from NATO friendly states. After heavy battles and a lots of cascualties, the USA had finally retaken Alaska with the help from Canada and is now preparing an invasion of eastern Russia, NATO forces are now advancing even deeper into Russia from the west. The Philippines retake lost territories and capture Taiwan. SCO was then on the brink of defeat and Russia was retreating from the Middle East. The capital of Russia was moved from Moscow to an unknown location. NATO friendly states invaded China from southeast Asia but was met with heavy resistance but progress is being made slowly.

2035

With help India had gotten back to its original territories and Pakistan immedately surrendered. Saudi Arabia and Iraq had almost capture Iran but Iran has sworn that they will never surrender. Central Asia is invaded by NATO friendly states. USA and Canada invades eastern Russia. NATO was getting ever deeper into western Russia and had captured Moscow. Many SCO alligned countries have surrendered. SCO is in a desperate situation. Turkey invaded Russia from the south. India ,with Australia's reinforcements, invaded China from the west and is making progess fast.

2036

Central Asia had been captured and Russia was crushed in a three front war. Iran had been captured. China surrenderd after having large parts captured by India, Australia,and Japan. Russia was then alone in the war and finally surrendered on November 11.

2037 and Beyond

After the war was over, NATO nations had installed democratic governments in all of SCO aligned countries and peace and stability (mainly in the war torn, Arabic countries in the middle east) had finally been achieved. Many new countries declared independence from Russia and China and some merged with nearby ones (ie. Tibet, parts of Siberia,Taiwan,Inner Mongolia,ect.) Afterwards United Nations was reinstated and the world entered a great era of rebuild, peace, and democracy.

2

Future of Network-Centric Warfare in Asia

The USA pioneered network-centric warfare (NCW) doctrine, or network-centric operations, in the 1990s. But first we must define NCW, as it can be a nebulous thing. Indeed, it is a theory of war rather than a collection of hardware.

A US Department of Defence release in 2005, entitled 'The Implementation of Network- Centric Warfare', defined NCW as "the combination of emerging tactics, techniques and procedures that a fully or even partially networked force can employ to create a decisive war-fighting advantage." The document highlighted three characteristics:

- NCW is first of all about human behaviour as opposed to information technology. The focus is on the verb 'to network' rather than on the noun 'network', which is just an enabler;
- NCW is a concept that, at the highest level, constitutes the military's response to the information age;
- NCW is an emerging theory of war because it identifies new sources of power (information sharing, information access, speed), how those sources relate to each other, how they are brought to bear to achieve the desired outcome, and how they link to political objectives.

The term 'network-centric warfare' first appeared in the US Department of Navy publication 'Copernicus: C4ISR for the 21st

Century' in 1997. NCW is essentially 'team warfare', where all military services integrate and synchronise to achieve joint warfare. It has four major tenets:

1. A robustly networked force improves information sharing.
2. Information sharing provides a common tactical picture and enhances the quality of information and shared situational awareness.
3. Shared situational awareness enables collaboration and self-synchronisation, and enhances sustainability and speed of command.
4. These, in turn, dramatically increase overall mission effectiveness.

The USA is the world's undisputed proponent of NCW, turning its vast information-gathering apparatus into a competitive advantage through robust networking of interconnected forces across the globe. This article offers a quick précis of NCW developments in the Asia-Pacific region. NCW involves three domains: (1) Physical domain where events occur and reality is perceived by sensors and individuals; (2) Information domain where collected data is transmitted; and (3) Cognitive domain that receives information so it can be assessed and acted upon. Because NCW encompasses many intangibles that are difficult to gauge, much of the following content focuses on new hardware being employed. In theory, such acquisitions should reflect more deep-seated NCW changes occurring within militaries.

Singapore has made the most progress regionally as it transforms into a 'Third-Generation Force' thanks to high levels of investment and an advanced technological base. The Singapore Army's newest vehicles such as the Terrex carry a battlefield management system (BMS) from ST Electronics. Vehicles possess two BMS terminals, while the Command, Control and Information System (CCIS) synchronises dismounted infantrymen fitted with the Advanced Combat Man System (ACM) to higher headquarters. The CCIS interacts with other ground-based systems and aerial platforms too. Another element aboard the Terrex is a Blue Force Tracking and Red Force Marking (BFT/RFM) system. Singapore's network-enabled force is the region's most advanced user of unmanned aerial vehicles (UAV) like the Heron 1 and Hermes 450. The Republic of Singapore Air Force (RSAF) has four Gulfstream G550 airborne early warning and control (AEW&C) aircraft fitted with an Elta EL/W-2085 Phalcon radar, and data from such platforms feed into Singapore's tactical picture.

In Malaysia, Sapura has commenced Phase 1A of the nation's Network-Centric Operations (NCO) contract. The two-year programme is due for completion in early 2014 and aims to integrate existing command, control, communications, computers and intelligence (C4I) systems and to study future capabilities. Phase 1B will be more comprehensive, probably adding capabilities like a BMS and integrating the Soldier Advanced Kombat Technology Integrated (SAKTI) programme. Thales, based on existing cooperation with Sapura, seems a likely foreign partner. Thales is also involved in fitting the Open Information Communication System (OICS) onto the AV8 armoured vehicle to allow internal/external information exchange and serve as a BMS platform.

In 2010, Northrop Grumman UK won a contract to create a Joint Operations Centre (JOC) in Brunei. Its heart is the company's International-Joint Operational Command and Control System. The contract provides both a static headquarters and deployable JOC. Common core software allows interoperability with regional partners. Phase 2 is believed to be under way, and it should implement tactical components such as a BMS. The network encompasses Harris Corporation Falcon II radios, but wideband networking radios and high-capacity line-of-sight (HCLOS) radios are an obvious future purchase.

In Thailand the Directorate of Signals is in charge of NCW technical aspects. Thailand employs commercial off-the-shelf (COTS) solutions alongside military-specific C4I systems as this proves more economical. In recent times the Royal Thai Air Force (RTAF) has made significant gains owing to a package of Saab JAS 39 Gripen fighters and Saab S100B Argus AEW&C aircraft. An integral part of the Swedish deal was installation of the StriC network, whose data-links connect Gripen and AEW&C aircraft into a complete air defence system. StriC, which greatly enhances the RTAF's networkcentricity was delivered in March 2011. Saab was subsequently requested to expand Thailand's air defence C2 system with a contract running from 2011-13.

Since 2001, Taiwan has invested heavily in its Lockheed Martin-derived Po Sheng ('Broad Victory') C4ISR system. The high-level Po Sheng system can quickly plug into the Joint Tactical Information Distribution System (JTIDS) of the USA's Pacific Command (PACOM). In the worst case of Chinese espionage in 50 years, authorities conceded Taiwan's C4ISR platform may have been compromised by Major General Lo Hsien-che before his arrest in 2011. The military has been hardening its communication system that is primarily based on a fibre-optic cable backbone connecting bases. There is now a need to extend it into an agile tactical network, and to add ISR capabilities. Furthermore, work is required to integrate Taiwan's Surveillance Radar Programme (SRP), a mountain-top missile early-warning radar, with Patriot PAC-3 and Po Sheng networks. Cyber-warfare is a threat to NCW, with Taiwan's National Security Bureau (NSB) revealing that, in the first half of 2012, hackers launched more than one million attacks on the NSB.

Over the years the author has observed increasing digitisation in China's People's Liberation Army (PLA), primarily through equipment being fielded in the elite Hong Kong Garrison. New assets include the Z-9ZH helicopter, a C2 platform with forward-looking infrared (FLIR) system and cabin command console. In addition, the garrison received the Type 07 6x6 Armoured Command Vehicle accommodating the latest radio equipment that can transmit/receive real-time data.

These platforms illustrate PLA advances in its drive towards NCW. 'Informationisation' is a fundamental goal, and in one sense, because the PLA was a late starter, it can take advantage of leapfrog technologies. C4ISR is crucial to China's blue-water naval presence, anti-access/area denial and missile capability. China has procured both KJ-2000 and KJ-200 AEW&C aircraft. China still has much to learn about gaining maximum benefit from them, plus their practicality is stymied by the fact that older fighters do not have digital data-links.

South Korea is rolling out its Tactical Information Communication Network (TICN) to replace its SPIDER communications system.

The USD3.8 billion TICN deal involving Samsung Thales, Huneed and LIG Nex1 has five subsystems such as High-Capacity Trunk Radio, Tactical Multiband and Multirole Radio, and Network Management System. Other important C4ISR projects include: (1) Korea Joint Command and Control System (KJCCS) to connect the Joint Chiefs of Staff to each service; (2) Military Information Management System (MIMS) to enable tactical-level cross-service interoperability; and (3) Joint Tactical Data Link System (JTDLS) to allow dissemination of digitised tactical information between all services.

South Korea knows it needs to improve C4ISR capabilities before it takes over wartime operational control (OPCON) of military forces on the peninsula in December 2015. Four Boeing 737 "Peace Eye" AEW&C aircraft have been inducted, plus it is contemplating RQ-4 Global Hawk UAVs, despite blanching at the USD1.2 billion price last year. The government has delayed any decision by at least a year, and is investigating cheaper alternatives. Since 2006, South Korea has been developing its Korea Air and Missile Defence (KAMD) system due for completion in 2015. Key components include Aegis-equipped KDX-III destroyers, EL/M-2080 Super Green Pine early-warning radars and Patriot missiles.

Japan is greatly concerned at North Korea's missile arsenal, as well as maritime territorial disputes with China. The Japan Air Self-Defence Force (JASDF) operates four Boeing E-767 AEW&C aircraft with JTIDS and 13 E-2C Hawkeyes. Missile defence incorporates four FPS-5 and seven FPS-4 radar installations, six Aegis-equipped destroyers, plus a series of communications and imagery satellites. Money is being invested in a new X-band satellite network. Initiated in 2009, the USD935 million Japan Aerospace Defence Ground Environment (JADGE) system, centralised at Yokota, brings a wider upgrade to conventional air defence and ballistic-missile defence systems. JADGE is closely interlinked to US systems. A JSDF C4 Systems

Command was established in 2008, while a far-reaching mobile communication network is promoting information sharing. However, the 2011 tsunami revealed communication capability gaps, leading to funding for the Next-Generation Field Communication System. The government stated the system "will enable the rapid creation of high-speed and wide-area communication networks and also be useful for disaster response."

Moving to a different continent, two years ago the author witnessed Elbit Systems' Battle Group and Below Command, Control and Communications (BGC3) system being trialled by Australia's 7th Brigade. This forms part of the $300 million LAND 75/125 programme awarded in 2010, with full operational capacity scheduled for late 2013. The Israeli system has two core software components: TORC2H and Tactical Intranet Geographic Dissemination in Real-time (TIGER). BGC3 was first installed on Bushmaster vehicles and used a layer of Harris radios. Australia has performed a lot of engineering to make it work with non-Israeli applications such as Raytheon's Advanced Field Artillery Tactical Data System (AFATDS) and Northrop Grumman's Force XXI Battle Command Brigade and Below (FBCB2) system aboard Abrams tanks.

The Royal Australian Air Force (RAAF) has six Boeing E-7A "Wedgetail" aircraft, and initial operational capability was declared last November. The RAAF instituted the Project Vigilare Network- Centric Command and Control System (NC3S) under AIR 5333, with new installations at RAAF Bases Tindal and Williamtown. Boeing helped develop NC3S along with an Air Defence System communications network integrating data from 45 different land, sea, air and space interfaces. It commenced operations on 2 September 2010.

Across the Tasman Sea, New Zealand is acquiring a Defence Command and Control System (DC2S) to support high-level decision-making as well as joint operations. Delivery is expected in 2015-16. The Network Enabled Army programme will deliver most of the tactical C4I capability from 2013-33, though it needs a new communications network and strategic links via the Strategic Bearer Network Project. India has high hopes for its

Tactical Communications Systems (TCS) though, as usual, movement has bogged down. Two local companies – Bharat Electronics Limited (BEL), and an L&T, Tata Power and HCL Infosys consortium – were shortlisted. An important step is a BMS for the Indian Army, but its delivery to a combat group is unlikely before 2015. Phase 2 should offer wider fielding of BMS from 2017-21, and the third phase would see upgrades in 2022-26. Total cost will be at least INR2.3 billion. It will also align with the Futuristic Infantry Soldier As a System (F-INSAS) programme.

The Combined Information & Decision Support System (CIDSS) has been stymied by the failed appearance of TCS as its key bearer. Last May the military ordered an investigation into the substandard CIDSS programme, though BEL is still working on it. CIDSS is one element of the army's Tac C3I system, with other elements being the Battlefield Surveillance System (BSS), Artillery Combat Command and Control System (ACCCS), and Air Defence Control and Reporting System (ADC&RS). India is essentially pursuing a bottom-up approach because of a lack of tri-service cooperation.

Cisco Systems helped the Indian Air Force inaugurate its fibre optic-based Air Force Network (AFNet) in September 2010. Riding on its backbone is the Integrated Air Command and Control System (IACCS) that provides connectivity and real-time transfer of voice, data and images between aircraft, satellites, UAVs, aerostats and ground bases. It also offers a ballistic-missile defence capacity. The Israel-launched RISAT-2 satellite is crucial to India's NCW capabilities, and the first element of the seven-satellite Indian Regional Navigational Satellite System (IRNSS) was launched in July.

IMPACTS OF INFORMATION AGE TECHNOLOGIES

To understand the future one needs to develop at least a broad conceptual understanding of the nature of the impacts that these technologies are likely to have. The impacts that these technologies are projected to have can be grouped into the following six areas.

First, the speed at which information can be transmitted, managed, manipulated, and interpreted will increase significantly. Information flows within and between organizations and among organizations and international actors will also accelerate, although at differing rates depending upon a host of factors. Increased speed will matter more for some uses than for others, and some international actors will benefit more from more rapid information flows than will others. But in general, the increased speed of information flow will increase the tempo of interactions within and between international actors.

Second, the capacity to transmit information will also increase significantly. Again, increased capacity will become available at different rates to different international actors. As with increased speed, greater information and communication capacity will benefit some organizations and international actors more than others. Here, however, the point to stress is that for many international actors, the ability to transmit and interpret greater amounts of information will mean that decision makers could have a greatly enhanced picture of the world, themselves, and others upon which to base their decisions.

Third, Information Age technologies will enhance the flexibility of information flows. Those needing information will be able to reach out and get it from more sources. Those needing to communicate with someone will find it ever more easy to do so quickly and directly. Put differently, these technologies will decrease the location-dependence of information and communication transactions. This greater flexibility will be available to some more quickly than to others, will matter more for some than for others, and will be embraced more quickly by some than by others.

Fourth, these technologies will provide more and more individuals greater access to more and more people, organizations, and information than ever before. This, some observers have argued, will lead to the democratization of information and communication flows throughout the world, that is, a decreased ability of a few (e.g. governments, businesses, and the other "haves") to dominate information and communication channels.

This will free information from the hierarchy, or in the case of the military, from the chain of command. Although this may be true, improved access will not occur—or in some cases, be permitted—at the organizations, societies, and international actors.

None of these anticipated impacts means that time, distance, or location no longer matter—they still do. Indeed, as pointed out several times above, Information Age technologies will be absorbed, diffused, and operationalized by different international actors in different ways and at different speeds. This will lead to different types and rates of change in different international actors. Factors that will influence the way and rate in which advanced technologies will be absorbed, diffused, and operationalized include but are not limited to:

1. purchase and upkeep cost;
2. age and utility of in-place technology;
3. an actor's social and cultural receptivity to new technology;
4. degree of insularity within an actor;
5. level and reliability of an actor's human, technical, and economic support infrastructures;
6. level and strength of traditional values and outlooks within an actor;
7. levels of concern over sovereignty on the part of states, and over control of decision-making processes on the part of the actors; and
8. many political, social, and economic factors idiosyncratic to each actor and therefore impossible to detail.

Despite these constraints on adoption, Information Age technologies are indeed lessening the role that time, distance, and location play in human interactions. It is also noteworthy—and fraught with implications for national security—that this process is uneven and will create new "gaps" and a new power relationship among players on the world stage.

Information Age

The Information Age (also known as the Computer Age, Digital Age, or New Media Age) is a period in human history characterized by the shift from traditional industry that theIndustrial Revolution brought through industrialization, to an economy based on information computerization. The onset of the Information Age is associated with the Digital Revolution, just as the Industrial Revolution marked the onset of the Industrial Age. During the information age, the phenomenon is that the digital industry creates a knowledge-based society surrounded by a high-tech global economy that spans over its influence on how the manufacturing throughput and the service sector operate in an efficient and convenient way. In a commercialized society, the information industry is able to allow individuals to explore their personalized needs, therefore simplifying the procedure of making decisions for transactions and significantly lowering costs for both the producers and buyers. This is accepted overwhelmingly by participants throughout the entire economic activities for efficacypurposes, and new economic incentives would then be indigenously encouraged, such as theknowledge economy.

The Information Age formed by capitalizing on computer microminiaturization advances.This evolution of technology in daily life and social organization has led to the fact that the modernization of information and communication processes has become the driving force of social evolution.

Internet

The Internet was conceived as a fail-proof network that could connect computers together and be resistant to any single point of failure. It is said that the Internet cannot be totally destroyed in one event, and if large areas are disabled, the information is easily rerouted. It was created mainly by DARPA on work carried out by British scientists like Donald Davies; its initial software applications were e-mail and computer file transfer. Though the Internet itself has existed since 1969, it was with the invention of the World Wide Web in 1989 by British scientist Tim Berners-Lee and its introduction in 1991 that the Internet became an easily accessible network. The Internet is now a global platform for accelerating the flow of information and is pushing many, if not most, older forms of media into obsolescence.

Progression

Library Expansion

Library expansion was calculated in 1945 by Fremont Rider to double in capacity every 16 years, if sufficient space were made available.He advocated replacing bulky, decaying printed works with miniaturized microform analog photographs, which could be duplicated on-demand for library patrons or other institutions. He did not foresee the digital technology that would follow decades later to replace analog microform with digital imaging, storage, and transmission mediums. Automated, potentially lossless digital technologies allowed vast increases in the rapidity of information growth. Moore's law, which was formulated around 1965, calculated that the number of transistors in a dense integrated circuit doubles approximately every two years.

The proliferation of the smaller and less expensive personal computers and improvements in computing power by the early 1980s resulted in a sudden access to and ability to share and store information for increasing numbers of workers. Connectivity between computers within companies led to the ability of workers at different levels to access greater amounts of information.

Information Storage

The world's technological capacity to store information grew from 2.6 (optimally compressed) exabytes in 1986 to 15.8 in 1993, over 54.5 in 2000, and to 295 (optimally compressed) exabytes in 2007. This is the informational equivalent to less than one 730-MB CD-ROM per person in 1986 (539 MB per person), roughly 4 CD-ROM per person of 1993, 12 CD-ROM per person in the year 2000, and almost 61 CD-ROM per person in 2007.

Information Transmission

The world's technological capacity to receive information through one-way broadcast networks was 432 exabytes of (optimally compressed) information in 1986, 715 (optimally compressed) exabytes in 1993, 1.2 (optimally compressed) zettabytes in 2000, and 1.9 zettabytes in 2007 (this is the information equivalent of 174 newspapers per person per day). The world's effective capacity to exchange information through two-way telecommunication networks was 281 petabytes of (optimally compressed) information in 1986, 471 petabytes in 1993, 2.2 (optimally compressed) exabytes in 2000, and 65 (optimally compressed) exabytes in 2007 (this is the information equivalent of 6 newspapers per person per day). In the 1990s, the spread of the Internet caused a sudden leap in access to and ability to share information in businesses and homes globally. Technology was developing so quickly that a computer costing $3000 in 1997 would cost $2000 two years later and $1000 the following year.

Computation

The world's technological capacity to compute information with humanly guided general-purpose computers grew from 3.0×10^8 MIPS in 1986, to 4.4×10^9 MIPS in 1993, 2.9×10^{11} MIPS in 2000 to 6.4×10^{12} MIPS in 2007.

Relation to Economics

Eventually, Information and Communication Technology—computers, computerized machinery, fiber optics, communication satellites, Internet, and other ICT tools—became a significant part of the economy. Microcomputers were developed and many businesses and industries were greatly changed by ICT.

Nicholas Negroponte captured the essence of these changes in his 1995 book, *Being Digital.* His book discusses similarities and differences between products made of atoms and products made of bits. In essence, a copy of a product made of bits can be made cheaply and quickly, and shipped across the country or internationally quickly and at very low cost.

Impact on Jobs and Income Distribution

The Information Age has affected the workforce in several ways. It has created a situation in which workers who perform tasks which are easily automated are being forced to find work which involves tasks that are not easily automated. Workers are also being forced to compete in a global job market. Lastly, workers are being replaced by computers that can do their jobs faster and more effectively. This poses problems for workers in industrial societies, which are still to be solved. However, solutions that involve lowering the working time are usually highly resisted.

Jobs traditionally associated with the middle class (assembly line workers, data processors, foremen and supervisors) are beginning to disappear, either through outsourcing or automation. Individuals who lose their jobs must either move up, joining a group of "mind workers" (engineers, doctors, attorneys, teachers, scientists, professors, executives, journalists, consultants), or settle for low-skill, low-wage service jobs.

The "mind workers" are able to compete successfully in the world market and receive high wages. Conversely, production workers and service workers in industrialized nations are unable to compete with workers in developing countries and either lose their jobs through outsourcing or are forced to accept wage cuts. In addition, the internet makes it possible for workers in developing countries to provide in-person services and compete directly with their counterparts in other nations.

This has had several major consequences, including increased opportunity in developing countries and the globalization of the workforce.

Workers in developing countries have a competitive advantage which translates into increased opportunities and higher wages. The full impact on the workforce in developing countries is complex and has downsides.

In the past, the economic fate of workers was tied to the fate of national economies. For example, workers in the United States were once well paid in comparison to the workers in other countries. With the advent of the Information Age and improvements in communication, this is no longer the case. Because workers are forced to compete in a global job market, wages are less dependent on the success or failure of individual economies.

Automation, Productivity, and Job Loss

The Information Age has affected the workforce in that automation and computerization have resulted in higher productivity coupled with net job loss. In the United States for example, from January 1972 to August 2010, the number of people employed in manufacturing jobs fell from 17,500,000 to 11,500,000 while manufacturing value rose 270%. Although it initially appeared that job loss in the industrial sector might be partially offset by the rapid growth of jobs in the IT sector, the recession of March 2001 foreshadowed a sharp drop in the number of jobs in the IT sector.

This pattern of decrease in jobs continued until 2003. Data has shown that overall, technology creates more jobs than it destroys even in the short run.

Rise of Information-intensive Industry

Industry is becoming more information-intensive and less labor and capital-intensive. This trend has important implications for the workforce; workers are becoming increasingly productive as the value of their labor decreases. However, there are also important implications for capitalism itself; not only is the value of labor decreased, the value of capital is also diminished. In the classical model, investments in human capital and financial capital are important predictors of the performance of a new venture. However, as demonstrated by Mark Zuckerberg and Facebook, it now seems possible for a group of relatively inexperienced people with limited capital to succeed on a large scale.

Innovations

The Information Age was enabled by technology developed in the Digital Revolution, which was itself enabled by building on the developments in the Technological Revolution.

Computers

Before the advent of electronics, mechanical computers, like the Analytical Engine in 1837, were designed to provide routine mathematical calculation and simple decision-making capabilities. Military needs during World War II drove development of the first electronic computers, based on vacuum tubes, including the Z3, the Atanasoff–Berry Computer, Colossus computer, and ENIAC.

The invention of the transistor in 1947 enabled the era of mainframe computers (1950s – 1970s), typified by the IBM 360. These large room-sized computers provided data calculation and manipulation that was much faster than humanly possible, but were expensive to buy and maintain, so were initially limited to a few scientific institutions, large corporations and government agencies. As transistor technologyrapidly improved, the ratio of computing power to size increased dramatically, giving direct access to computers to ever smaller groups of people. Along with electronic arcade machines and home video game consoles in the 1980s, the development of the personal computers like theCommodore PET and Apple II (both in 1977) gave individuals access to the computer. But data sharing between individual computers was either non-existent or largely manual, at first using punched cards and magnetic tape, and later floppy disks.

Data

The first developments for storing data were initially based on photographs, starting with microphotography in 1851 and then microform in the 1920s, with the ability to store documents on film, making them much more compact. In the 1970s, electronic paper allowed digital information appear as paper documents.

Early information theory and Hamming codes were developed about 1950, but awaited technical innovations in data transmission and storage to be put to full use. While cables transmitting digital data connected computer terminals and peripherals to mainframes were common, and special message-sharing systems leading to email were first developed in the 1960s, independent computer-to-computer networking began with ARPANET in 1969. This expanded to become the Internet (coined in 1974), and then the World Wide Web in 1989.

Public digital data transmission first utilized existing phone lines using dial-up, starting in the 1950s, and this was the mainstay of the Internet until broadband in the 2000s. The introduction of wireless networking in the 1990s combined with the proliferation ofcommunications satellites in the 2000s allowed for public digital transmission without the need for cables. This technology led to digital television, GPS, and satellite radio through the 1990s and 2000s.

Computers continued to become smaller and more powerful, to the point where they could be carried. In the 1980s and 1990s, laptops first allowed computers to become portable, and PDAs allowed use while standing or walking. Pagers existing since the 1950s, were largely replaced by mobile phones beginning in the 1980s, giving mobile networking ability to a few at first. These have now become commonplace, and include digital cameras. Starting in the 1990s, tablets and then smartphones combined and extended these abilities of computing, mobility, and information sharing.

Information Age Strategic Environment

The Information Age, like the agricultural and industrial ages which preceded it, is a global phenomenon. Global communications are virtually instantaneous, computers and other Information Age technologies are found in even the most underdeveloped states, and almost every country has least one system connected to the Internet.

However, again like the preceding agricultural and industrial ages, changes being introduced by the Information Age are not equally pervasive everywhere. Change induced by Information Age technologies is taking place in different countries at different rates of speed, with different impacts, different organizational characteristics, and with different strategic implications. As pointed out earlier, different societies absorb, diffuse, and operationalize Information Age technologies at different rates because of cost and cultural considerations. These factors include the age and utility of in-place technology; a society's social and cultural receptivity to new technology; the degree of insularity of a society; the level and reliability of a society's human, technical, and economic support infrastructures; the level and strength of a society's traditional values and outlooks; the level of education within a society; the degree of technical sophistication of users and potential users of Information Age technology within a society; the level of concern over sovereignty on the part of states, and over control of decision-making processes on the part of a society's leadership elites; and many other political, social, and economic factors idiosyncratic to each society and therefore impossible to detail.

What, then, will the emerging strategic environment look like? Here, we will begin with the view of Alvin and Heidi Toffler as a point of departure. This view is criticized by some as being too simplistic and by others as overlooking important historical facts. However, it is a widely recognized view that provides a common reference point, one whose assumptions can be "tested" in a systematic way.

To the Tofflers, the world is moving toward a global socio-economic revolution that will lead to the development of a global "trisected power structure." This new strategic environment will entail a trisected global power structure that will supersede the Industrial Age's bisected structure in which states that developed industrial "smokestack" based economies enjoyed economic, social, and military superiority over more primitive agriculturally based societies.

In the Information Age, the Tofflers argue, those states that use and benefit most from Information Age technologies will be at the apex of a new three-tiered global power structure dominated by knowledge and knowledge-related "intangibles." They will be superior in capabilities to those states that remain dependent on either an industrial or agricultural economy.30 In an effort to gain the advantages afforded by Information Age technological capabilities, some states may even attempt to bypass the industrial stage of development, moving directly from an agricultural economy to an information economy. But all three types of societies, with many countries not fitting clearly into one or another of the three dominant types, will coexist even as they coexist in today's bisected power structure.

Countries at the apex of this trisected global power structure will be more dependent on the technologies of the Information Age than will those states that remain with an industrial or agricultural economy. Because of this greater dependency, they as societies will be more vulnerable than industrial or agricultural societies to any alteration, disruption, or destruction of the technologies upon which they rely (e.g., information or critical infrastructure warfare), much the same way as industrial societies are more vulnerable to the disruption or destruction of energy and fuel supplies than are agricultural societies. Despite the enhanced economic and military capabilities that flow from the technologies of the Information Age, the security equation for post-industrial states will be complicated because of this vulnerability, which we will discuss later.

At the same time, as the trisected global power structure emerges, the capabilities provided by the technologies of the Information Age are likely to further blur the boundaries between domestic and international affairs. In the emerging strategic environment, the combination of increased speed, capacity, and flexibility of information flow combined with greater access to, more types of, and heightened demand for information will make it increasingly difficult for states to control inward and outward information flows. Some states will try to control access to freely available information, as China has with access to Internet sites.31 However, few will succeed unless they are willing to impose truly draconian social or technological solutions to their perceived problem. Such solutions might include capital punishment or long-term imprisonment for accessing information sites deemed unacceptable, restricting Internet access via licenses to only a few loyal subjects, or otherwise restricting access to advanced information and communication technologies. States that apply such solutions, while perhaps maintaining control of information flows, will suffer other social and economic losses, including limiting their ability to move from agricultural or industrial level to an information based level of economic development.

Because of the capabilities that they provide, the technologies of the Information Age are also likely to increase the role that non-state actors play in the international system. Multinational corporations have long been major actors in the international scene, but they are likely to grow even more influential as businesses becomes increasingly regionalized and globalized.

Already, taking advantage of opportunities afforded by advanced information and communication technologies to increase the speed, capacity, and flexibility of information flows, many businesses have made geography and national borders less relevant as they have created an international marketplace and increased profitability by moving their labor intensive back room operations to countries where labor costs are low.

Similarly, nongovernmental organizations (NGOs) have proliferated, increasing in number from perhaps four thousand such organizations in the late 1970s to perhaps as many as thirty thousand in the late 1990s. A significant but uncertain percentage of this growth is undoubtedly due to the ability that like- minded or like-interested people now have on a global base to share information and to collaborate. Thus, the emerging strategic environment will be more complex than the one that exists today.

If this analysis is substantially correct, more fissures of change and potential conflict will divide the global community than in the past.

Inevitably, the technologies of the Information Age will continue to be absorbed, diffused, and operationalized at different speeds and with different results in different countries. Without denying that states will, for the foreseeable future, remain the dominant type of international actor, more types of actors, and more actors of each type, will gain importance on different issues. Given the potential provided by Information Age technologies for collections of individuals to articulate and perhaps act on their viewpoints, the strategic environment of the Information Age may well be far more complex than that which preceded it. This view is contrary to those who argue that the Information Age will drive us to global homogeneity.

There are at least four views about the speed with the Information Age will usher in changes to the strategic environment, and about how extensive those changes may be. A few voices urge caution about leaping to conclusions that the Information Age is truly upon us. These analysts do not deny that change is taking place nor that advanced technologies provide humankind with capabilities far beyond those previously available, but they are skeptical that, in the final analysis, much other than capabilities will change. This perspective is not widely shared, but it can not be overlooked.

One such skeptic is Frank Webster, who has observed that there are immense difficulties in measuring what is meant by an Information Age.32 He also warns that information by itself means nothing, and that humankind must take into consideration the meaning and quality of information, not just its quantity.

Even with the proliferation of information-related technologies, Webster wonders whether society has or will change profoundly enough to warrant calling the near term future an Information Age.

While Webster and others with similar perspectives fully admit that information technologies provide humankind with capabilities that were unimaginable a few short years ago, their premise is that little in human interrelationships or organizations has changed fundamentally or is likely to change fundamentally as a result of advanced information and communication technologies.

What does this imply for national security affairs? If Webster's view is accurate, this means that new and emerging technologies will continue to enhance military capabilities, but that the strategic environment will change little. Military systems, weapons platforms, and kill mechanisms may grow more capable, more lethal, more accurate, and obtain greater reach, but national security planners and strategists will be able to proceed with their planning as if little else other than capabilities have changed.

A second perspective sees strategic change taking place in an evolutionary rather than revolutionary way. Without denying that the cumulative impact of new technologies will be revolutionary, this school nonetheless sees change occurring in a paced and evolutionary manner. Advocates of this school of thought accept that future human and organizational relationships will be fundamentally different from past relationships, but that these changes will unfold over time, permitting individuals and organizations to adjust slowly or coevolve.

INDIAN ARMY DEVELOPS NCW CAPABILITY

The Indian Army has launched an ambitious programme for transforming itself into a net centric force. It has over the period evolved a doctrine for integrating various components of C4I2 (command, control, communication, computers, information and intelligence) together with an Information Warfare (IW) doctrine, given the growing nature of threat in the neighbourhood. However since these two components on their own do not create NCW transformational thinking, particularly in the absence of integrated doctrines and inter-service synergy, it is now in the process of developing a comprehensive net centric warfare doctrine, that aims to close the loop between sensors that pick up information, decision-makers and shooting platform that aim to reduce what is generally called 'sensor to shooter' time in other words speedier engagements and enhancement of tempo of operations.

The fulcrum of net-centricity being developed by the Indian Army is actually what is generally referred to as the Tac C3I System (Tactical Command, Control, Communications and Information System). Under the overall rubric of Tac C3I, sub-systems like the CIDSS (Command Information Decision Support System), ACCCS (Artillery Command, Control & Communication System), BSS (Battlefield Surveillance System), ADC&RS (Air Defence Control & Reporting System), BMS (Battlefield Management System) are in various stages of development, trials and fielding.

In an exercise carried out last year somewhere in the desert sectors the efficacy of these systems was tested providing much needed assurance to the field formations.

An effective communication provides the backend of sensor connectivity to generate synergistic effect. Within this construct army is developing a Tactical Communication System, providing both the bandwidth for data sharing and seamless connectivity.

According to Army's Signal Officer-in-Chief Lt General S P Kochhar, "The need for a state-of-the-art Tactical Communication System (TCS) has been long felt. The TCS being conceived for the force will bridge the gap between existing and contemporary technologies in the sphere of military communication". The Indian Army is following what can be termed as the bottom up approach for developing NCW capability, rather than an evolutionary model adopted by both the Americans and more recently the Chinese. There are two important reasons for this.

In the absence of integrated and synergistic oversight that could only happen if there is a Chief of Defence Staff or Permanent Chairman Chiefs of Staff Committee there is little tri-service integration with each service evolving their own path with a working perspective of their eventual integration.

A vital requirement in a networked system is not only interoperability of the system under development but also facilitation of information sharing among systems that were not originally designed to talk to each other. For inter-Services interoperability, there is requirement of a comprehensive and well documented tri-service model which forms the basis for reference at the conceptual and development stage. Finalisation and adoption of standards and protocols, mutually compatible database structures, development/deployment of interfaces between systems using disparate platforms and commonality of hardware are challenges which need to be overcome. Harmonising standards and protocols for the three Services is a gigantic task.

Despite the above systemic problems, the Army is closely looking at various software components of the system which are vital to its functional efficacy which include; policy on data handling and data storage, policy and responsibly for cyber security together with plans to set up Army Information Assurance Agency under the Director General Systems.

Areas where the Army has yet to draft credible policy perspectives include; policy on simulation and war-gaming, enunciation of bandwidth requirements in synch with increasing net-centricity. Understandably these shortcomings and at times turf battles have resulted in inordinate delay in developing the Tactical Communications System (TCS).

Another important component of the Indian Army's transformational perspective is developing capacities for "cyber warfare". It is a potent instrument of war with means to weaken enemy capabilities even before battle is joined. Security of information and assets is vital to a military where networked infrastructure involves country-wide WANs and numerous smaller networks in a network of networks concept. The endeavour to prevent an attack or contain it and affect swift recovery is important aspects of cyber warfare.

Malware penetrating the systems or embedded at manufacturing stage can be disastrous in military networks. Hence there is a requirement of fool-proof mechanisms to check our system for malware, particularly so as all computer parts and some software are imported including mostly from a country notorious for its "botnets". The US military concerned by repeated Chinese hacking and venomous attacks is raising a Cyber Command, it may be prudent for India to expedite creation of such a command which has been recommended by the Naresh Chandra committee on Defence Reforms.

Air Force's IACCCS (Integrated air Command, Control and Communications System)

Like the Army the Indian Air Force is in the advance stages of developing an integrated network in terms of a layered, hardened and in-depth air defence command, control and communications network, called IACCCS. The complete system is being established under a two-phase programme costing Rs 160 billion designed as a robust, survivable network-centric C4I3 infrastructure that will receive direct real-time feeds from existing space-based overhead reconnaissance satellites, ground-based and aerostat-mounted ballistic missile early warning radars and high-altitude-long-endurance unmanned aerial vehicles, and manned airborne early warning & control (AEW & C) platforms.

The IACCCS will also coordinate the early warning and response aspects of a layered, ground-based, two-tier ballistic missile defence (BMD) network that is now at an advanced stage of development. The fibre-optic network-based AF Net, on the other hand, replaces the IAF's troposcatter-based communications network. Developed at a cost of Rs 10.77 billion in collaboration with US-based Cisco Systems Inc, HCL Infosystems Ltd and

Bharat Sanchar Nigam Ltd (BSNL), the AF Net incorporates the latest traffic transportation technology in the form of internet protocol (IP) packets over the network using multi-protocol label switching (MPLS).

A large voice-over-internet-protocol (VoIP) layer with stringent quality of service enforcement will facilitate robust, high quality voice, video and conferencing solutions.

With these two critical elements now in place, the way ahead is now clear for plugging into the IACCCS a large number of new-generation ground-based radars that are now in the process of being delivered, be it for airspace surveillance in search of airborne targets (like manned aircraft, ballistic and cruise missiles, attack helicopters and unmanned aerial vehicles), or coastal surveillance or ground surveillance.

BMD Integration

The most challenging and contentious part of the IACCCS' implementation roadmap, however, remains the two-tier BMD component. While the ground-based, airborne and space-based systems required for giving early warning of inbound hostile ballistic/cruise missiles are already being acquired from both indigenous sources and abroad (primarily Israel), acquisition of the active 'hard-kill' component—anti-ballistic missiles and their fire-control systems—looks set to be a long drawn-out affair due to the differing perceptions of BMD among the three armed services.

The initial components of such a two-tier BMD network, comprising both endo-atmospheric and exo-atmospheric missile interceptors, are not likely to be commissioned until 2015.

For fire-control purposes the BMD system uses ELTA Systems-built EL/M-2080 'Green Pine' ground-based active phased-array L-band long-range tracking radar (LRTR), an initial two of which were supplied in late 2001 under the US$50 million 'Project Sword Fish' to the DRDO by the ELTA Systems Group subsidiary of Israel Aerospace Industries.

It is of significance that nearly three million lines of software code were written in India for the Battle Management/Command,

Control, and Communications & Intelligence (BM/C[3]I) centre, the hub of software and hardware systems. Transmission links to the interceptor missile are based on jam-proof CDMA technology and multiple data transmission links have been set up so that if one is jammed the others could function. Israeli inputs were sought and received for designing and fabricating the BM/C[3]I centre, which not only acts as the DRDO's primary BMD engagement simulator, but is also being used for evolving BM/C[3]I concepts, for defining BMD goals and developing BMD doctrine, for evaluating candidate systems architectures, for serving as the principal prototyping-cum-validation tool for the BMD's BM/C[3]I algorithms, and for defining the human role in the BMD battle. The BMD's endo-atmospheric element makes use of the THALES Raytheon-supplied S-band Master-A engagement radar.

Enhancing Space based Domain Awareness: IRNSS

The Indian Regional Navigational Satellite System (IRNSS) is an autonmous regional GPS based satellite navigation system being developed by the ISRO. The project was approved in May 2006 at a total project outlay of Rs 16 billion. The projeect was due for completion by the end of last year. The IRNSS will comprise a constellation of seven GPS navigational satellites placed in a geo-stationery orbit that will provide an absolute accuracy of around 10 metres or better throughput India and region extending upto 2000 kilometres around India. This system is likley to be operational by 2015 -16.

Geographical Information Systems (GIS)

GIS plays a crucial role in operational planning, execution and monitoring progress of operations by showing all entities of interest in the context of a map. The GIS provides spatial information platform such as digital maps, digital elevation maps and satellite images to visualise the operational scenario. This enable the disposition of enemy deployments and better planning of own forces' deployment.

Most of the GIS applications used by Indian armed forces are based on commercial off-the-shelf (COTS) software. These COTS GIS come with strict licensing policy and are prone to technology denial. Their interoperability with other GIS systems for exchange of spatial information is limited.

To overcome these challenges and pitfalls of COTS GIS, the Centre for Artificial Intelligence and Robotics (CAIR) has developed a home-grown GIS software for military applications, christened as INDIGIS."The INDIGIS is a suite of GIS components which are customisable, scalable and data centric to meet the specific GIS requirements of a collaborative defence environment. It offers a common platform for display, analysis and decision support involving spatio-temporal data for Net Centric Operation (NCO) systems," Indigenous GIS kernel has been developed as a library of software components to cover the following major function.

They are: a) processing of geo-spatial data in various formats of interest to Indian military; b) creation and management of a portable military symbol library; c) geo-spatial data exchange, analysis and visualisation with various Tactical Command Control Communication and Intelligence (TacC3I) systems; d) analysis and visualization of data from military sensors like GPS, digital compass, Battlefield Surveillance Radar, echo-sounder and unmanned aerial vehicles; e) support for all the usual features of COTS GIS including analysis and visualization of geo-spatial data in 2D and 3D.

Naval Plans for Net Centric Operations

Indian navy plans to create and sustain a three dimensional, technology enabled network centric system to transform itself into a formidable sea power. Navy is aware that the key to harnessing the full potentials of such an advanced technology driven system lies in enhanced maritime domain awareness based on availability of "satellite resources" on an uninterrupted basis. Indian navy's radical shift in its strategic outlook is clearly exemplified by the fact that it is aiming for a global reach from being a regional sea power focussed only on the threats from China and Pakistan.

To boost its strike capability, Indian navy is quite keen to link up its long range missiles, radars and air defence systems on all the sea bed assets to a centralised and a dedicated satellite network. Unlike the US Navy that is in a position to dominate a large part of oceanic waters through its "sustained and creative" reliance on a variety of advanced space based platforms including satellites meant for communications and navigation as well as reconnaissance and surveillance. The Indian navy in the immediate future is not looking at the kind of a sophisticated spacecraft system capable of penetrating oceanic thermal layers to monitor the movement of undersea objects.

The Indian navy's immediate requirement is essentially to acquire a dedicated, conventional satellite system to ensure a smoother, faster and a secure communications link for a better coordination of its assets. However, Navy is fully well aware that ocean watch satellites snooping on the naval movements, electronic ferret satellites gathering data on radio frequencies, meteorological satellites predicting weather to facilitate an effective use of the weapons systems, navigation satellites guiding lethal weapons to designated locations with unfailing accuracy, reconnaissance satellites providing vital data on the strength of the potential adversaries and communications satellites ensuring a real time link up for the effective use of the resources are all essential elements in creation off an effective maritime domain awareness system. As a long term vision, Indian navy is keen to operate an exclusive satellite supported by a constellation of spacecraft to meet the challenges lying ahead. Of course, for well over five years now, media reports have been suggesting Indian navy's plan for a dedicated satellite system. And everything going as planned, the Indian navy, the youngest of the Indian defence services, will get its first exclusive satellite system for a "secure and reliable" communications sometime during this year. The multi band communications satellite dubbed Gsat-7, will be designed, developed and launched by the Indian Space Research Organisation (ISRO).

NETWORK WARFARE: ARMED FORCES AND NCW

Network centric warfare or NCW is redefining the future battle-space. In the information age, power is increasingly derived from information sharing, information access and speed. The Indian armed forces are moving fast in this direction. The usage of information technology as a force multiplier in warfare stems from the belief that information advantage leads to information superiority eventually enhancing combat effectiveness of platforms.

This is achieved by "networking" of sensors, decision-makers, and shooting platforms, thereby creating shared awareness, speed of command, high-tempo manoeuvre, close coordination and synchronisation during operations resulting in greater lethality, and enhanced combat capabilities. The primary objective of applying modern information technology is to enhance battle-space awareness between operational and command elements.

Within the above concept "Battlefield Management Systems (BMS)" act as force-enablers. It gives combat-advantage to Armed Forces, enabling a state-of-the-art networked theatre in a spit-fire battlefield environment. The recognition of information dominance in future wars is based on the success of information dominated military command and control, in influencing outcome of the battle.

Since the 1980s, Indian defence scientists in general, and specialists at the Centre for Artificial Intelligence and Robotics (CAIR) in particular, have been playing back-room role in enabling the transformation of Indian armed forces. "Third generation war focuses on using speed and surprise to bypass the enemy's lines and collapse their forces. Essentially, this means the end of linear warfare at the tactical level, with units instead of seeking frontal contact attempt to out-manoeuvre each other to gain the greatest battlefield advantage. The impact of C2 capabilities have kept increasing with each generation of warfare and have become an essential ingredient of third generation warfare and beyond.

Integrated command and control (C2) capabilities are essential to meet the complexities of third generation warfare and spearheaded the digitisation of the battle space. Hence, the sensors and weapon interfaces, together with the communication infrastructure have migrated to digital technology. These developments have been driven by the adoption of Information and Communication Technologies (ICT) for supporting the C2 chains. The units enabling the above are collectively called Battle Management Systems (BMS) or C4I2SR (command, control, communication, computers, information, intelligence, surveillance and reconnaissance) systems.

The C2 process has been characterized as a series of sequential and interactive steps by a US Air Force strategist Col John Boyd, who termed it the Observe-Orient-Decide-Act (OODA) loop. The central tenet of modern BMS is the OODA loop (see image below). An entity that can process this cycle quickly, by observing and reacting to unfolding events more rapidly than an opponent, can thereby get inside the opponent's decision cycle and gain operational advantage. In the last two decades, armed forces have been investing in the design and development of various C2 systems.

3

Future of World War III in Asia

WORLD WAR III

Claims that World War III has already started reverberate relentlessly across the media landscape. It's become a persistent drumbeat that is steadily gaining momentum. From Pope Francis's declaration that "we must not be afraid to tell the truth, the world is at war" to Russian claims that NATO's Operation Anaconda in 2016 was a precursor to an invasion of Russia and all-out war with the West.

The symbolism of German tanks traveling across Poland toward the Russian frontier for the first time since 1941 was not lost on Vladimir Putin who declared, "you people do not feel a sense of the impending danger...that the world is being pulled in an irreversible direction." Critics of Donald Trump have already warned that given the 45th President's penchant for unpredictability, a twitter storm could inadvertently precipitate a confrontation that would quickly escalate into a military clash.

Certainly, the intent of the new administration to challenge the status quo, from trade policy with China to the value of NATO, the disarray of the European Union, the relentless spread of jihadist terror and its consequences into every aspect of life in Europe and North America, the spread of violence around the world underscored by never-ending wars in Afghanistan, Syria,

Libya and Yemen; all underscore the sense that the world is untethered, that international institutions are increasingly impotent, that the global order is coming apart as it descends into ever greater chaos and disorder.

At the height of the Cold War the possibility of a Third World War was a real and frightening possibility. Pentagon strategists gamed possible conflict scenarios and how they might evolve, think tanks opined on optimal nuclear force structures, strategic deployments and response strategies. Novelists and screen writers mined the topic for countless thrillers. Professional historians wrote "contra-factual histories" of how the war had started, played out and its ultimate consequences.

With the end of the Cold War the prospect of a Third World War seemed to recede from the playbook of potential conflicts. Armchair strategists speculated about possible U.S.-China conflicts or even a limited U.S.-Russian clash over Eastern Europe and the former Soviet states. The novelist Tom Clancy even postulated a Sino-Russian war that would see the U.S. intervene on behalf of Russia, Moscow joining NATO, and culminating in a rogue nuclear missile attack launched by Beijing against the United States. A bit farfetched given the current state of American relations with Russia. I guess that's why they call it fiction.

It was always assumed, however, that a Third World War would be fought between the United States and the Soviet Union, and that it would represent a heating up of the Cold War that would ultimately lead to a military clash over Western Europe. Conflict would breakout all over the world, hence the designation "Third World War," but it would be in Europe that the main confrontation would be played out.

The Soviet Union is no more. Although Russia still retains a significant military force and the largest nuclear arsenal in the world (7,000 Russian warheads versus 6,800 for the United States), it lacks the breadth and depth of forces to engage the United States and its NATO allies on a worldwide basis. The current impression of Russian ascendency and the restoration of a bipolar world is owed more to clever Russian diplomacy than it does to a restoration of Russian military power.

In the meantime, there is another very real war that is being fought worldwide. The United States, supported by various NATO members and assorted Arab governments, has fought two wars in the Gulf, one to expel Iraqi forces from Kuwait and one to create a regime change in Baghdad, and another war in Afghanistan. It has been engaged in a long running conflict with various jihadist groups, most notably al-Qaida and, in the last several years, Islamic State. Over the last two decades, U.S. forces intervene directly and indirectly in a broad stretch of Muslim countries from Mali to Pakistan and, in particular, in civil wars in Syria and Libya and, to a lesser extent, in Yemen as well. In addition, the U.S. finds itself increasingly confronted by Iran and its Shia proxies throughout the Middle East.

At the same time, both al-Qaida and Islamic State have spread their operations around the world, collectively creating more than 75 "franchises" in various countries in the Muslim world and setting up cells throughout Europe, North America and Australasia. In the process, they have demonstrated a capacity to radicalize "lone wolf jihadists" and spur them to stage low level, terrorist attacks throughout Europe and North America.

Since 9/11, there have been 48 separate attacks of jihadist violence in the United States that have claimed the lives of 139 Americans. There have been scores of planned terrorist attacks, some admittedly bordering on the comical, that have been thwarted by law enforcement authorities. The FBI has identified and opened active investigations on more than 1,000 would-be American jihadists, spanning all 50 states.

According to the website thereligonofpeace.com, worldwide, there have been a total of 30,000 incidents of jihadist inspired violence since the attack on September 11, 2001. In December 2016 alone, there were a total of 1,378 deaths and 1,737 injured from 188 incidents of jihadist terror in 27 countries. Another study by the BBC and the International Center for the Study of Radicalization and Political Violence at the University of London suggested the numbers were even higher. To put these statistics in perspective, in a typical year there are 9,000-gun related homicides in the United States.

Just in 2016, Europe experienced three major terrorist attacks and scores of additional jihadist incidents. Between the Brussels suicide bombings, the Nice truck attack and the Berlin Christmas market attack, there were a total of 134 people killed and 830 injured. Since 2015, there have been a total 35 terrorist attacks and an additional 25 planned attacks that were thwarted across Europe. What is more troublesome, is that Interpol estimates that around 10,000 EU passport holders have trained and fought with jihadist organizations throughout the Middle East. Many of these have already returned.

One of the ironies of Europe's war against jihadist terror occurred after theParis attacks of 13-14 November 2015. Following the attacks, which killed 130 people and injured another 368, French police, supported by national police forces in Belgium, Holland and Germany, launched a massive manhunt to identify the ringleaders of the Paris attacks. The mastermind, Abdelhamid Abaaoud, was finally cornered in an apartment in the Paris suburb of St. Denis. He was subsequently killed following a shootout with French police.

Western reporters correctly identified St. Denis as a predominantly Muslim neighborhood and dutifully quoted French police admonitions that the neighborhood was prone to crime and unsafe at night. They missed, however, a most sublime irony. The neighborhood of St. Denis is home to the Basilica of St. Denis, an imposing medieval abbey church that dates to the 12th century, which was the final resting place for all but three of France's kings and queens.

Buried there also, in a modest grave, is Charles Martel. Charles the Hammer was never crowned a king of France but his exploits, at the Battle of Tours in 732, in defeating the Moorish armies that crossed the Pyrenees intent on expanding the Muslim empire into Western Europe, laid the foundation of the Carolingian dynasty and its reassertion of European power under his grandson Charlemagne. It is a supreme irony that one of the men considered most responsible for defending the remnants of Christian Europe from the Muslim onslaught of the 8th century would today find his grave located in a Muslim neighborhood.

Who said that history's muse doesn't have a sense of humor? The historical analogies can, however, be overplayed. It is tempting to see the current conflict between Islamic jihadists and the Western world as little more than the next round in a clash of civilizations that have been at war with each other for the better part of a millennium. It is a struggle that has waxed and waned across Europe and the Mediterranean world since the 8th century, a struggle that has twice seen Muslim armies on the verge of overrunning Europe and that has seen Europe respond in-kind.

From the 18th century on, especially after the battle of Navarino in 1827, the Muslim world and the Ottoman Empire, which was its leading edge, had been on the defensive gradually seceding territory to Europe's powers until World War I finally broke the Ottoman Empire and the Sykes-Picot treaty divided its remaining lands among the European victors.

Jihadist iconography with its references to avenging the Christian crusades as well as past Muslim defeats, from the sieges of Vienna and Malta to the Battle of Lepanto; its repudiation of the Sykes-Picot boundaries; its incorporation of the mythology of epic Islamic victories at Qadisiyyah or Yarmouk; and its declarations that jihadists will reconquer the lost lands of the historic Muslim empires of the 9th to the 12th centuries, further reinforce this impression–so does the jihadist practice of singling out Christians, especially clergy, among its prisoners for immediate execution.

Nonetheless it would be incorrect to see the current jihadist violence as simply a continuation of the Christian-Muslim struggle of the past Millennium. For one thing, Europe today is largely a secular society. The targets of jihadist violence have, to a large degree, been secular symbols of Western society–a free press, tourism sites, music halls, etc. There have not been many attacks against symbols of Christian culture in Europe, such as churches, even though such locations are undefended and would represent very soft targets of attack. At least not yet, although it's hard to believe that there isn't some jihadist group intent on attacking St. Peter's Basilica at the Vatican. In the Middle East, however, Christian churches and landmarks have often been singled out for attacks. There are probably around 50,000 to 100,000 active jihadists in the world today, of which around 10,000 to 20,000 represent a core leadership group. There could be as many as 100,000 to possibly 200,000 additional militants that have had some training or some battlefield experience, that are committed jihadists, but are not necessarily active. This latter group is a sort of a strategic reserve that can be called upon, on a regional basis, when needed, and that are available to whichever jihadist group will pay to hire them. Truthfully, intelligence agencies are not certain how many jihadists there are in the world, how many are simply active sympathizers or wannabes, and how many actually pose a lethal threat.

Intelligence agencies estimate that there are probably 10,000 to 20,000 jihadists and committed supporters in Europe, of which around 5,000 to 10,000 are in France and Belgium. There is probably half that number in the United Kingdom. In the United States that number is believed to be between 1,000 and 2,000 militants.

In addition, there is a significant pool of sympathizers who identify with the jihadist movement, will support it financially, and are generally in agreement with their aims, even though they themselves will not actively participate in jihadist violence and may even condemn the more brutal examples of jihadist terror. This is perhaps the hardest group to identify. Several recent surveys suggest that this last group may amount to between five percent, to as much as twenty percent, of the world's Muslim population.

It's hard to be entirely sure because it's impossible to know to what extent respondents game pollsters by giving politically correct answers depending on who they perceive the questioner to be. Assuming that the five percent to twenty percent figure is reliable, then these sympathizers represent a pool of supporters of between 75 million to 300 million people. It's possible that the number of sympathizers is greater, but it's unlikely that the number is smaller.

So where does that leave us? The conflict with jihadist organizations is certainly a worldwide struggle. Jihadist inspired violence has occurred on every continent in the world. The only exception being Antarctica. A significant portion of the worldwide response to jihadist violence has been in the form of military operations carried out by national military forces. A struggle against a quasi-military force numbering between 100,000 and 300,000 combatants that are in turn supported by between 75 million and 300 million non-combatants certainly feels like a war.

On the other hand, conventional military operations against the Islamic State and other jihadist organizations notwithstanding, the vast majority of jihadist incidents in the West are handled by national police forces, even if sometimes these involve paramilitary police or elite police units, and the vast majority of jihadist violence has been against civilian noncombatants. In that regard, jihadist violence seems less like a military conflict than it does a criminal conspiracy, albeit a worldwide one with an overtly political agenda.

Moreover, while we can reject the characterization of jihadist violence as a Christian-Muslim struggle, much less a continuation of the historic Christian-Muslim enmity that lasted from the 8th century through the 19th century, the fact remains that these jihadists are explicitly targeting and see their opponent as Western culture and civilization in both its Christian and secular forms. What they are advocating is a replacement of Western culture by an explicitly Islamic alternative and in this endeavor, that they have the sympathy and varying degrees of support of literally millions of the world's Muslims.

The struggle with jihadism is in fact a world war; one with multiple front lines scattered across the world's major cities. That conclusion is inescapable. It is not the Third World War, because it has little in common with the first two, and while conventional military forces will play a role, this conflict will involve national police forces to an unprecedented extent. It is therefore possible to say that this is the first "World War" fought by asymmetric forces simultaneously across the globe that involves both civil and military forces.

There have been other conflicts fought by asymmetric forces. Indeed there is nothing new about such wars. The conflict between the Irish Republican Army (IRA) and Great Britain or that between the United States and the Vietcong are examples of such clashes. What is different about the jihadist conflict is that it is being fought on a worldwide basis. IRA violence was almost entirely carried out in Northern Ireland and England. The conflict with the Vietcong was fought in Vietnam and to a lesser extent Cambodia and Laos. The Vietcong never attempted to stage attacks against civilians in San Francisco or against U.S. military installations in Europe. In the struggle with jihadism there are no targets off the table, no theater of operation that is off limits or beyond reach.

Finally, the fact also remains that the jihadists identify themselves as Muslims, utilize Islamic iconography and its symbolism, and wrap themselves in its traditions and sacred scriptures to justify their actions. Moreover, in doing so they have the support of a sizable number, even if they remain a minority overall, of other Muslims around the globe. We can characterize their beliefs as a corruption of the Islamic faith and point out that an overwhelming majority of the world's Muslims do not agree with them and that they simply wish to live in peace with their non-Muslim neighbors. Nonetheless, it doesn't change the fact that a Muslim identity, albeit a corrupted one, is at the core of the jihadist movement.

This is what world war looks like in the 21st century. It is not a conventional global war like World War I and II, although it certainly involves the deployment of military forces around the globe. It has both the elements of a conventional battlefield and an insurgency, but an insurgency fought simultaneously across the globe in multiple independent theaters where the target of opportunity might just as easily be a local shopping mall as it is a military target half a world away. Jihadist violence might be the result of a centrally organized operation or unscripted, random acts of violence by local, self-radicalized militants. The enemy can be a combatant on the other side of the world or your seatmate on the local subway, they can be everywhere and they can be equally impossible to find. We have never fought a war like the one we are fighting now. We lack a comprehensive doctrine of how such a war should we fought or a coherent strategy to defeat our opponents.

We have relied predominantly on military operations, even though it is clear that in a war of ideas military force will never be a complete solution. Our government leaders are unwilling to admit this is going to be a multigenerational war that will require significant spending and sacrifice. We expect our military personnel to carry out never ending deployments while politicians treat the notion of mandatory military service as the third rail of American politics.

Instead those same politicians look for any pretext to hang out the "mission accomplished" sign. They can put it away because it is unlikely that they will have a legitimate reason to use it in our lifetime. Even as we roll back the Islamic State, new and old jihadist organizations are standing by ready to assume the mantle of jihadist leadership. The defeat of Islamic State and its militants won't end jihadist violence in the world, it will simply morph into new organizations and actors articulating the same storyline.

This is a war for nothing less than the heart and soul of secular Western civilization, a war in which the old rules of combat and strategic protocols no longer apply. We cannot win this war with the tactics and strategy of the last World War, we cannot win it with our current half-hearted attempts, we cannot win it with tactics devised and judged on a template of political correctness, and we cannot win this war if we are unwilling to admit we are already fighting it.

WORLD WAR III COULD START IN 2017

The Trump administration enters office in an unsettled time. For a variety of reasons (some directly connected to Trump's rhetoric), the great powers face more uncertainty than at any time in recent memory. In the first few months of Trump's presidency (indeed, perhaps even before his presidency begins) the United States will have to navigate several extremely dangerous flashpoints that could ignite, then escalate, conflict between the US, Russia, and China.

Korean Peninsula

Reportedly, President Obama suggested to President Trump that North Korea policy would represent the first big test of his administration. North Korea continues to build more and more effective ballistic missiles, as well (most analysts suspect) to expand its nuclear arsenal. While the economy and political system remain moribund, the state itself has shown no inclination to collapse.

Moreover, South Korea has mired itself in a serious political crisis of its own. Conflict could erupt in any of several ways; if the United States decides to curtain North Korea's ballistic missile programs with a preventative attack, if North Korea misreads US signals and decides to preempt, or if a governance collapse leads to chaos. As was the case in 1950, war on the peninsula could easily draw in China, Russia, or Japan.

Syria

Recent Russia victories in Syria appear to have paved the way for the Assad regime to shift the civil war to a new phase. The United States declined to intervene in defense of Aleppo, instead concentrating its forces on Iraq and the fight against ISIS. The Obama administration will not contest Russia's support of Assad, and there is little to indicate that the Trump administration will seek confrontation.

But while the most dangerous moments may have passed, US and Russian forces continue to operate in close proximity of one another. The US airstrike near Deir al-Zour, which killed sixty-two Syrian troops, derailed the prospect for US-Russian cooperation in Syria. A similar event, launched either by Russian or American forces, could produce retaliatory pressures in either country. Moreover, the presence of spoilers (terrorist groups and militias on either side, as well as a variety of interested states) serves to increase complexity, and the chances for a miscalculation or misunderstanding.

WORLD WAR III: WHY RUSSIA WILL BURY THE WEST

In June 2014, the Pentagon conducted a "table top" exercise – a sort of war game between Russia and NATO. The scenario was Russian pressure on NATO member Estonia and Latvia. Would NATO be able to defend those countries?

"The results were dispiriting," Julia Ioffe writes in Foreign Policy. Even if all US and NATO troops stationed in Europe were dispatched to the Baltics – including the 82nd Airborne, which is supposed to be ready to go on 24 hours' notice – the US would lose. "We just don't have those forces in Europe," explains a senior US general. "Then there's the fact that the Russians have the world's best surface-to-air missiles and are not afraid to use heavy artillery."

The Russian 'victory' was not a one-off. The Americans conducted the exercise as many as 16 times, under various scenarios, all favourable to NATO, always with the same conclusion. The Russians were simply invincible.

In this backdrop, Turkey's rash act of shooting down a Russian Air Force jet portends grave tidings for NATO. Because Turkey is a NATO member, if the Russian Air Force pounds the living daylight out of the Turks, at least in theory all the other members of the US-led military bloc are treaty-bound to come to its defence.

Although the chances that the Americans will risk New York for Istanbul are smaller than small – which leaves a very nervous Turkey on its own – one can never rule out the possibility of a NATO hothead wanting to attack Russia.

A nuclear exchange will undoubtedly have catastrophic consequences for both sides – and perhaps the entire planet – but there are certain factors that could skew the fighting field in Russia's favour.

Megaton capability

According to data exchanged on October 1, 2014 by Moscow and Washington, Russia has 1,643 deployed strategic warheads, compared with 1,642 for the US. Marginal difference in numbers but Russian land-based strategic forces have an explosive yield that is an order of magnitude greater than anything in the US armoury.

Moscow's primary deterrent weapon is the mighty SS-18, a single one of which can destroy an area the size of New York – the state, not just the city. To get an idea of the destructive power of the SS-18, just look at the nuclear weapon the US used to destroy the Japanese cities of Hiroshima and Nagasaki in 1945. The Hiroshima bomb was a primitive 15 kiloton warhead and yet it wiped out a city of 70,000 in a few seconds. The SS-18 – code named Satan by NATO – carries 10 warheads, each having a yield of 750 to 1000 kiloton). Some of these missiles carry a single 20,000 kiloton warhead – that's 1333 times Hiroshima.

At the same time, 80 per cent of the American population resides on the eastern and western seaboards, so a few well-aimed nuclear missiles can end all human life in these densely populated coastal strips. Russia has a population only half of the US but it's dispersed widely across the country's massive landmass so that pockets of human inhabitation can survive both a first as well as a second strike.

Russia has another trump card up its sleeve – its supersonic bomber fleet of Tupolev Tu-160s. These Mach 2 plus aircraft can take off from well-defended airbases located deep in the heart of Russia, fly over the North Pole, launch nuclear-tipped cruise missiles from safe standoff distances over the Atlantic, and return home to watch the destruction on CNN.

That's assuming CNN will be around. For, the Russian strategic bomber fleet can singlehandedly wipe out every major city in the US.

It is because the Americans know the capability of Russia's nuclear forces that they have tried hard to eliminate the doomsday weapons like the SS-18 through arms limitation talks.

Tactical warheads

Before the use of strategic weapons, Russia could cripple forward NATO bases with tactical – or battlefield – nukes.

Russian military doctrine emphasises the use of small-yield nuclear weapons as a war fighting tool early on in a conflict in order to stun and confuse NATO forces, impacting their ability to think and act coherently.

After tactical nuclear artillery decimates forward deployed NATO military troops, Russia could deliver small-yield warheads via intermediate range missiles that could devastate the next line of military bases, while limiting civilian casualties. At this point the US would be faced with the option of retaliating with strategic weapons and face a devastating response from Moscow. A good guess is the option won't be used.

For, no American president would risk a single US city for a dozen European ones. John F. Kennedy didn't risk it in 1962 for the same reason – the loss of even one city was too many.

State of US strategic forces

How reliable is the US Strategic Nuclear Command? If you are an American, you won't feel so reassured after reading that Presidents Jimmy Carter and Bill Clinton both "reportedly lost the launch code cards that presidents are expected to have on them at all times – Clinton for months, according to a former chairman of the joint chiefs of staff. Carter allegedly sent his out with a suit to the cleaners".

In any conflict – more so in a high stakes nuclear standoff – morale, training and discipline are key factors. Russian officers who have the job of deciding when and where to aim their nuclear missiles include PhD holders who are required to think on their feet. On the other hand, American personnel who have the same role are beset with alcoholism, depression and cheating.

Nothing can sugar coat the crisis plaguing the US strategic forces. In October 2013, Major General Michael Carey, responsible for the command of 450 nuclear missiles, was fired after drunken behaviour on a visit to Russia. Days earlier, another military officer, Vice Admiral Tim Giardina, with high-level responsibility for the country's nuclear arsenal, was relieved of his duties after he was caught using counterfeit gambling chips at an Iowa casino.

Think that's frightening? Check this out. A US Air Force general who supported the command mission to provide nuclear forces for the US Strategic Command was an alcoholic. General David C. Uhrich kept a vodka bottle in his desk and repeatedly drank on duty, so much so that another officer told investigators that "if he did not have his alcohol, the wheels would come off".

The rot has trickled down to US missileers who have a culture of cheating on competency tests, endangering the readiness off American ICBMs. Again, in February 2014, the US Navy revealed it was looking into allegations that enlisted sailors cheated on tests involving the nuclear reactors that power its submarines and aircraft carriers.

The US strategic forces are also suffering from systemic neglect, with its ICBM bases in North Dakota and Montana reporting "leaking roofs". The missileers, who work in blast-proof bunkers located 60 feet underground, are forced to defecate in buckets and urinate in jugs, and bring it all back up at the end of 24 hours. How ready these personnel will be when they have to react to a Russian missile strike is questionable.

On the other hand, Russian Strategic Forces are treated as the very elites in the military. The quality of Russian personnel can be deduced from the actions of Russian strategic forces officer Lt Colonel Stanislav Petrov. On September 26, 1983, a Russian early-warning satellite indicated five US nuclear missile launches. Tensions were high between Washington and Moscow after the downing of a South Korean airliner weeks earlier, and Petrov had only minutes to respond. With little additional information to go on, he deemed the readings a false alarm, reasoning that "when people start a war, they don't start it with only five missiles".

This is precisely why highly qualified personnel matter. When you're placed squarely in the cross hairs of the enemy's nuclear missiles and you're holed up in a bunker 60 feet below the earth's surface, then nervousness, insomnia and depression are part of your daily life. Unable to cope, less educated personnel will abuse alcohol and drugs and even exhibit criminal behaviour. On the other hand, educated and motivated officers will keep their cool even in the event of a thermonuclear showdown.

For, a nuclear war may not necessarily involve a quick exchange of ballistic missiles. According to War Scare: Russia and America on the Nuclear Brink, by Peter Vincent Pry, Director of the US Nuclear Strategy Forum, the Russian Strategic Forces are trained to "launch pre-emptive or retaliatory nuclear strikes, survive a hammer blow from a massive enemy nuclear attack, launch follow-on nuclear strikes, and supervise military operations in a protracted nuclear war, expected to last weeks or months". In such a drawn out, harrowing scenario, Russia's nuclear warfare specialists clearly have the edge.

WEAPONS OF WORLD WAR III: HOW NEW TECHNOLOGY WILL AFFECT THE NEXT GREAT CONFLICT

During a panel this week at South by Southwest Interactive 2015, authors Peter Singer and August Cole discussed their collaboration on Ghost Fleet, a novel about the next great superpower conflict. Part of the reason they wrote the book is to be able to paint a picture, in fiction, of how big future wars might be fought — and it can be pretty scary to think about.

First, a bit of background: Peter Singer is a former Brookings Institution Fellow now with think tank NewAmerica.org, and consults to both government security agencies and the private sector. August Cole is a senior fellow at the Atlantic Council, and has covered defense issues and the defense industry for both *The Wall Street Journal* and Marketwatch.com. Dave Anthony, the director and producer of the Call of Duty video game franchise, moderated the panel.

As the authors mentioned — and it was a bit of a theme elsewhere at SXSW — there is a long history of works of science fiction predicting the future. Jules Verne's classic *20,000 Leagues under the Sea* sparked the public imagination in submarines. Arthur C. Clarke proposed geostationary satellite communication in 1945, and Isaac Asimov's *I, Robot* series of short stories in the 1940s prefaced the fear of modern smart robots running amok.

The authors drew some historical reference with how each great conflict radically improved previous technology and introduced new ones. In World War I, the tank was invented, and while fearsome when it first rumbled past the trenches, it wasn't mobile enough, and also came too late to be a factor in the ground war. Airplanes also first saw large-scale use in combat in this war, but again air power did not prove to be a decisive factor in the outcome.

By World War II, both the tank and airplane were radically improved, and both proved huge factors in the war, in large part because equally spectacular advances in mass production enabled them to be deployed at incredible scale. In the initial stages of the war in Europe, the German army — while not necessarily having a vast superiority in the technology — gained shockingly rapid victories in Poland and France by innovating in the tactics using tank technology and air power. Airplanes saw huge development in speed and range.

Aside from fighters, the development of the long-range bomber brought the ability to bring war rapidly — for the first time — to civilian populations and the manufacturing centers for making the weapons and supplies of war. The new technologies that World War II ushered in — jet propulsion for airplanes, self propelled missiles, and the nuclear bomb — help shape the balance of power in today's world.

So what could the next great war look like? The authors say that two new domains will figure prominently: space and cyberspace. While war will still be fought on land, sea, and air, war in (and from) space and in cyberspace could, like the long range bomber and the missile in World War II, prove another way to bring the effects of war to any population on any continent on the planet. While the technical abilities of the NSA and other U.S. agencies in cyber tactics is extremely strong, Singer pointed out that the United States may be vulnerable due to the sheer size of cyber attacks we could face. Think of an army of thousands of hackers from another country conducting zero-day attacks on a variety of government and private systems. The recent Sony hack caused huge economic loss and problems for Sony. If that were multiplied many times in a war scenario, economic activity could grind to a halt.

Each new weapons technology in wars past brought moral, ethical and political considerations in their use. Singer and Cole noted that in World War I, the Germans' sinking of the passenger liner Lusitania brought worldwide outrage about the use of submarines in war. In World War II, shortly after Pearl Harbor, the US adopted the German tactic and declared unlimited submarine warfare on Japan. The same essentially happened with bombing non-strategic parts of civilian cities. Today's new weapon is the drone, which has been used with great success in targeted situations by the U.S. The next step in its evolution is the autonomous drone. The next generations of drones will use artificial intelligence (AI) to identify unfriendly targets among friendly ones, and learn and adapt from what it runs into — much the same way Google's autonomous car does. The thought of turning loose machines that can "think" — and control — themselves in war will give political leaders and many others pause. But it is very likely to happen as we continue to try to limit the risk of human casualties.

In the same vein as drones, autonomous robots are also on the horizon. And since we already have very smart drones, the Air Force is experimenting with unmanned fighters and bombers. The refinement of the technology with today's drones will enable those much more complex machines to be controlled remotely as well. Like how the driverless car can cause a major rethink of what a car does and how it's designed, a pilot-less fighter could cause the same for airplane design.

Part of the technical challenge will be the risk of a major failing of part of the backbone that our fighting forces rely on, like the GPS infrastructure. Today we all rely on GPS satellite information in daily life and perhaps forget that it was initially build for military purposes. If it was infiltrated in cyberwar, and an army of drones, missiles, and other weapons were given the wrong information, chaos could ensue. The initial fallings of Apple Maps would pale by comparison. Other infrastructure, like the Internet, is also vulnerable. As most of the world now runs on open source software, the knowledge to modify a system for nefarious purposes is fairly well known. As the recent Shellshock scare points out, many of the devices and systems that we rely on every day need to be adequately protected, because if taken over they have the ability to severely affect the use of the Internet. In today's hyper connected world, the general public with multiple connected devices might learn something is happening faster than government officials. A great example is the well known story of the Pakistani IT consultant who live-tweeted the secret raid on Osama Bin Laden's compound in 2011. The Islamic extremist organization ISIS has social media feeds in 23 different languages. The ability to shut down or damage the communication capabilities of enemies will be as important as always, but much harder with the easy availability of today's technologies. Distributed networks can use easily available strong encryption, and even new peer-to-peer networking technologies, to make it harder to shut down centralized control.

From a political standpoint in democratic countries, the power of social networks, as witnessed by some of its effect in the so-called Arab Spring, could have far reaching implications in the next conflict. From disseminating certain news about the war that the government and traditional media may not want to deal with, to giving voice to dissenting opinions at great scale, Facebook, Twitter, Instagram, and other networks could drive political opinion in ways not seen before.

Bio hacking is another new set of technologies that could also play a role. Loosely defined, it refers to an augmentation of our basic biology to give us supernatural powers and skills. Today our smartphones can give us some of these powers (or perhaps we like to believe that), from being our off board memory by enabling us to look up practically any piece of information, to guiding us in an unfamiliar place. Embed that power in a chip, as Moore's law shows no sign of abating, and implant that computing power in a human, and the enhanced capabilities could make the next generation's ultimate computing platform. Enhanced vision through embedded retinal implants and processors, software that controls nanobots with drugs released into the body at the right time to combat fatigue or fear, and software controlled exoskeletons, are all technology that can make a class of super-warriors like Robocop and Terminator closer than we think.

Today's art, in movies and video games, often shows us some of these new weapons and technology years before the reality. Call of Duty: Advanced Warfare featured a weapon called the Railgun, which is a revolutionary electric-powered weapon that can shoot a projectile at 5,000 miles an hour, without that projectile needing any explosive. It is slated for testing by the US Navy in the next year or two, and could revolutionize firepower in its deadliness, range, and cost to manufacture.

Lastly, a couple of other interesting concepts were brought up. One is that we are very dependent on technology that we don't understand very well. Perhaps it is a facet of living in today's modern high tech world, but there was a time when people knew more about their cars, radios, and appliances, and could at least attempt to fix basic problems with them. Our cars, computers, and devices are so complex now that it usually takes specialists to fix them. In a future war, the lack of skill at understanding how the technology we rely on works could be a weakness. Much of that complexity comes from the information technology that is now embedded in them.

That the US ranks 27th in the world among developed countries in STEM (science, technology, engineering, math) graduates should be a worrisome fact. In a future war, there will be many roles to be played behind the front lines that involve very advanced skills in software, mechanical engineering, electrical engineering, bioengineering, and advanced manufacturing methods, to mention just a few. Our collective skill set may be just as important to our security as it is to economic competitiveness.

WORLD WAR III WILL BE FOUGHT ON THE INTERNET

After Republicans pressured President Obama to label the Sony hack as "terrorism" and news broke that North Korea's internet had been "disrupted," it started to look a lot like we were trading shots across a digital bow. The Sony hack certainly isn't terrorism — or cyberwarfare, as some have daringly painted it — but it could be a look into a future where we fight each other with ones and zeros, not sticks and stones. The next world war may well be fought on the internet — and the major players are likely to include the United States, Russia, China, Iran, and North Korea, in some configuration or another.

Within the last 100 years, the face of warfare has evolved dramatically, and rapidly. In the First World War, soldiers were dragging themselves through muddy trenches and dodging mortars. In the Second World War, V-2 rockets and atom bombs made the news — and in Russia, Italian soldiers faced off against Russian troops for the last significant cavalry charge in history. The Gulf Wars brought us long-range missiles and, ultimately, drones. Today, we're facing an entirely different kind of battlefield and a different brand of weaponry.

Over the course of history, war has become more and more abstract, not just in terms of its aim, but the weapons used. Close-quarters fighting has grown unusual, as have battles fought over obvious and tangible resources like land. Today, wars are about politics, and the tools we use to fight them distance warriors from each other — a soldier in Arizona can command a drone strike in Pakistan, while a hacker in Russia can execute code thousands of miles from a target.

We have lost the immediacy of warfare, which, in a way, seems to make it more inevitable. Isolation from the consequences of war is a one-way ticket to boosting confidence in waging it. In the case of cyberwar, those consequences could be huge. This isn't a matter of corporate hackings and embarrassingly leaked emails, accurately defined as "vandalism" by the Obama Administration. This is a case of oil pipeline explosions,shutdowns of power grids, nuclear reactor meltdowns, sabotage of weapons systems, and other events that could cause substantial damage, and significant fatalities.

"Cyberwar" has been thrown around in the wake of the attacks on Sony, which are not necessarily linked to North Korea at all, despite claims from the FBI and suggestions from the administration — which, notably, has failed to provide concrete proof of such arguments. This betrays a fundamental lack of understanding about what cyberwar really is, which is critical to comprehending why the next world war is likely to take place online.

The Pentagon identifies cyberwar as an event involving government actors — either members of the government itself or agents of organizations funded by the government — who use cyberspace to achieve military objectives. That can involve active attacks (manipulating power grids to cut power to vast sections of a country, say), defense (securing nuclear power plants against penetration), or exploitation (taking advantage of vulnerabilities). The Pentagon is actively involved in training U.S. soldiers in the art of cyberwar, developing long-term strategies intended to give the U.S. an advantage on the playing field of the internet.

It's distinct from terrorism, and it's not the same thing as vandalism, either. Cyberwarfare is also not hacktivism, created by disruptive social groups like Anonymous: It is, very specifically, an act of government against government, intended to create military advantages. The attack on Sony might give the economy a small hit, and the result carries loaded implications for freedoms of speech in the U.S., but it wasn't an act of war, especially if it was conducted by individuals, not a government.

A world war fought in physical space is unlikely at this juncture. As the United States has learned, painfully, land wars result in casualty numbers deemed unacceptable by citizens at home, and can involve substantial political and social implications. The U.S. is likely to be mired in the Middle East for decades — and it's too smart to ponder similar involvement in Russia, North Korea, or China, three restless nations currently posing national security threats.

That means turning to the cyber realm, but that, too, will come at a cost — and that cost will be the likely creation of another world war. Should the United States delve into a full frontal attack on an enemy nation, that nation will likely be supported by allies — China, for example, has a vested interest in protecting North Korea. The United States, in turn, would draw upon allies in NATO as well as further afield, potentially embroiling the entire globe in a bitter digital battle that could extend over years or even decades.

Don't mistake a cyberwar for a fake war, though — this is a prospect with very real ramifications, and it's already happening. Nations on all sides are likely to use tools that will result in attacks like the Syrian Electronic Army's attempts against multiple targets in 2013.

The organization, believed to be supported by President Bashar al-Assad and his government, although they have officially denied it, took on any and all possible sources criticizing the Syrian regime. That same year, Iran purportedly attacked U.S. energy companies, which may have been a penetration test that could have long-term consequences — compromising a corporation is one thing, but kneecapping our energy supply is another.

Earlier this year, an attack some accuse Russia of orchestrating singled in on diplomats and embassies in former Eastern Bloc countries. With no clear profit motive, the attack clearly demonstrated an interest in gathering intelligence — exactly the kind of military advantage Russia would need in the event of more outward warfare. In Iran, Stuxnet appears to be attacking nuclear facilities, and the United States, along with Israel, may be behind it.

One of the most perturbing things about cyberwar may be the fact that it is an uncharted frontier. In the First World War, German forces rained mustard gas, phosgene, and chlorine gas down on enemy trenches, leaving soldiers gasping for air in agonizing, painful deaths — the new and distant face of warfare. In 1925, the world collectively agreed that such weapons should never be used again, creating the Geneva Protocol. Follow up conventions and agreements have strengthened the global position on chemical weapons. Similarly, the Geneva Protocol bans a number of other human rights abuses in war — including torture.

Such ethics, enforced and abided by or not, don't exist for cyberwar; like mustard gas, it's something no one imagined until it started happening. It's an entirely new playing field for both targets and participants alike, and in a world without ethics, anything goes. Cyberwar could create opportunities for exploiting loopholes in existing treaties and agreements, in addition to creating an entirely new landscape of horrors. Using chemical weapons is a violation of international law, but what if cyberwarfare creates a spill at a chemical facility? The use of nuclear weapons is controversial, but what about the exploitation of vulnerabilities at nuclear power plants or nuclear weapons facilities?

Cyberwar could open the world to possibilities like shutting down the power supply and record-keeping at hospitals — even though attacking hospitals, medics, and doctors is barred under international law. It would also represent an escalation of attacks on civilians, as when war is so distant, it becomes difficult if not impossible to distinguish combatants from ordinary civilians. Just as Brits feared the streets of London in the Second World War, citizens of a nation at cyberwar would have to fear every component of their lives that could possibly be exploited or manipulated through cyber means.

This is no small worry. For better or for worse, we live in a world where a substantial percentage of our lives is overseen electronically. The financial system, the grid, the water supply, medical facilities, and more are all at the mercy of cyberattacks, which is precisely why the prospect of cyberwar is so appealing to aggressors and so terrifying to defenders.

For those at the helm, it also involves minimal investment. Weapons systems can cost billions of dollars, with constantly escalating costs as other nations develop counterattacks. Storage, transport, and deployment of such weapons is also extremely costly. For the budget-conscious military — if such a thing ever exists — cyberwarfare is the perfect opportunity to produce maximum damage with minimum spending. In fact, a country's own weapons systems could be used against it, in what may be the most cruel and ironic attack of all.

With escalating diplomatic tensions worldwide, the question to ask ourselves isn't if we'll see another world war, but when — and the medium will be digital when it happens.

4

The Military Intelligence Function in Future War

The *Indian Army Doctrine* accepts Intelligence as "an addition to the widely accepted principles of war because of its pre-eminence in any future conflict." This clearly brings out the great emphasis placed on this function by the military and rightly so in light of India's historical experience of both success and shortcomings. Instances of inadequacy include the 1947 tribal bid for Kashmir even as India remained sanguine with its Standstill Agreement. The surprises of 1962 and the Kargil War are examples. The materialisation of an additional armoured division in the 1965 War on the Pakistani orbat was also unexpected. This has been the case with Operations Other than War also such as the limitations in tactical intelligence in the Golden Temple and Jaffna battles. Consensus on future wars being that they would be short and lethal, the luxury of time and resources to regain the initiative lost due to faulty intelligence would not exist. Therefore, to prevent history from repeating itself, there is a need to incorporate the additional and fresh areas of intelligence interest brought on by the asymmetric and nuclear dimensions of future conflict. This commentary dilates on the implications of these features of conflict on the intelligence function in future conflict.

The foremost lesson of recent conflicts is that irregulars would form part of the opposition armies in hostile territory. This is not a new phenomenon given Napoleon's experience in Spain and later in Russia. But the dimension has changed exponentially since the Iraqi and al Qaeda challenge to US stabilisation operations in Iraq War II. Even the Israelis faced an unconventional foe in both their recent forays into Lebanon and Gaza. The 'lessons learnt' of both armies needs critical study, not necessarily for replication since their way of war is very different, but incorporation of best practices suitably modified for Indian conditions.

Since conventional conflict may arise in fairly short order in case of a punitive Indian response to future 26/11 type situations, it behoves its military to ready itself for these. Implementation of the 'Cold Start' strategy may involve broad front offensives to limited depth. These would not only be contested by defenders but their action will be supplemented by employment of irregulars as force multipliers. In which case, the military needs to employ its intelligence resources as also task the Research and Analysis Wing to spot possible prior preparations and the latent networks that would be activated. Pakistan has not only promised an unconventional counter but is also known to have trained fighters for the purpose. Areas such as southern Punjab in Pakistan, in which may figure future military objectives, have of late inclined towards fundamentalism. Across the Line of Control, numbers of irregulars familiar with the terrain and irregular methods can be expected to be much more. Thus, cannon fodder would be readily available to complicate India's offensives and its immediate and longer term aftermath.

In addition, a sociological profile of prospective areas of offensive thrusts needs to be built up so that the occupation for howsoever brief a duration is successfully conducted. This effort would help in countering insurgency during stabilisation operations and fulfilling the duties of an occupying power. Follow on forces tasked to restore order in the communication zone need to have personnel with language skills and training in psychological war.

Next, since perception management is an intelligence function, the intelligence community would require formulating responses to likely scenarios that would develop. These include putting the lid on collateral damage that would be inevitable both in developed terrain and in the heavily populated Line of Control and explaining the benefits of cooperation. The Israeli discourse in the wake of the Goldstone Report may have pointers. It is a separate matter that the Report would be more useful reading for those conducting operations, particularly on the imperative of fighting within the laws of armed conflict; the instrumental logic being that lesser collateral damage would mean quicker stabilisation and easier the temporary occupation.

The second expanded dimension of the intelligence function is nuclear related. An interesting aspect here is that while in peacetime nuclear information security is equivalent to security of crown jewels, in war there would be a need for an element of transparency on both sides. This is because of the need to reassure the enemy against any move towards pre-emption. The requirements of nuclear signalling may also necessitate a deliberate showing of one's hand. This could be for instance done by discreetly displaying a heightened nuclear alert status.

Intelligence agencies would require awareness of the nuances of this game in order that the intelligence assets are suitably tasked to search for and pick up the required information. This means a degree of integration between military intelligence, RAW and NTRO doing this overseen by the JIC, NSCS and the HQs, Strategic Forces Command. Given that nuclear decision making would be a high tension exercise in real time, less ambiguity would make for rational decision making. This aspect needs inclusion in exercises involving multiple agencies and war gaming of the staff and decision makers.

Arriving at an understanding with and networking foreign intelligence agencies on this score would be crucial, given that the United States in particular is known to have privileged access to information. The channel can also be used for making escalation pressures recede. Such interaction would be particularly useful in case of a face off against China. While technical means are improving, their system would be considerably more impervious. Therefore, assistance from foreign intelligence agencies could help. This obviously requires to be pre-programmed.

The problem would be less with collection of information than with analysis. For instance, if preparation for missile launch has been picked up, it cannot by default be taken as nuclear related. Likewise, detecting a change in nuclear alert status should not trigger pressures for pre-emption. Alarming instances of misreading information occurred during the Cold War. Some analysts opine that this is accentuated in the South Asian setting in which technology is less capable and flight times are shorter. Coping with these problems require being sensitive to the possibility as a first step.

More importantly, given that non-state actors can have an autonomous agenda, an accurate reading of the source of a strike would be critical in determining the violence of response.

The 'insider-outsider' threat to the Pakistani nuclear complex has been in evidence over the past few years. It bears recall here that India's No First Use is liable to be reconsidered in case of a 'major' attack by chemical and biological weapons also. The link to state sponsorship of terrorist action as exploding a radiological device would require to be discerned for appropriate response.

The nuclear intelligence dimension needs special effort at foregrounding in India.

This owes to the possibility of being lulled into a false sense of complacency by two oft-repeated views. One is that nuclear weapons are political weapons.

Second is that the Pakistani threshold is likely to be a high enough for India to prosecute conventional military operations, albeit informed by the Limited War concept. That the nuclear initiative would be with Pakistan, which may think differently, is a sobering thought. The scenario of the Cold Start offensives overstepping predetermined lines in the fog of war is a case in point. Therefore, alert intelligence and competent analysis is vital in order that Indian forces do not inadvertently nudge the nuclear threshold. Picking up signals of nuclear preparation can help in timely reversing of provocative military action and in establishing communication and contact with the opposite side to defuse in-conflict nuclear crisis. For the greater good, incidental exposure of the source of the information should not come in way of preventive action.

MILITARY PHILOSOPHY, EDUCATION AND THE 21ST CENTURY WARRIOR

In warfare, American soldiers, sailors, airmen and marines traditionally rely on a limited set of values to guide them with difficult choices found only in war. On the battlefield, country, unit, family, faith and self, drive men and women. Modern warfare found within the 21st Century requires the United States invest further in educating their recruits ensuring they are raising warriors, professional individuals capable of thinking beyond country, unit, family and faith.

For a traditional military, serving for 2-4 years then out is acceptable during a *draft*, and then only for career fields that do not require extensive training such as gate guard or cook This is unacceptable with a special operations community, or an all-volunteer force, where there are fewer recruits with far greater responsibilities and required training than generations prior.

In addition, it takes years to recruit, train and develop shadow warriors. Modern American military brings changes in demographics where there is more diversity and over half the force is married with children finally college educated. Career individuals have increased risk of facing true conflict or war. America's national security rides on the backs of these people.

In today's battlefields, the entire world demands these individuals be capable of a wide variety of sophisticated decisions under incredible stresses, where a poor decision – or even a good decision with a poor outcome – can have substantial national security impacts (e.g. the death of civilians, offending a local potentate). Never forget how their current foe moves freely not dressed in traditional uniforms, or follows basic laws of armed conflict. Even worse, todays and tomorrow's adversaries now emerge within civilian populations further muddying the waters of societies. Educating warriors beyond the conduct of hostilities has much potential to reduce unnecessary violence, trauma and innocent death.

Warfare is never simple, and changes with each generation. This paradigm shift in raising warriors operating alone and autonomously requires people trained in the arts, philosophy, critical thinking and leadership. The fact is how country, unit, family and faith are a limited support system. When confronted by an adversary where man faces death or takes the life of another human being, going against nature, demands individuals capable of compartmentalizing yet thinking at light speed considering option. Additionally, the more exposure to real-world combat, the more difficult compartmentalizing becomes.

21st Century American warfare should rely on professional warriors capable of moving in small *clusters of pods even swarming around one's adversary from all directions or immediately dispersing to survive*(Arquilla 2002).

This modality requires both very sophisticated swarm situational awareness, and refined, small, secure communications (including displays) that are not yet fully developed. (Kohler 2011). These individuals will require and demand awareness to make complicated even troubling decisions with potential for catastrophe.

Fewer warriors with far greater access to intense firepower and situational awareness, capable of unimaginable devastation yet expected to perform with precision. American warriors must become experts in their fields wielding power yet be broad enough in mindset to become warrior diplomats capable of operating with balance and restraint when it counts.

With strategic knowledge, awareness enables us to make the right decisions under a wide variety of circumstances. Precisely what is demanded of individual special operations non-commissioned and junior officers who face near insurmountable obstacles, which threaten their lives or others, even national security.

To overcome frictions of modern warfare while operating autonomously, *special operations Non-Commissioned Officers and Junior Officers must be capable of thinking and behaving likeground force commanders.*

To be successful and reach full potential raising the level of awareness, improving intelligence and cognitive capabilities modern militaries must integrate critical thinking and philosophy studies to develop warriors.

Our philosophy is our motivation. Teaching history and military philosophy is good for warriors. However one must study with balance, taking in more than one view point. Where Clausewitz encourages defeating adversaries with all out violence yet at times, disregards the need for intelligence, Sun Wu impresses the idea of restraint emphasizing intelligence to outwit one's adversary.

More than one source of military philosophy is required to broaden the minds of professional warriors ultimately reducing risks on modern battlefields, increase confidence and improve survivability. Lessons learned through military philosophy are how one cannot solely study the "Art of warfare". To balance oneself and be responsible with the tools of warfare, one must study math, sciences and arts. If not, one is certain to go to extremes drunk from the power of military art.

TWENTY FIRST CENTURY, AN AMERICAN RENAISSANCE

A Mature, Aware, Efficient and Sustained Force

What once known as the home of red headed stepchildren or career suicide, SOCOM is now America's gold standard in warriors. The problem is how special operations are a minority within the DoD. So much so, since World War II, the American special operations community has always reduced even disbanded following every military campaign.

With the drawdown of troops in Iraq and Afghanistan, as we speak, in 2011, American special operations will continue to be cut. This choice is a major barrier to American and coalition to national security. The problem is how raising and fielding a special operations capability on average, takes decades.

The lesson learned is 21st Century nations cannot afford to be ignorant and repeat this mistake. If disbanded, every new campaign or action will result in nations forced to rebuild even recreate a special operations capability. To remain independent and mature *breaching* new levels of performance, even reaching full potential, *US SOCOM must have the following*.

Cabinet Secretary of US SOCOM: *Doctors, lawyers, engineers and American warriors*.

Joint Chiefs of Staff SOCOM 4 Star General: *Guidance and Interference*.

US intelligence agencies never mixed well with each other or the military. Despite intelligence budgets emphasizing military purposes, their (agencies) fierce independence creates unnecessary barriers to national security.

The front line American warrior must not be distracted by intelligence. To be effective and focused on their mission, warriors must be one-step ahead of their adversaries. The mistake made believes raw intelligence is only for authority figures, negating the needs of front line operators and decision makers. No longer should warriors expend unnecessary energy and precious time collecting raw data from multiple sources of intelligence. Modern warriors should be pushed relevant intelligence, not only pull it.

In the 21st Century, there must be the DoD, SOCOM to include every agency, all collaborating for the same purposes...the war fighter and national security. Competition must remain, however reality of real world conflicts and global awareness demands operations be intelligent, collaborative, even self-healing when attacked. Integration must be capable of transforming real time.

Virtual Intelligence Agency (VIA)

Jan 11, 2011: NSA Breaks Ground on Utah 'Spy Center' Data Center CIO: Network World – The National Security Agency is building one of the largest and most expensive data centers as a place to gather and analyze intelligence data. At $1.2 billion, this is the largest Department of Defense construction project underway. Officials broke ground at the site 25 miles south of Salt Lake City Thursday, and it will give NSA diversity with a separate data center beyond the one it has in Ft. Meade, Md., says NSA Deputy Director J. Chris Inglis.

Simply put, higher fidelity information and data will improve the mission of warriors and decision makers.

The office of Director of National Intelligence (DNI) is not the ideal solution required for true national security. A more technical solution is demanded to harness competition between the "16" key intelligence agencies, yet collaborate between all agencies, the US DoD, SOCOM, finally America's closest allies (Britain, Canada, Australia and New Zealand).

Weapons of choice for the 21st Century will not only be fourth, fifth generation fighter jets, aircraft carriers or unmanned aircraft and innovative integrated communications. Instead, nations must field*highly skilled special operations* vs. armies. Most importantly, *military grade fusion centers* designed to withstand threats and damage caused by new forms of warfare. Warfare such as CYBER attacks, or hacking nation's most secure networks. Finally, fusion centers are constructed to feed intelligence to operators.

Fusion centers or data centers, are weapons systems that provide many capabilities to include cloud computing or web based storage resembling Google, Amazon.com, Apple, Rackspace and Dell. A fusion center takes in information and or data from multiple sources (16 agencies) where intelligence will be collect, analyze and disseminate it to front line warriors and key decision makers.

A fusion center is effective by removing *stovepipes* enabling every source to collect raw intelligence on communications, travel, relationships, geo-locations, funding, etc. To be effective, data centers must not be only under one intelligence agency...they must integrate. The VIA is an integrated user interface for one purpose...intelligence.

The concept of a VIA should be in the form of a *fusion center* that will become a *technical* solution providing *glue* between interests, operations and information shared between every agency. The first mission or priority of the VIA is *collaboration*; next is autonomous information operations even CYBER warfare capabilities.

Collaboration does not simply mean a memorandum of understanding or agreement to share in operations and logistics. True collaboration is a single memo of understanding and agreement to pool the best resources and share crucial data, yet somehow preserve the competitive nature of intelligence. All done to gather as much relevant data to study and observe adversaries, finally disseminate that awareness to front line decision makers.

"In the near future swarming intelligence techniques that operate independently without a central command authority will rely on technologies such as the proposed VIA for its current and real-time intelligence. An independent swarm will collectively converge on an effective solution without the need for a *decision maker*, otherwise known as *emergent behavior*. Smart, small, independent is the name of the game". (Sotzen 2011).

Construct fusion centers to collaborate and exploit intelligence and the CYBER domain. Support decision makers, but most importantly, provide a deep pipe of relevant intelligence to special operations warriors. Study, observe and take action against adversaries by dominating the information or "CYBER" domain.

Fielding the first SOCOM fusion center will help further efforts with other near peers. With robust fusion centers, nations can look in more than one direction at the same time.

The objective is to create a robust network of multiple fusion centers capable of self-healing and harness its power for the defense of a nation's position all over the world. Fused intelligence and CYBER warfare is real and a current threat to all nations. This is not the sky is falling, instead its common sense.

Coalition Unconventional Battlefield Exploitation (CUBE)

The May 1st, 2011 covert mission where American intelligence and special operations crossed Pakistan's borders without permission to capture or kill Bin Laden was the work of professionals. The August 6, 2011 fatal crash of a *conventional* CH-47 Chinook carrying an entire troop of warriors was a tragic loss to their families and American national security. Similar to Somalia in 1993, a simple rocket propelled grenade launcher shot down this quick reaction force. Extreme military and intelligence operations such as counter-terrorism or CT missions demand a highly skilled force capable of carrying out a nation's most demanding operations. This small CT community requires a course of instruction enabling independent and creative thinking capable of preparing students for unpredictable scenarios...increasing chances of success and survival. CT training and operations require flexible standards for complex missions threatening the lives of not only the operators involved, but *civilians* impacted by any CT action.

Since 9/11, CT operations have skyrocketed. What conventional leadership once disrespected because it never understood CT, is now a specialty demanded to find and capture High Value Targets (HVT). CT is not only small teams breaching a structure to capture or kill individuals. CT can collect time sensitive intelligence even conducts offensive operations or preemptive strikes responding to find sources of CYBER warfare.

The 21st Century standard for CT operations to include both American and allied tactics, techniques and procedures (TTP) is CUBE. In training and with operations, the concept of a CUBE means a small team, a form of instruction; finally, it is another term for national CT operations. To work effectively, a CUBE is a special operations team integrated with every source of relevant intelligence and domain (Amphibious, Ground, Space, Airpower and CYBER).

When deployed, teams formed into *cubes* will respond to global threats. To an adversary, where units are composable or fractionated (Kohler, 2011), CUBE is confusing where no team is the same. The idea is CT teams or Cubes constantly learn; evolve even transform real-time becoming intelligent. SOCOM and allied teams will experience the entire life-cycle of evolution real-time transforming and improving the more they train and operate.

By teaching the McRaven art of warfare, CUBE will emphasize how following the simple principles of purpose, simplicity, security, repetition, speed, and surprise will achieve relative superiority. In his book titled "Spec Ops", Admiral McRaven analyzes case studies of history's most daring CT missions; CUBE will be CT training integrating operational expertise from not only the US, but also international standards breaking free of*Cold War* TTP's.

In training, CUBE ensures students see and experience every aspect of CT operations. Examples include integrating Combat Search and Rescue (CSAR), reconnaissance, media considerations, Sniper teams, communications, aviation (TAC, insertion/ extraction, C4ISR), weather, space assets even CYBER capabilities, and so on. Practicing CUBE will enable US SOCOM and allies to evolve and transform collaborating to master current tactics yet rehearse to develop new solutions.

Current CT operations execute too fast to capture lessons learned meant for evolution. During training and operations, automated Intelligent Joint after Action reports will capture the smallest details in TTP's where both instructors and students learn from each other. Secure internet communications will enable vital *operational* information and best knowledge of operations and lessons learned are shared with SOCOM and coalition teams across the globe.

Where the US Air Force has the Air Warfare Center in Nevada, this document argues how US SOCOM must have their specialized *Joint* Special Operations Warfare Center at Hurlburt Field/Eglin AFB or Ft. Bragg, North Carolina.

The concept of CUBE was created back in 2003 (Kubik, 2003), but only now presents itself as a vehicle for maturing even advancing SOCOM and allied forces. US SOCOM Special Tactics communities initiate CUBE because only ST forces experiences both US Navy and Army even allied TTP's. The best chances of collaboration and success is through sharing knowledge and expertise reaching levels of learning, adapting, evolving even transforming.

SINGULARITY OR CIVIL WAR? THE FUTURE OF ARTIFICIAL INTELLIGENCE

On the one side are optimists, who believe in the limitless possibilities of technology to liberate humanity. On the other side are pessimists, who believe that artificial intelligence will lead to war, political strife, and even a *Terminator*-style battle between machines and men. Then there are the skeptics, who believe the predictions of both sides to be hyperbolic nonsense.

It's a debate that will grow louder as the pace of technological change increases. Recently, IBM hired 2,000 new consultants to build and sell services from its "Watson" supercomputer, arguably the closest thing humanity has to genuine A.I. Watson is the same machine that astonished onlookers in 2011 when it beat two humans on a special episode of *Jeopardy!* It has encyclopedic knowledge, superhuman data analysis skills, and is capable of both understanding and talking in natural language. As its *Jeopardy!* win shows, it's also capable of unravelling complex verbal puzzles, analysing words and connecting them to millions of possibilities in its vast bank of data at superhuman speeds.

IBM is a firm believer in the potential of Watson-like machines to solve everything from the problems of a local retail business to global healthcare challenges. Their new investment is the first consultancy dedicated to what they call "Cognitive Computing" – another word for artificial intelligence.

The company predicts that demands for the problem-solving abilities of supercomputers will grow rapidly in the next five years. Stephen Pratt, global leader of the new IBM consulting branch, says, "Before long, we will look back and wonder how we made important decisions or discovered new opportunities without systematically learning from all available data."

As the age of intelligent machines dawns, it will add fuel to a previously esoteric between philosophers, scientists, and fururists about what the future will look like. On the one hand are optimists, who believe in the limitless capacity of smart machines to solve problems including ignorance, disease, and even death itself. They believe that artificial intelligence will one day surpass human intelligence, and in the process overcome all the challenges that humanity has yet to conquer. To them, IBM's recent investments in cognitive computing are just further proof that utopia is on the way.

Pessmists, by contrast, do not doubt the limitless possibilities, but they forsee much grimmer implications for humanity: political strife, violence, and the possible obsolescence of humanity. Some even believe that the divide between pro-A.I factions and anti-A.I factions in society could lead to widespread civil wars.

Skeptics, meanwhile, believe both sides of the debate are barking mad and wildly overestimate the potential of A.I.

The Optimists

If the optimists have a prophet, it's Google's commander-in-chief of A.I.: futurist and inventor Ray Kurzweil. Kurzweil worked on one of the very first computers in the 1950s and went on to pioneer advances in machine intelligence, including the first computer program capable of recognising human text in any font. He later combined this technology with a text-to-speech synthesizer to create the Kurzweil Reading Machine, the first machine allowing blind people to have written text read to them by a computer.

Beyond his impressive track record, what makes Kurzweil an icon to optimists is his range of Nostradamus-like predictions about the future of humanity. Many of these seemed bizarre and outlandish when they were originally made but were late proven correct. Kurzweil predicted that by the early 2000s, internet use would be widespread (correct), and that by the late 1990s, a computer would beat a grandmaster at chess (correct – IBM's "Deep Blue," a predecessor of Watson, defeated Gary Kasparov at chess in 1997.) Kurzweil's predictions even have their own Wikipedia page.

Kurzweil's most controversial prediction is that a "Technological Singularity" will occur within the next half-century. Kurzweil believes that exponential growth in the processing power of computers will by 2045 lead to a moment of accelleration where machine intelligence speeds past that of humanity, with unpredictable results. Kurzweil believes that once machines have moved past human intelligence in this manner, it will only be a matter of time before they tackle the problems that human minds are incapable of solving: war, disease, political conflict, and – most controversially – mortality.

Once again: Kurzweil believes that humans, with the assistance of machines, will become immortal within the next century. It's hard to imagine a more optimistic prediction.

In other circumstances, these predictions would sound like the ramblings of a madman or a sci-fi writer having a brainstorm. But because Kurzweil has so often been correct in his predictions, and because of his ironclad credentials as one of America's leading technological pioneers, he has not been dismissed as a madman.

Indeed, a whole network has emerged in preparation for the Singularity. "Singularity University," set up in 2008, says its aim is to "educate, inspire and empower leaders to apply exponential technologies to address humanity's grand challenges." The Machine Intelligence Research Institute, while not mentioning the Singularity directly, acknowledges that "researchers largely agree that A.I. is likely to begin outperforming humans on most cognitive tasks in this century."

There are even signs of an ideology forming around this optimistic vision of the future. Zolstan Istvan, a futurist, philosopher, and sci-fi author, is currently running for President of the United States on the first "Transhumanist Party" ticket. Istvan has stated that if elected, his primary goal would be to help scientists and technologists "overcome death and aging within 15-20 years, a goal an increasing number of leading scientists think is reachable." CNET calls Istvan "The only Presidential candidate promising immortality."

5

ISIS War in Syria

Conflict in Iraq and Syria has seen ISIS seize vast territory. Charting the group's rise, Peter Welby says that future dangers lie in the appeal to Islamists worldwide of their claims to a caliphate.

The resounding successes of the Islamic State of Iraq and al-Sham (ISIS) in the summer of 2014 were shocking. Cities fell to ISIS forces a fraction of the size of their defenders; soldiers were ordered to abandon their posts; and those soldiers who were captured were massacred. Buoyed by its advance, the group declared a caliphate, a move that has split the jihadi world despite long being the aspiration of such organisations. Reeling from its string of defeats, it took until March 2015 for Iraqi forces to start their counter-attack in earnest, and even then, ISIS remained in a position to seize Ramadi in May 2015. But unprecedented as these advances were in scale, they fit into a pattern that the group has set since its foundation.

ISIS can trace its roots back to 2002, when Abu Musab al-Zarqawi – a Jordanian who was to gain notoriety in the Iraqi insurgency from 2003-6 – founded a jihadi organisation called *Tawhid wal-Jihad* in the north of Iraq. Zarqawi had been linked with al-Qaeda while in Afghanistan in the late '90s, but was not a member of the group and disagreed with the tactic of focusing on the 'far enemy' (the West) as opposed to the 'near enemy' (rulers in the Islamic world). Following the 2003 invasion of Iraq, Zarqawi's organisation grew more active and affiliated itself to al-Qaeda in 2004, becoming al-Qaeda in Iraq (AQI).

Despite the tactical differences, this made a useful alliance of convenience: Zarqawi's organisation gained the recruiting and resourcing benefits of being part of a global and credible jihadi organisation, while al-Qaeda gained an affiliate in Iraq, already by that stage the global centre of jihad.

Zarqawi's AQI was an influential actor in Iraq's descent into chaos between 2003 and 2007. It had an explicit policy of stoking sectarian violence with the aim of rallying the Sunni community around Sunni jihadi groups, a tactic that ISIS is replicating now. This gained criticism from al-Qaeda's leaders, who felt that the indiscriminate and brutal violence risked alienating their supporters. However, it continued to support Zarqawi in public until he was killed in an airstrike in 2006.

In late 2006 AQI joined with eight other Islamist insurgent groups to form the Islamic State of Iraq (ISI), without permission from the al-Qaeda leadership. The name chosen for this new group indicated its ambitions: it was more than a mere jihadi group, but an embryonic caliphate, governed by Islamic law, to which all Muslims within its territory owed allegiance.

As the US surge took hold in 2007 and the so-called 'Anbar Awakening' or *sahwa* – the cooptation of Sunni tribes in Anbar province in the fight against the insurgency – diminished the group's support base, the notion of the Islamic State's 'territory' was a tenuous one. Successive ISI leaders were killed in airstrikes, and the group's capacity to launch attacks was severely diminished.

But the accession in 2010 of its current leader, Abu Bakr al-Baghdadi, coincided with a change in the external pressures the group faced. The USA withdrew its forces in 2011 and the promised integration of the Anbar militias into the armed forces was abandoned, removing a significant counter to insurgent activity. Absent American restraint, Prime Minister Maliki gave vent to his more sectarian impulses, creating grievances that the Islamic State was quick to exploit. Moreover, the start of the Syrian civil war created a fertile new cause and battlefield for the group's recruitment, and moulded it into the military force it has become.

The Syrian war also facilitated the Islamic State's final break with al-Qaeda. Since 2006, the group's relationship with al-Qaeda had been ambiguous, possibly deliberately so: the mutual benefits that had first prompted Zarqawi to affiliate to the organisation remained. In 2011, Baghdadi created a Syrian subsidiary, Jabhat al-Nusra (JN), under Abu Mohammad al-Jolani, in order to gain a toehold in the war. In 2013, with JN showing unwelcome signs of independence, he announced their reabsorption into the expanded Islamic State of Iraq and al-Sham – 'al-Sham' being the Arabic name for Greater Syria, with connotations of earlier caliphates. However, Jolani appealed to al-Qaeda's central command, which ruled in his favour, ordering Baghdadi to confine his group to Iraq.

The alliance between al-Qaeda and ISIS was no longer convenient. ISIS could now claim a history and a support base that established its credibility, and al-Qaeda's central leadership was weak. An ISIS spokesman declared that al-Qaeda's leader, Ayman al-Zawahiri, was sinful, and Jolani nothing less than a traitor. Shortly afterwards, Zawahiri announced that ISIS had nothing to do with al-Qaeda.

In subsequent fighting in Syria, much of it with other rebels including JN and other jihadi groups, ISIS has gained and held significant amounts of territory. It captured the city of Raqqa from other rebels in early 2014, using it since as a base to launch attacks in Syria and Iraq. In Iraq, the group exploited botched Iraqi military operations in Fallujah in January 2014 to gain control of the city. Control of sparsely populated transport corridors allowed them to advance rapidly in the kind of surprise attacks that delivered them Mosul, among other cities, in June of the same year.

However, 2015 has brought setbacks for the group, with Kurdish forces, comprising mainly the Popular Protection Units (YPG) in Syria and the Peshmerga in Iraq, emerging as key opponents. A hard-fought four month battle for the city of Kobane, on the Syrian-Turkish border, culminated in victory for the YPG in January 2015 – though ISIS has maintained a presence nearby. In September 2014, the US began a military campaign against ISIS in Iraq and Syria, supported by more than a dozen European and Arab states. Extensive airstrikes have supported the operations of Kurdish and Iraqi ground troops in making strategic gains. In Iraq, the Peshmerga were able to dislodge ISIS from key areas around Mount Sinjar in December 2014. Furthermore, Iraqi security forces, aided by Shia militias supported by Iran, in March 2015 launched the first major government offensive against ISIS since June 2014, in Tikrit.

Regardless of these defeats, ISIS' development since 2013 changed the nature of the group. It is no longer a mere terrorist group, but an army that can hold and administer territory. It governs according to harshly interpreted principles of Islamic law, including the imposition of *dhimmi* pacts on minorities – guaranteeing protection in exchange for the payment of a tax and the acceptance of second-class citizenship.

Minorities, including Shia Muslims, have been subject to severe human rights abuses, including massacres and forced conversion, and the persecution of minorities in northern Iraq has been particularly brutal. ISIS has also provoked shock and condemnation worldwide for its brutal execution of foreign journalists and humanitarian aid workers, as well as captured combatants from opposing forces.

While the quality of its governance is questionable – a 2006 paper produced by the group stated that improving the quality of the people's religion was more important than improving the quality of their lives – it can broadly coerce the consent of the people it governs.

Meanwhile, a further danger lies in the group's appeal beyond the borders of Iraq and Syria. While other jihadi groups, both in these countries and elsewhere, seek to establish an Islamic caliphate, ISIS claims to be one. Baghdadi has declared himself "Caliph Ibrahim," and goes by the title "Commander of the Faithful." In the language of his speeches and in his titles, he lays claim to a form of authority from the earliest days of Islam. This combined with the supposedly just cause of the fight against Assad in Syria has proved to be a powerful draw to young Islamists across the world, spread by means of an adept use of social media, and slickly presented propaganda such as the monthly magazine *Dabiq*. Some of these recruits will eventually return to their homes, taking with them their experiences as members of the most brutal jihadi group in the conflict. By claiming responsibility for the November 2015 attacks in Paris and the downing of a Russian plane in Egypt, ISIS gives the impression that the group, ordinarily focused on targeting the near enemy, is keen to convey a broadening of its operational strategy and the pursuit of targets further afield.

The danger is not limited to individuals attracted to ISIS' flag. In November, Baghdadi demanded that all Islamist and jihadi movements across the world be dissolved or absorbed into his 'caliphate.' Many groups have taken up the call, and new ones continue to do so. While some were previously unknown, others, including Boko Haram in Nigeria and Ansar Beit al-Maqdis in Egypt, have long been prominent actors in their own countries' conflicts. Moreover, the appeal of the universal caliphate is fracturing established groups that have not declared allegiance.

A focus on ISIS should not underestimate the unpredictable nature of this conflict: sudden changes in fortune have been a hallmark of the Syrian civil war, and in Iraq the concerted action of Shia militias and the military – not to mention Iranian interests – may yet turn the tide. Moreover, as the development of ISIS shows, jihadi groups can fracture suddenly and dramatically. However, bolstered by state-of-the-art equipment seized from Iraqi bases and resources from oil fields in its territory, by reported extensive assets, and by an Iraqi army that, whatever its current momentum, melted before them in June 2014, ISIS will not be defeated without a hard fight.

The US-led campaign against ISIS, known as Operation Inherent Resolve, has launched over 6,000 airstrikes against ISIS and is killing about 1,000 militants every month, roughly the same number believed to be joining the group, leaving the group's manpower strength effectively capped at 30,000 to 40,000. ISIS has had to adopt a different strategy since the commencement of aerial attacks on the group in Iraq and Syria, no longer having the freedom of movement it once enjoyed. With Russia entering the foray and reportedly carrying out airstrikes against ISIS targets, the group's capabilities will be further diminished.

MILITARY ACTIVITY OF ISIL

The military of ISIL is the fighting force of the Islamic State of Iraq and the Levant (ISIL). The total force size has been estimated from tens of thousands to over two hundred thousand. ISIL's armed forces grew quickly during 2014. The ISIL military, including groups incorporated into it in 2014, openly operates and controls territory inIraq, Syria, multiple cities in Libya, and Nigeria. It also has made border clashes and incursions into Lebanon, Iran, and Jordan. ISIL-linked groups operate in Algeria,Pakistan, the Philippines, and in West Africa (Cameroon, Niger, and Chad). In January 2015, ISIL was also confirmed to have a military presence in Afghanistan and in Yemen. Additionally, in early February 2015, it was reported that ISIL was smuggling fighters into the European Union, by disguising them as civilian refugees.An ISIL representative said that ISIL had successfully smuggled 4,000 fighters, and that the smuggled fighters were planning attacks in Europe to retaliate for the airstrikes carried out against ISIL targets in Iraq and Syria. However, experts believe that the ISIL claim of 4,000 was exaggerated to boost their stature and spread fear, although they acknowledged that some of the Western countries are aware of the smuggling. A significant number of ISIL fighters are from outside Iraq and Syria.

Their military is based on mobile foot militant units using light vehicles such as gun equipped pick-up trucks (technicals), motorbikes and buses for fast advances. They also use artillery, tanks and armored vehicles captured from the Iraqi and Syrian Armies. It is alleged that the ISIL military had gained control of 3 aircraft from the Syrian Army and are flying them over Syria, although two of these were reportedly shot down by Syria.

ISIL has a long history of using truck and car bombs, suicide bombers, and IEDs. They have also deployed chemical weapons in Iraq and Syrian Kurdistan. Other terror tactics include genocide, mass executions (including beheadings), psychological operationsthrough sophisticated propaganda, widespread torture of prisoners, and organized sexual violence and slavery.

Command Structure

According to the Institute for the Study of War, ISIL's 2013 annual report reveals ametrics-driven military command, which is "a strong indication of a unified, coherent leadership structure that commands from the top down". Middle East Forum's Aymenn Jawad Al-Tamimi said, "They are highly skilled in urban guerrilla warfare while the new Iraqi Army simply lacks tactical competence."

Little is known about the military command structure of ISIL. Sources indicate that Abu Muslim al-Turkmani (Deputy Leader in Iraq – Killed in Action) was an Iraqi Army General and Abu Ali al-Anbari (Deputy Leader in Syria) was also an Iraqi Army Major General, both under the Saddam Hussein government. Georgian born fighter Abu Omar al-Shishani is a prominent figure in the ISIL military and it has been speculated that he may have become the military chief for the Islamic State of Iraq and the Levant following the death of Abu Abdul-Rahman al-Bilawi al-Anbari in Mosul in June 2014. Reports indicate that the military is organized into brigades such as a female unit tasked with policing religious laws. According to battle reports ISIL often operates in small mobile fighting units.

ISIL's fighters are reportedly organised into seven branches: infantry, snipers, air defence, special forces, artillery forces, the "army of adversity", and the Caliphate Army.

This force structure is largely replicated in each of its designated provinces, with the most skilled fighters and military strategists in each area serving in the special forces unit, which is not allowed to redeploy to other provinces. Parallel to this structure is the Caliphate Army, which is directed by ISIL's central command rather than its provincial leadership. Made up overwhelmingly of foreign fighters, it is deployed to assist in battles across ISIL controlled territory.

The group also operates outside areas it largely controls using a cell structure. An ISIL-linked senior militant commander in

Sinai told Reuters, "They [ISIL] teach us how to carry out operations. We communicate through the internet,... they teach us how to create secret cells, consisting of five people. Only one person has contact with other cells. They are teaching us how to attack security forces, the element of surprise. They told us to plant bombs then wait 12 hours so that the man planting the device has enough time to escape from the town he is in."

MILITARY MEASURES TAKEN BY ISIS IN SYRIA AND IRAQ

In June 2014 ISIS began a military campaign in Iraq whose objective, in ITIC assessment, was to take over most of the territory of northern and western Iraq to launch an attack on Baghdad. At the same time it waged campaigns for the control of various districts in eastern and northern Syria and to weaken its rivals and enemies (the Syrian regime, the Al-Nusra Front, the Kurdish militias and the other rebel organizations). Its military achievements so far have enabled it to create a supranational territorial continuum of the vast area under its control, where it is actively working to establish the rule of its self-declared Islamic Caliphate.

To date ISIS' military campaign in Iraq has had three stages: ISIS captured the oil city of Mosul from the Iraqi army. The Iraqi army, in whose establishment and training the United States invested enormous resources for years, collapsed and fled. An ISIS force also captured the Mosul Dam with its hydroelectric plant (north of the city on the Tigris), driving out the Kurdish Peshmerga force defending it. (An ISIS force also tried to capture the Haditha Dam on the Euphrates, the second largest dam in the country, but was met with resistance from the Iraqi army stationed there.) ISIS also took control of the city of Tikrit, Saddam Hussein's birthplace and a former stronghold of the Iraqi Ba'ath party.

Containment and halt (second half of August – September 2014): During the second half of August and September 2014 (when the United States began its pinpointed aerial attacks) ISIS' advance was halted. The Kurdish Peshmerga forces, the Iraqi army and the Shi'ite militiasretook the Mosul Dam. The Iraqi army drove ISIS forces from the large Haditha Dam and the oil city of Baiji (an important logistic passage besieged by ISIS). ISIS enemies saved the lives of minority groups considered "infidels" by ISIS and targeted for harassment, attack and slaughter: Yazidi refugees were rescued from Mt. Sinjar (in northern Iraq) and the siege of the predominantly Shi'ite-Turkmen town of Amerli (south of Kirkuk) was lifted.

Establishment of control over the Al-Anbar province, possibly a step in a campaign against Baghdad (end of September – mid-November 2014): ISIS forces cleared pockets of resistance in the Al-Anbar province (Iraq's largest Sunni district) and advanced towards the capital city of Baghdad. At the same time, ISIS carried out a series of suicide bombing attacks in Baghdad, mainly in Shi'ite neighborhoods. The news agencies reported ISIS forces located several dozen miles from the city and fighting in the city of Abu Ghraib, west of Baghdad. However, the Iraqi army, the Shi'ite militias and the Kurdish forces had several military achievements, the most prominent of which was relieving the siege of Baiji.

So far ISIS has not yet taken full control of the Sunni Al-Anbar province. In ITIC assessment, in the future ISIS is planning to take over Baghdad, but apparently the campaign will be far more difficult than the easy conquest of Mosul, because its operatives are liable to encounter fierce resistance from the Shi'ite militias and the Iraqi army, which will have Iranian support and aerial cover from the American-led coalition. It is also likely that ISIS' rivals will cooperate against it. In can be expected that ISIS will attempt to overcome resistance by besieging Baghdad and disrupting life in the city (by firing rockets and mortar shells, and detonating IEDs and car bombs). During October and to mid-November 2014 hundreds of civilians were killed in Baghdad, most of them Shi'ite, in suicide bombings and car bomb attacks, for at least some of which ISIS was responsible.

While launching military campaigns, ISIS has firmly established its grip on extensive areas of eastern and northern Syria. It has expelled its rivals and enemies (among them other rebel organizations, the Al-Nusra Front and the Syrian army), and attempted to gain control of new key areas (as of this writing the campaign for the Kurdish region of Qobanê near the Turkish border has not yet ended). It established its control over Al-Raqqah, turning it into its "capital city" in Syria, and solidified its control over the local population.Its accomplishments are funded by the enormous sums of money pouring in from its control of the country's infrastructure, especially the sale of petroleum products from the fields in eastern Syria (although its profits have decreased since the Americans and their allies began aerial attacks).

The Significance and Main Implications of ISIS' Achievements in Syria and Iraq

The foothold gained by ISIS in Syria and Iraq has far-reaching local, regional and international significance and implications: Iraq: ISIS conquests in the summer of 2014 accelerated the disintegration of Iraq into religious and ethnic components. It can be said that Iraq no longer functions as a nation state. Three quasi-entities arose: a Sunni district controlled by ISIS in western and northern Iraq; an autonomous Kurdish region in the north and a Shi'ite region in the center and south affiliated with the Shi'ite regime in Baghdad. The borders between them are blurred and unstable, and ISIS, which is gaining strength, can be expected to continue its efforts to enlarge the areas under its control at the expense of the other entities, which are currently on the defensive.

Syria: In Syria as well ISIS' increase in strength contributed to deepening the country's de facto division. ISIS secured its control over the northern and eastern parts of the country and weakened its various rivals (the Syrian regime, the Al-Nusra Front and the other rebel organizations). However, ISIS has not been able to break the Syrian regime's hold on Damascus and other core areas in the north and west, or of the rebel organizations on the southern part of the country (including most of the area of the Golan Heights along the border with Israel). The strengthening of ISIS and the American-led campaign against it increased the existing complexity of the Syrian civil war and made the situation more volatile, making it more difficult to resolve the Syrian crisis in the foreseeable future.

The establishment of the global jihad in the Middle East: ISIS' successes in Syria and Iraq turned them into a new focus for the global jihad, inheriting the place of Afghanistan and Pakistan. As opposed to the era of Osama bin Laden, today there are two principal hostile, rival jihadi organizations: one, ISIS, affiliated with the global jihad but at odds with the Al-Qaeda leadership of Ayman al-Zawahiri; and the other, the Al-Nusra Front, a branch of Al-Qaeda in Syria. Between the two are global jihad networks within the Middle East and beyond. Some of the jihadi networks in the Middle East, mainly the Egyptian-based Ansar Bayt al-Maqdis, have already taken a stand and sworn allegiance to ISIS, which is gaining power against the Al-Qaeda leadership. In addition, in the future ISIS' potential for subversion and terrorism is liable to destabilize countries in the Middle East and to export jihadi terrorism to Israel and the West.

Regional Middle East significance: The foothold gained by ISIS and the global jihad in Syria and Iraq reflects and may aggravate the regional upheaval in the Middle East: the flashpoints include the tensions, schisms and hostility among the various ethnic, religious and tribal groups, especially between the Sunnis and Shi'ites; the political weakness of the nation states created and forced upon the region by the French and British after the First World War; the loss by the key states in the Middle East of their ability to govern; and the establishment of alternative ideologies and governance in the places where nation states collapsed. The establishment of the Salafist-jihadi organizations in Syria and Iraq are manifestations of the power of radical Islamic ideology to attract followers and present itself as a magical solution for the ongoing distress and basic ills that have plagued the nation states since their inception.

Thus additional instability and volatility were injected into the already unstable situation in the Middle East by the establishment of ISIS and the global jihad organizations' power base in Syria and Iraq. They are liable not only to accelerate the disintegration of Syria and Iraq but to filter into the entire region.

In the foreseeable future ISIS can be expected to continue its military occupation of Syria and Iraq, establish its control and oppose the campaign the United States is waging against it. However, in the long run, as it establishes itself more firmly in Syria and Iraq, its influence may gradually spread to other Arab states; its growing cooperation with the Ansar Bayt al-Maqdis is proof thereof. Veterans of the fighting in Syria who return to their countries of origin in the Middle East are liable to become "carriers" of terrorism and subversion, whether at ISIS instigation or on their own initiative, thereby contributing to political instability in their own countries (as has already happened in Darnah in eastern Libya, taken over by a jihadi network which expressed its support for ISIS).

The American movement against ISIS and the ISIS Comeback

ISIS' dramatic successes in the summer of 2014 were a strong blow to American foreign policy in Iraq. America's objective was to establish a democratic Iraqi regime that would fight terrorism and provide the country with a stable administration. That proved to be completely unrealistic. The Iraqi army, in whose establishment the United States invested enormous resources, was exposed as weak, as was the Shi'ite-affiliated central regime in Baghdad supported by America.

Moreover, the Americans regarded the rapid establishment of ISIS and the Al-Nusra Front in Syria and Iraq as threatening the stability of Middle Eastern countries (among them Jordan, Egypt, Saudi Arabia, Lebanon and the Gulf States). In addition, there was a significant rise in the number of foreign fighters who fought in the ranks of ISIS and other jihadi organizations in Syria and Iraq and who might endanger the security of America and other Western countries when they returned to their countries of origin.

During the first three years of the Syrian civil war the United States did not attach great significance to ISIS and the Al-Nusra Front, and tended to regard them as part of the general chaos created in Syria and Iraq after the regimes in both countries disintegrated. The change in American policy began in the summer of 2014 with the fall of Mosul, the declaration of the Islamic Caliphate and the significant increase in the number of foreign fighters. The media-documented slaughter and executions carried out by ISIS horrified and enraged American and Western public opinion and also contributed to the change in American policy.

The United States altered its policy from underestimating ISIS to demonizing it and representing it as a significant regional and international threat.

The change in concept required an American response, which was given in two stages: the first (June – August 2014) consisted of "pinpointed" responses intended to support the local forces in Iraq in halting the momentum of ISIS attacks. The pinpointed responses mostly involved sporadic aerial attacks, the dispatch of a small number of advisors and providing besieged minorities with humanitarian aid. However, it quickly became clear that pinpointed responses were ineffective and did not provide a satisfactory answer to the challenges to American interests posed by the successes of ISIS.

For that reason, the second stage was formulated as a comprehensive strategy for a campaign against ISIS, as noted in a speech given by President Obama on September 10, 2014. The objective of the new strategy was to "degrade and ultimately destroy" ISIS in the following ways: massive aerial bombings in Syria and Iraq; reinforcing the local forces in Syria and Iraq (the Iraqi army, the Kurdish forces, the so-called moderate rebel organizations in Syria); damaging the sources of ISIS' power (especially its financial resources); improving the United States' and the international community's deterrent capabilities against the foreign fighters and deepening international collaboration against them. President Obama and spokesmen for the American administration repeatedly stressed that the new strategy did not include sending a significant ground force to fight in Syria or Iraq, the so-called "boots on the ground."

To implement the strategy, in a relatively short period of time the United States established an international coalition of Western and Arab countries. The Western allies (most importantly

France and Britain) participated in the aerial attacks on Iraq while some of the Arab states (Saudi Arabia, the UAE, Jordan and Bahrain) joined the aerial attacks on Syria. By the end of October 2014 the United States and its allies had carried out 632 aerial attacks against ISIS' military and economic infrastructure in Syria and Iraq (286 in Syria and 346 in Iraq). The attacks have continued into November.

In ITIC assessment, the new American strategy suffers from a series of weaknesses, which are detailed in this study.

The main among them are that its political objectives, both declared and undeclared, seem unrealistic; it is extremely difficult to destroy an organization with a Salafist-jihadi ideology such as ISIS; there are limits to what military force can achieve against jihad organizations in general and ISIS in particular; the local forces in Syria and Iraq that America is counting on are weak; and the coalition is heterogeneous, composed of countries with different interests and internal constraints that are liable to make it difficult for them to provide the United States with effective support.

Beyond the inherent weaknesses in the American strategy, societal and political situations in Syria and Iraq are complex and fluctuating. They cannot be fundamentally changed through military action, limited or even extensive. That is because ISIS and other Salafist-jihadi terrorist organizations arose from the chaos in security and the societal and political disintegration of Syria and Iraq, and because of the drastic changes caused by the regional upheaval. Iraq and Syria are a swamp in which ISIS and other jihadi organizations thrive. Rooting out ISIS will be impossible until the swamp has been drained, and that is currently not on the horizon.

However, ISIS has its own inherent weaknesses, which are examined in this study. If the United States learns to exploit them the campaign against ISIS may have positive results, although perhaps less far-reaching than expected by President Obama. The American-led military, economic and political campaign, if continued with determination, may eventually weaken (although not destroy) ISIS; its spread throughout Syria and Iraq may be halted (with the campaign of Baghdad still on the agenda); and the Iraqi army and local organizations/militias within Syria and Iraq hostile to ISIS can be strengthened. The campaign against ISIS may also improve the way the United States and its allies deal with the foreign fighters who return to their countries of origin.

As to ISIS' responses to the American campaign, ISIS has publicly beheaded five abductees, three American and two British. On September 21, 2014, ISIS called on its supporters around the globe to use a variety of methods to kill civilians in the United States and its allied countries. It is possible that a number of terrorist attacks, including the vehicular and shooting attacks in Canada, the planned beheading of Australians and attacks in other countries were the first responses to the call.

The Israeli Feature

The establishment of ISIS is part of the larger picture of the establishment of global jihad organizations in Syria and Iraq, such as the Al-Nusra Front. For Israel the situation holds several threats and dangers: The Golan Heights and the Sinai Peninsula might be turned into active terrorist fronts:As of today, the Golan Heights are controlled by rebel organizations, the most prominent of which is the Al-Nusra Front, Al-Qaeda's branch in Syria.

While ISIS does not currently have a significant presence there, the dynamics can easily change the Golan Heights from a relatively quiet area into an active terrorist front where the Al-Nusra Front may be dominant. In the Sinai Peninsula ISIS-affiliated Ansar Bayt al-Maqdis (which has become the Sinai province of the Islamic State) is expected to launch terrorist attacks against Israel, although its strategic priority is its campaign against the Egypt regime.

ISIS support for jihadi organizations and networks in the Middle East, especially the countries bordering on Israel: ISIS is a terrorist organization with semi-state capabilities: it has advanced weapons and technology captured from the Iraqi and Syrian armies; it earns enormous amounts of money from oil fields and other resources; it has supporters in the Middle East and worldwide who help it enlist foreign fighters; it has an advanced media network which brands ISIS and the global jihad. To date those capabilities are mainly exploited for internal purposes (fighting enemies in Iraq and Syria). However, they may filter into jihadi organizations and networks in the Middle East, including countries and entities bordering on Israel, and strengthen the operational capabilities of local jihadi organizations.

Terrorist attacks in Israel and against Israeli and Jewish targets abroad: In the foreseeable future ISIS strategy will continue focusing on gaining a firmer foothold in Syria and Iraq.

However, in view of the American aerial attacks and the competition between the jihadi organizations, ISIS may encourage or initiate attacks within Israel from inside the country or from its borders, or against Israeli and/or Jewish targets abroad. They may receive help and support from the veterans of the fighting in Syria and Iraq who returned to their countries of origin and/ or from local operatives and networks that support ISIS.

Cooperation between the United States-led coalition and Iran: Despite Iran's basic hostility towards the United States, and despite Iran's subversion of American interests in the Middle East, it might collaborate with the United States against ISIS and global jihad in Syria and Iraq, the common enemy. Such collaboration might occur at Israel's expense and harm its vital interests (for example, Iran's concessions on the nuclear issue). In addition, collaborating against ISIS might increase Iranian influence in Syria and Iraq, and might also strengthen Hezbollah's status in Lebanon, possibly strengthening the Iranian-led radical camp in the Middle East.

There are potential dangers both to the West and to Israel in regional politics caused by the subversive potential of the increasing strength of Al-Qaeda and the global jihad in Syria and Iraq. The influence of a strong Al-Qaeda and global jihad in those countries might filter into the entire Arab world, including pro-Western countries such as Jordan and Saudi Arabia, which so far have shown themselves strong enough to survive the regional upheaval. It might also give more power to the global jihad organizations and networks in countries peripheral to the heart of the Middle East which have failed regimes (such as Libya and Yemen) or weak regimes (such as Tunisia).

Methodology

ISIS (sometimes ISIL) is an acronym for The Islamic State in Iraq and Greater Syria. Once the Caliphate was declared ISIS began calling itself the "Islamic State (IS)" or the "Caliphate State." However, this study refers to the organization as ISIS, the term usually used by the international community, the Arab and Western media, and even by "Islamic State" supporters.

In preparing this study the ITIC dealt with a number of challenges: Turning a large amount of information into a comprehensive picture: When ISIS became a regional and international threat, individual bits of information became a daily flood. One of the challenges in preparing this study was turning them into a comprehensive research whole that examined the various aspects of ISIS' rise: its historical and causal background; its Islamic and Salafist-jihadi roots; its objectives; its military, political, administrative and financial capabilities; and the Iraqi, Syrian, Middle Eastern and international environments in which it operates.

Frequent changes in the situation on the ground in Iraq and Syria: During the past half year dramatic developments occurred in Iraq and Syria, with the regional upheaval in the background. In addition, ISIS is basically a dynamic organization, continually seeking to change the status quo both in the areas in which it operates against a large number of local enemies, and against the international campaign currently being waged against it. That forced the ITIC staff to update the study continually, understand the significance of tactical developments and examine and reexamine the situation on the ground. That situation is still in flux, so this study may be considered an interim report, which will have to be updated in the future.

The need to integrate information from various disciplines and fields: ISIS cannot be analyzed and examined only as a terrorist organization operating within a local national framework. A study of ISIS necessitates integrating various fields of knowledge, among them the history of Islam (including the Sunni-Shi'ite schism); the Salafist-jihadi movement from which ISIS sprang; the changes in Al-Qaeda and the global jihad; the developments in the civil wars in Syria and Iraq and the various aspects of the Middle Eastern upheaval. In preparing the study the ITIC used the existing literature and studies, and received support from experts in the various fields.

Problematic sources of information: In preparing the study we used primary sources from ISIS and other jihadi organizations. ISIS frequently posts information on the Internet about itself and its activities, but it is self-glorifying propaganda meant to sully the reputations of its rivals, threaten its enemies and deflect accusations. There is also a vast amount of information posted by ISIS' many rivals, which tend to defame the organization and sometimes manipulate the extent of its potential threat. In preparing this study we used investigative reports from correspondents (some of them Western) who had been allowed into areas under ISIS control. However the information to which they were exposed was sometimes directed and supervised by ISIS and intended to serve its political and propaganda objectives. Because of the awareness of the problem and because of the lack of trustworthy sources of information, all sources were treated carefully and critically.

Extremely valuable sources of information used in preparing this study were the continuing reports and basic research work published by experts and think tanks working in various disciplines and following ISIS and the developments in Syria and Iraq (primarily in the United States, Britain and Israel). Other important sources were reports from news agencies and the global media following ISIS and the developments in Syria and Iraq.

UPRISING AND CIVIL WAR IN SYRIA

Small protests began in Syria on 28 January 2011. Mass protests erupted on 15 March in Damascus and Aleppo, and spread in the following days to more cities, while growing in size. The week of 15–21 March is considered by news media as the beginning of the Syrian uprising. On 18 March, the protests turned bloody when the Syrian government reacted with deadly violence. On 20 March in Daraa, after security forces opened fire on the protesting crowd, protesters burned the local Ba'ath Party headquarters, the town's courthouse and a telephone company building. That day 15 demonstrators and 7 policemen were killed in Daraa. By 25 March, 90 civilians and 7 policemen had been killed in Syria.

The protesters' demands until 7 April were predominantly democratic reforms, release of political prisoners, "freedom", abolition of emergency law and an end to corruption. After 8 April, the emphasis in demonstration slogans gradually shifted towards the call for overthrowing the Assad government. Protests spread: on Friday 8 April, they occurred simultaneously in ten cities. By Friday 22 April protests occurred in twenty cities. On 25 April, the Syrian Army started a series of large-scale deadly military attacks on towns, using tanks, infantry carriers, and artillery, leading to hundreds of civilian deaths. By the end of May 2011, 1,000 civilians and 150 soldiers and policemen had been killed and thousands detained; among the arrested were many students, liberal activists and human rights advocates. In his March 2011 speech addressing the protests, Assad claimed that an international terrorist conspiracy sought to topple his government. During this time, Assad released extremists from the Sednaya prison; extremists with no association to the uprisings. These fighters would go on to lead militant groups such as ISIS and al-Qaeda affiliate Jabhat al Nusra.

Significant armed rebellion against the state began on 4 June in Jisr al-Shugur, a city in Idlib Governorate near the Turkish border, after security forces on a post office roof had fired at a funeral demonstration. Protesting mourners set fire to the building, killing eight security officers, and then overran a police station, seizing weapons from it. Violence continued and escalated over the following days. Unverified reports claim that a portion of the security forces in Jisr defected after secret police and intelligence officers executed soldiers who had refused to fire on civilians. Later, more protesters in Syria took up arms, and more soldiers defected to protect protesters. Both sides in the conflict used propaganda to promote their own righteousness and their opponents' wickedness. By the end of July 2011, around 1,600 civilians and 500 security forces had been killed and 13,000 arrested.

Escalation (November 2011 - March 2012)

In early November, clashes between the FSA and security forces in Homs escalated as the siegecontinued. After six days of bombardment, the Syrian Army stormed the city on 8 November, leading to heavy street fighting in several neighborhoods. Resistance in Homs was significantly greater than that seen in other towns and cities, and some in opposition have referred to the city as the "Capital of the Revolution". Unlike events in Deraa and Hama, operations in Homs have thus far failed to quell the unrest.

November and December 2011 saw increasing rebel attacks, as opposition forces grew in number. In the two months, the FSA launched deadly attacks on an air force intelligence complex in the Damascus suburb of Harasta, the Ba'ath Syrian Regional Branch youth headquarters in Idlib Governorate, Syrian Regional Branch offices in Damascus, an airbase in Homs Governorate, and an intelligence building in Idlib. On 15 December, opposition fighters ambushed checkpoints and military bases around Daraa, killing 27 soldiers, in one of the largest attacks yet on security forces. The opposition suffered a major setback on 19 December, when a failed defection in Idlib governorate lead to 72 defectors killed.

In January 2012, Assad began using large-scale artillery operations against the insurgency, which led to the destruction of many civilian homes due to indiscriminate shelling. By this time, daily protests had dwindled, eclipsed by the spread of armed conflict. January saw intensified clashes around the suburbs of Damascus, with the Syrian Army use of tanks and artillery becoming common.Fighting in Zabadani began on 7 January when the Syrian Army stormed the town in an attempt to rout out FSA presence. After the first phase of the battle ended with a ceasefire on 18 January, leaving the FSA in control of the town, the FSA launched an offensive into nearby Douma. Fighting in the townlasted from 21 to 30 January, before the rebels were forced to retreat as result of a government counteroffensive. Although, the Syrian Army managed to retake most of the suburbs, sporadic fighting continued. Fighting erupted in Rastan again on 29 January, when dozens of soldiers manning the town's checkpoints defected and began opening fire on troops loyal to the government. Opposition forces gained complete control of the town and surrounding suburbs on 5 February.

On 3 February, the Syrian army launched a major offensive to retake rebel-held neighborhoods. In early March, after weeks of artillery bombardments and heavy street fighting, the Syrian army eventually captured the district of Baba Amr, a major rebel stronghold. The Syrian Army also captured the district of Karm al-Zeitoun by 9 March, where activists said that government forces killed 47 women and children. By the end of March, the Syrian army retook control of half a dozen districts, leaving them in control of 70 percent of the city. By 14 March, Syrian troops successfully ousted insurgents from the city of Idlib after days of fighting. By early April, the estimated death toll of the conflict, according to activists, reached 10,000.

Ceasefire attempt (April–May 2012)

Kofi Annan was acting as UN–Arab League Joint Special Representative for Syria. His peace plan provided for a ceasefire, but even as the negotiations for it were being conducted, Syrian armed forces attacked a number of towns and villages, and summarily executed scores of people. Incommunicado detention, including of children, also continued. In April, Assad began employing attack helicopters against rebel forces.

On 12 April, both sides, the Syrian Government and rebels of the FSA entered a UN mediated ceasefire period. It was a failure, with infractions of the ceasefire by both sides resulting in several dozen casualties. Acknowledging its failure, Annan called for Iran to be "part of the solution", though the country has been excluded from the Friends of Syria initiative. The peace plan practically collapsed by early June and the UN mission was withdrawn from Syria. Annan officially resigned in frustration on 2 August 2012.

Rebel offensives (November 2012 - April 2013)

After Brahimi's ceasefire agreement officially ended on 30 October, the Syrian military expanded its aerial bombing campaign in Damascus. A bombing of the Damascus district of Jobar was the first instance of a fighter jet being used in Damascus airspace to attack targets in the city. The following day, Gen. Abdullah Mahmud al-Khalidi, a Syrian Air Force commander who was described by the state media as one of the country's top aviation experts, was assassinated by opposition gunmen in the Damascus district of Rukn al-Din. In early November 2012, rebels made significant gains in northern Syria. The rebel capture of Saraqib in Idlib governorate, which lies on the strategic M5 highway, further isolated Aleppo from government-controlled areas of the country. Due to insufficient anti-aircraft weapons, rebel units attempted to nullify the government's air power by destroying landed helicopters and aircraft on air bases. On 3 November, rebels launched an attack on the Taftanaz air base, a core base for the Syrian military's helicopter and bombing operations.

On 18 November, rebels took control of Base 46 in the Aleppo Governorate, one of the Syrian Army's largest bases in northern Syria, after weeks of intense fighting with government forces. Defected General Mohammed Ahmed al-Faj, who commanded the assault, hailed the capture of Base 46 and stated that nearly 300 Syrian troops had been killed and 60 had been captured, with rebels seizing large amounts of heavy weapons, including tanks. On 22 November, rebels captured the Mayadeen military base in the country's eastern Deir ez-Zor Governorate. Activists said this gave the rebels control of a large amount of territory east of the base, stretching to the Iraqi border. On 29 November, at approximately 10:26 UTC, the Syrian Internet and phone service was shut off for a two-day period. Syrian government sources denied responsibility and blamed the blackout on fiber optic lines near Damascus becoming exposed and damaged; Edward Snowden in August 2014 claimed that this Internet breakdown had been caused, though unintendedly, by hackers of the NSA during an operation to intercept Internet communication in Syria.

In mid-December 2012, American officials said that the Syrian military had resorted to firing Scud ballistic missiles at rebel fighters inside Syria. Reportedly, six Scud missiles were fired at the Sheikh Suleiman base north of Aleppo, which rebel forces had occupied. It is unclear whether the Scuds hit the intended target. The government denied this claim. Later that month, a further Scud attack took place near Marea, a town in a rebel-held area north of Aleppo near the Turkish border. The missile appeared to have missed its target. That same month, the British *Daily Telegraph* reported that the FSA had now penetrated into Latakia Governorate's Mediterranean coast through Turkey, and that the Syrian government's forces were unable to repel the FSA invasion thus far. In late December, rebel forces pushed further into Damascus, taking control of the adjoining Yarmouk and Palestine refugee camps, pushing out pro-government Popular Front for the Liberation of Palestine-General Command fighters with the help of other factions. Rebel forces launched an offensive against army positions in Hama governorate, later claiming to have forced army regulars to evacuate several towns and bases, and stating that "three-quarters of western rural Hama is under our control." Rebels also captured the northern town of Harem near the Turkish border in Idlib governorate, after weeks of heavy fighting.

On 11 January 2013, Islamist groups, including al-Nusra Front, took full control of the strategic Taftanaz air base in the northern Idlib governorate, after weeks of fighting. The air base, one of the largest in northern Syria, was often used by the military to carry out helicopter raids and deliver supplies. The rebels claimed to have seized helicopters, tanks and multiple rocket launchers, and other military equipment, before being forced to withdraw by a government counter-attack. The leader of the al-Nusra Front said the amount of weapons they took was a "game changer". On 11 February, Islamist rebels captured the town of Al-Thawrah in Ar-Raqqah Governorate and the nearby

Tabqa Dam, Syria's largest dam and a key source of hydroelectricity. The next day, rebel forces took control of Jarrah air base, located 60 kilometres (37 mi) east of Aleppo. The base had been used to launch bombing raids in Aleppo governorate, and had served as an important supply line for the Assad government. On 14 February, fighters from al-Nusra Front took control of Shadadeh, a town located in Al-Hasakah Governorate near the Iraqi border.

On 20 February, a car bomb exploded in the Mazraa neighborhood of Damascus near the Ba'ath Syrian Regional Branch headquarters, killing at least 53 people and injuring more than 235. None of the organized groups on either side in the conflict claimed responsibility. On 21 February, the FSA in Quasar began shelling Hezbollah positions in Lebanon. Prior to this, Hezbollah militants had been shelling villages near Quasar from within Lebanon. A 48-hour ultimatum was issued by a FSA commander on 20 February, warning the militant group to stop the attacks or face retaliation.

On 2 March, intense clashes between rebels and the Syrian Army erupted in the north-central city of Raqqa, with many reportedly killed on both sides. On the same day, Syrian troops regained several villages along the highway near Aleppo. By 3 March, rebels had overrun Raqqa's central prison, allowing them to free hundreds of prisoners, according to the SOHR. The SOHR also stated that rebel fighters were now in control of most of an Aleppo police academy in Khan al-Asal, and that over 200 rebels and government troops had been killed fighting for control of it.

On 4 March, rebel forces launched an offensive to capture Raqqa outright. By 6 March, the rebels had captured the entire city, effectively making Raqqa the first provincial capital to be lost by the Assad government. Residents of Raqqa celebrated by toppling a bronze statue of his late father Hafez Assad in the centre of the city. The rebels also seized two top government officials. On 18 March, the Syrian Air Force attacked rebel positions in Lebanon for the first time. The attack occurred at the Wadi al-Khayl Valley area, near the border town of Arsal. On 21 March, a suspected suicide bombing in the Iman Mosque in Mazraa district killed as many as 41 people, including the high profile pro-Assad Sunni cleric, Sheikh Mohammed al-Buti. On 23 March, several rebel groups seized the 38th division air defense base in southern Daraa governorate near a strategic highway linking Damascus to Jordan. On the next day, rebels captured a 25 km strip of land near the Jordanian border, which included the towns of Muzrib, Abdin, and the al-Rai military checkpoint.

On 25 March, rebels launched one of their heaviest bombardments of Central Damascus since the revolt began. Beginning in Kafr Sousehdistrict, mortars reached Umayyad Square, where the Ba'ath Party headquarters, Air Force Intelligence and state television are located. On 26 March, near the Syrian town of al-Qusayr, rebel commander Khaled al Hamad, who commands the Al Farooq al-Mustakilla Brigade and is also known by his nom de guerre Abu Sakkar, ate the heart and liver of a dead soldier and said "I swear to God, you soldiers of Bashar, you dogs, we will eat from your hearts and livers! O heroes of Bab Amr, you slaughter the Alawites and take out their hearts to eat them!" in an apparent attempt to increase sectarianism. Video of the event emerged two months later and resulted in considerable outrage, especially from Human Rights Watch which classified the incident as a war crime. According to the BBC, it was one of the most gruesome videos to emerge from the conflict to-date. On 29 March, rebels captured the strategic town of Da'el after days of fierce fighting. The town is located in Daraa Governorate, along the strategic highway connecting Damascus to Jordan. On 3 April, rebels captured a military base near the city of Daraa.

Government and Hezbollah offensives (April–June 2013)

On 17 April, government forces breached a six-month rebel blockade in Wadi al-Deif, near Idlib. Heavy fighting was reported around the town of Babuleen after government troops outflanked weakened rebel positions with troops attempting to secure control of a main highway leading to Aleppo. The break in the siege also allowed government forces to resupply two major military bases in the region which had been relying on sporadic airdrops. On 18 April, the FSA took control of Al-Dab'a Air Base near the city of al-Qusayr. The base had no aircraft and was being used primarily to garrison ground troops. Meanwhile, the Syrian Army re-captured the town of Abel. The SOHR director described the loss of the town by saying that it will hamper rebel movements between al-Qusayr and Homs city. According to him, the capture of the airport would have relieved the pressure on the rebels in the area, but their loss of Abel made the situation more complicated. The same day, rebels reportedly assassinated Ali Ballan, who was head of public relations at the Ministry of Social Affairs and a member of Syria's relief agency, in a restaurant at Mazzeh district in Damascus. On 21 April, government forces captured the town of Jdaidet al-Fadl, near Damascus.

In April, government and Hezbollah forces launched an offensive to capture rebel-held areas near al-Qusayr. On 21 April, pro-Assad forces captured the towns of Burhaniya, Saqraja and al-Radwaniya near the Lebanese border. By this point, eight villages had fallen to the government offensive in the area. On 24 April, after five weeks of fighting, government troops re-took control of the town of Otaiba, east of Damascus, which had been under rebel control for the previous eight months, serving as the main arms supply route from Jordan. Meanwhile in the north of the country, rebels took control of a key position on the edge of the strategic Mennagh Military airbase, on the outskirts of Aleppo. This allowed them to enter the airbase after months of besieging it.

On 2 May, government forces captured the town of Qaysa in a steady push north from the city's airport. Troops also retook the Wadi al-Sayeh central district of Homs, driving a wedge between two rebel strongholds. SOHR reported a massacre of over 100 people in the coastal town of Al Bayda, Baniyas, when the Syrian army stormed the town. However, this could not be independently verified due to movement restrictions on the ground. Yet the multiple video images that residents said they had recorded in Bayda and Ras al-Nabeh – particularly of small children, were so shocking that even some government supporters rejected Syrian television's official version of events, that the army had simply "crushed a number of terrorists." On 3 May, the Syrian army backed by the Shabiha reportedly committed a massacre of civilians near the city of Baniyas. The Syrian Observatory for Human Rights said that at least 50 people – and possibly as many as 100 – were killed and that dozens of villagers were still missing.

On 8 May, government forces captured the strategic town of Khirbet Ghazaleh, situated along the highway to the Jordanian border. Over 1,000 rebel fighters withdrew from the town due to the lack of reinforcements and ammunition. The loss of the town also resulted in the reopening of the government supply-route to the contested city of Daraa. The rebels continued to withdraw from other towns so as to not face the Army's advance along the highway. On 11 May, the rebels managed to cut a newly build desert road used as an Army supply route between central Syria and Aleppo's airport. On 12 May, government forces took complete control of Khirbet Ghazaleh and secured the highway near the town. By mid-May, due to the recent Army gains in retaking modest, but strategically important locations, military analysts pointed out that the government would have a major advantage in any future peace talks with the opposition and the West. Analysts on both sides credited the government advances to the major restructuring of their forces, which they filled with thousands of militia irregulars trained, at least in part, by Hezbollah and Iranian advisers in counter-insurgency operations. The government's success was also credited to the shift by the Army from conducting counter-insurgency operations to holding on to strategic areas and not trying to recapture the whole country and crush the rebellion.

On 13 May, government forces captured the towns of Western Dumayna, Haidariyeh, and Esh al-Warwar allowing them to block supplies to the rebels in al-Qusayr. On 16 May, rebels stated that they recaptured the town of Al-Qisa after launching a unified counter-offensive. On 17 May, rebels captured four villages in Eastern Hama, including the Alawite town of Tulaysiah. The villages were abandoned by its residents days before the rebels arrived. On 19 May, government forces captured the rebel-held town of Halfaya in Hama governorate. The Syrian army also launched its offensive against the rebel-held town of Qusayr after taking control of surrounding villages and countryside. A military source reported that the Army entered Qusayr, capturing the city center and the municipality building. One opposition activist denied this, but another confirmed it and stated the Army was in control of 60 percent of the city. During the day's fighting, Hezbollah commander Fadi al-Jazar was killed.

An anonymous opposition source told the Associated Press that the attack was launched from the east and the south and that Hezbollah fighters took control of the town hall within a few hours and that by the end of the day, rebel units were pushed out of most of Qusayr.

He added that the fighting was then concentrated in the northern part of the city. The attack appeared to surprise the rebels, who expected the army to push by the north on several rebel-controlled villages before attacking the city. The turning point of the offensive was reached when Hezbollah fighters took control of the Al Tal area overlooking Qusayr. Several rebels fighters accused some commanders from fleeing the Al tal area at the last minute.

Meanwhile SOHR reported that the Syrian army was at the area by the western neighborhood of al-Quseir in order to lay siege on the city itself. On 23 May, rebels captured a military base near the town of Nairab. By 29 May, government forces captured the al-Dabaa air base, north of al-Qusayr. On 1 and 2 June, after heavy fighting, the Syrian Army recaptured three of the Alawite villages that had been previously captured by the rebels in Eastern Hama governorate, after rebel forces retreated from the area. On 5 June, rebel forces withdrew from al-Qusayr, and the Syrian military and its allies took full control of the town. The following day, government forces captured the nearby village of Dabaa.

On 6 June, rebels attacked and temporarily captured the Quneitra border crossing which links the Israeli-occupied Golan Heights with the rest of Syria. However, the same day, government forces counter-attacked with tanks and armoured personnel carriers, recapturing the crossing. On 7 June, Syrian troops backed by Hezbollah captured two villages north of al-Qusayr: Salhiyeh and Masoudiyeh. The next day, they captured the village of Buwaydah, the last rebel-held village in the al-Qusayr region. Between 7 and 14 June, Army troops, government militiamen, and Hezbollah fighters launched operations in Aleppo Governorate. Over a one-week period, government forces had advanced both in Aleppo city and the countryside around the city, pushing back the rebels. However, on 14 June, according to an opposition activist, the tide had started reversing, after rebels managed to halt an armoured reinforcement column from Aleppo city for two government-held Shiite villages northwest of the city. As of 16 June, the rebels had been holding back the column for two days. Rebels claimed they destroyed one tank and killed 20 government soldiers northwest of the town of Maaret al-Arteek.

Before the column was stopped, government forces had captured the high ground at Maaret al-Arteek, threatening rebel positions. Government forces also managed to make some advances in the southern part of Aleppo governorate, capturing the village of Ain-Assan village. During the fighting in Aleppo city itself, on 13 June, government forces managed to temporarily advance into the rebel-held Sakhour district from two directions, but were soon repelled. Some described it as just simply another skirmish or possibly a probing attack and not a full assault.

On 10 June, Shia pro-government fighters from the village of Hatla, east of Deir al-Zour, attacked a nearby rebel position, killing four rebels. The next day, in retaliation for the attack, thousands of rebels attacked and captured the village, killing 60 residents, fighters and civilians, according to SOHR. 10 rebel fighters were killed during the attack.

At dawn on 13 June, rebels seized an Army position on the northern edge of the town of Morek, which is located on the strategic north-south highway, in fighting that killed six soldiers and two rebels. Later in the day, the Army shelled the base and sent reinforcements in an attempt to recapture the post. On 14 June, the Al Nusra front captured a military barracks near Idlib city, after three days of fighting. On 15 June, the Syrian Army captured the Damascus suburb of Ahmadiyeh near the city's airport. Rebels said fighting began after rebels entered the town to use it as a position to launch mortars on the Damascus airport. They added that fighting was ongoing. On 22 June, the Syrian Army captured the rebel stronghold town of Talkalakh. Four days later, the Army captured the town of Al-Qariatayn, also in Homs governorate.

Fighting between ISIS and other rebel groups (January - March 2014)

Tension between moderate rebel forces and ISIS had been high since ISIS attacked and captured the border town of Azaz from FSA forces on 18 September 2013. Conflict was renewed over Azaz in early October and in late November ISIS captured the border town ofAtme from an FSA brigade. On 3 January 2014, the Army of the Mujahideen, the Free Syrian Army and the Islamic Front launched an offensive against ISIS-held territory in Aleppo and Idlib provinces. A spokesman for the rebels said that rebels attacked ISIS in up to 80% of all ISIS held villages in Idlib and 65% of those in Aleppo.

By 6 January, opposition rebels managed to expel ISIS forces from the city of Raqqa, ISIS's largest stronghold and capital of the Raqqa province. On 8 January, opposition rebels expelled most ISIS forces from the city of Aleppo, however ISIS reinforcements from the Deir Ezzor province managed to retake several neighborhoods of the city of Raqqa. By mid January ISIS fighters retook the entire city of Raqqa, while rebels expelled ISIS fighters fully from Aleppo city and the villages west of it.

On 29 January, Turkish aircraft near the border fired on an ISIS convoy inside the Aleppo Provence of Syria, killing 11 ISIS fighters and 1 ISIS emir. In late January it was confirmed that rebels had assassinated ISIS's second in command, Haji Bakr, who was al-Qaeda's military council head and a former military officer in Saddam Hussein's army. By mid-February, the Al-Nusra Front joined the battle in support of rebel forces, and expelled ISIS forces from the Deir Ezzor province. By March, the ISIS forces fully retreated from the Idlib province. On 4 March, ISIS retreated from the Aleppo-Turkey border town of Azaz and other nearby villages, choosing instead to consolidate around Raqqa in an anticipation of an escalation of fighting with Al Nusra.

Continued Government and Hezbollah offensive (March 2014)

On 4 March, the Syrian army took control of Sahel in the mountainous Qalamoun region. On 8 March, government forces took over Zara, a strategic town in Homs province, further blocking rebel supply routes from Lebanon.

On 11 March, Government forces andHezbollah took control of the Rima Farms region, positioning themselves directly facing Yabrud. On 16 March, Hezbollah and government forces captured Yabrud, after Free Syrian Army fighters made an unexpected withdrawal, leaving the Al Nusra Front to fight in the city on its own. On 18 March, Israel used artillery against Syrian Army base, after four of its soldiers had been wounded by a roadside bomb while patrolling Golan Heights.

On 19 March, the Syrian army captured Ras al-Ain near Yabrud, after two days of fighting and al-Husn in Homs province, while rebels in the Daraa Province captured Daraa prison, and freed hundreds of detainees. On 20 March, the Syrian army took control of the Krak des Chevaliers in al-Husn. On 29 March, Syrian army took control of the villages of Flita and Ras Maara near the border with Lebanon.

Continued fighting (March - May 2014)

On 22 March, rebels took control of the Kesab border post in the Latakia Province. By 23 March, rebels had taken most of Khan Sheikhoun in Hama. During clashes near the rebel-controlled Kesab border post in Latakia, Hilal Al Assad, NDF leader in Latakia (who also founded the NDF) and one of Bashar Al Assad's cousins was killed by rebel fighters. On 4 April, rebels captured the town of Babulin, Idlib, located on the main highway. On 9 April, the Syrian army took control of Rankous in the Qalamoun region. On 12 April, rebels in Aleppo stormed the government-held Ramouseh industrial district in an attempt to cut the Army supply route between the airport and a large Army base. The rebels also took the Rashidin neighbourhood and parts of the Jamiat al-Zahra district. On 26 April, the Syrian army took control of Al-Zabadani. According to SOHR, rebels took control of Tell Ahrmar, Quneitra. Rebels in Daraa also took over Brigade 61 Base and the 74th battalion.

On 26 April, the FSA announced they had begun an offensive against ISIS in the Raqqa province, and had seized five towns west of Raqqa city. On 29 April, activists said that the Syrian army captured Tal Buraq near the town of Mashara in Quneitra without any clashes. On 7 May, a truce went into effect in the city of Homs, SOHR reported. The terms of the agreement include safe evacuation of Islamist fighters from the city, which would then fall under government control, in exchange for release of prisoners and safe passage of humanitarian aid for Nubul and Zahraa, two Shiite enclaves besieged by the rebels. On 18 May, the head of Syria's Air Defense, General Hussein Ishaq, died of wounds sustained during a rebel attack on an air defense base near Mleiha the previous day. In Hama governorate, rebel forces took control of the town of Tel Malah, killing 34 pro-Assad fighters at an army post near the town. Its seizure marked the third time rebels have taken control of the town.

Presidential election (June 2014)

Syria held a presidential election in government-held areas on 3 June 2014. For the first time in the history of Syria more than one person was allowed to stand as a presidential candidate. More than 9,000 polling stations were set up in government-held areas. According to the Supreme Constitutional Court of Syria, 11.63 million Syrians voted (the turnout was 73.42%). President Bashar al-Assad won the election with 88.7% of the votes. As for Assad's challengers, Hassan al-Nouri received 4.3% of the votes and Maher Hajjarreceived 3.2%. The Interior Ministry said there were 15.8 million eligible voters, both inside and outside Syria. Tens of thousands of Syrians abroad voted in the week leading up to the 3 June election day, although many of the more than 2.7 million Syrian refugees across the region either abstained or were excluded by voting laws. Belgium, Canada, Egypt, France,

Germany, Saudi Arabia, Turkey, UAE and the United States did not allow the elections to be held in the Syrian embassy. The vote did not take place in 40-60% of Syria, due to the areas being under rebel control. The areas under Kurdish militia control also did not allow voting, though some people still traveled to government held areas to vote. Rebels threatened attacks to disrupt the polls in government-held areas. The civilian death toll from shelling from the rebel side was at least 12. Syrian government warplanes bombed rebel areas while elections were held.

There were observers from more than 30 countries including Bolivia, Brazil, Cuba, Ecuador, India, Iran, Iraq, Nicaragua, Russia, Pakistan, South Africa and Venezuela. This delegation of observers, according to the The Guardian led by the government's chief international supporters, said Syria's election was transparent and free and the delegation blamed the US and its allies for 'crimes committed against the Syrian people.' Many critics of the Syrian government have denounced the election as "rigged" and "a farce", There were no independent monitors stationed at the polling stations. State employees were told to vote or face interrogation.

Continued fighting (June 2014 - July 2014)

Starting on 5 June, ISIS forces seized swathes of territory in Iraq in addition to heavy weapons and equipment from the Iraqi army, some of which they brought into Syria. Government airstrikes targeted ISIS bases in Raqqa and Hasakah in coordination with an Iraqi army counteroffensive. On 14 June, government forces retook the border town of Kessab in northern Latakia province, while rebels took over Tall al-Gomo near the town of Nawa in the Daraa Governorate, as well as reentering the Qalamoun area.

ISIS offensive and continued fighting (July 2014 - ongoing)

According to the Syrian Observatory for Human Rights, on 17 July 2014 Islamic State took control of the Sha'ar oil field, killing 90 pro-Assad forces while losing 21 Islamic State fighters. In addition, 270 guards and government-aligned fighters were missing, captured, or killed. About 30 government persons managed to escape to the nearby Hajjar field. On 20 July, the Syrian Army managed to secure the field, although fighting continued in its outskirts.

On July 25, the Islamic State took control of Base 17 near Raqqa.

On 7 August, Islamic State forces took the 93rd brigade Syrian army military base in Raqqa. ISIS used weapons captured from their offensive in Iraq to carry out the attack. Multiple suicide bombs also went off before the base was stormed.

On 13 August, IS forces took the towns of Akhtarin and Turkmanbareh from rebels in the Northern province of Aleppo. Islamic State forces also took a handful of nearby villages from other rebels. The other towns seized include Masoudiyeh, Dabiq and Ghouz. Rebels are now concerned about supply routes.

Also on 13 August, around 31 rebel fighters and eight Islamic State fighters were killed in fierce clashes in Aleppo province. On 14 August, Free Syrian Army commander Sharif As-Safouri admitted working with Israel and receiving anti-tank weapons from Israel and FSA soldiers also received medical treatment inside Israel. On 14 August, the Syrian army as well as Hezbollah militias retook the town of Mleiha. The Supreme Military Council of the FSA denied claims of Mleiha's seizure, rather the rebels have redeployed from recent advances to other defensive lines. Mleiha is strategically located just outside Damascus and has been held by the Islamic Front. Rebels had used the town to fire mortars and shell government held areas inside Damascus.

Meanwhile ISIS forces in Raqqa were launching a siege on Tabqa airbase, the Syrian government's last military base in Raqqa. Kuwaires airbase in Aleppo also came under fierce attack by ISIS.

On 16 August, the Kurdish and Syrian News Agency reported that 22 people were killed in the Southern village of Deraa by a car bomb which was detonated outside a mosque. The bomb was thought to be detonated by ISIS. Also on 16 August, fighters from the Islamic State seized the village of Beden in Aleppo province from rebels.

On 17 August, fighter jets from the Syrian air force carried out airstrikes on Islamic State positions in Ar Raqqa killing and wounding dozens of fighters. Several of the airstrikes targeted IS military councils. Also, the Syrian Army told all residents to leave the Lebanese village of Tfail because the Syrian army would be shelling it soon. On 18 August there were reports that the US Air force had carried out airstrikes on Islamic State militants in Raqqa Province. The Syrian military denied that there were any US air strikes in Syria.

On 19 August, a senior figure in the Islamic State who had prepared planned car and suicide bombs across Syria, Lebanon and Iraq was killed. Some reports said that he was killed when a bomb was detonated which was attached to his car by Hezbollah fighters. There were also several reports that he was killed by the Syrian army in the Qalamoun region, near the border with Lebanon.

On 19 August, American journalist James Foley was executed by ISIS, who claimed it was in retaliation for the United States operations in Iraq. Foley was kidnapped in Syria in 2012 by Shabiha militia, and later held in an airforce intelligence complex in Damascus. ISIS also threatened to execute Steven Sotloff, who was kidnapped at the Syrian-Turkish border in 2013. There are reports ISIS captured a Japanese national, two Italian nationals, and a Danish national as well. Syria has become the most dangerous country in the world for journalists; at least 70 have been killed covering the war, and more than 80 kidnapped, according to the Committee to Protect Journalists.

On 21 August, the Syrian army killed more than 140 Islamic State fighters in an ambush in Ar-Raqqa province during ISIS's siege of Tabqa airbase. Around seven Syrian soldiers were also killed. The Syrian air force also carried out around 15 airstrikes in Raqqa province. Also on 21 August, the Syrian army claimed to have taken back a village from Islamic State fighters in Raqqa province.

On 22 August, the Syrian army killed an Islamic State press officer in Raqqa province. The IS press officer was named as Abu Mosa.

On 22 August the Al-Nusra Front also released a video of captured Lebanese soldiers and demanded that Hezbollah withdraw from Syria under threat of their execution.

On 23 August, more than 24 ISIS fighters were killed in the battle for Tabqa airbase and 150 IS fighters were injured during clashes with the Syrian Army. On the same day, the Tabqa airbase was no longer encircled by IS fighters and the Syrian army had taken back M-42 Highway from IS fighters. This highway leads to the city of Salamiyyah in the Hama Governate. The highway will now allow key supplies to reach the Syrian army as they continue their assault on ISIS in Raqqa province. Also in Raqqa, the Syrian army took control of the town of Al-Ejeil. Also on 23 August, several senior UK and US figures urged Turkey to stop allowing ISIS to cross the border and go and fight in Syria and Iraq. There were also reports that IS was sending reinforcements to the Syrian province of Raqqa. The fighters were taken out of Iraq and sent to Syria. This came after days of fighting which left several IS fighters dead as they battled the Syrian army in Raqqa. The Syrian Observatory for Human Rights said at least 400 IS fighters had also been wounded in the previous five days in clashes with the Syrian Army and National Defense Force in Raqqa alone.

On 24 August, 32 rebels were killed in a land mine ambush performed by the Syrian army in Deraa.

On 24 August, the Islamic State seized Tabqa airbase from regime forces after days of bloody fighting. Prisoners taken by IS forces were executed a couple of days later and a video from the mass killing was posted on YouTube. The death toll varies from 120 to 250, depending on source.

On 26 August, the Syrian Air Force carried out more than 12 airstrikes against IS fighters and targets in the province of Deir-Ezzur. This was the first time the Syrian armed forces attacked IS in Deir-ezzur as the Syrian army pulls out of Raqqa and shifts to Deir-Ezzur in a bid to seize its oil and natural gas resources as well as strategically splitting IS territories into separate pieces.

On 27 August, an artillery shell fired from the Syrian army from Qunetira moderately injured a Israeli army officer. Also on 27 August, rebel forces captured the Syrian side of the Quneitra Israel-Syria border pass after heavy fighting.

On the 1st of September, the Syrian army had advanced in the Damascus suburb of Jobar after a intensive shelling campaign. Also, the Syrian army began shelling Al-Nusra positions in the Qunetira border post near Israel in a bid to free the captured UN peacekeepers. On the 2nd of September, Senior regional analysts and reporters said that "the force that is most able to challenge IS, is the Syrian armed forces and therefore the west will need to work with president Bashar Al Assad to combat the more serious threat of IS".

DESTRUCTION OF SYRIA'S CHEMICAL WEAPONS

On 9 September 2013, Russia urged Syria to put its' chemical weapons stockpile under international control. The initiative was expressed in the wake of American threat of attacking Syria after the chemical attack of 21 August. On 14 September, US and Russia announced in Geneva that they reached a deal on how Assad should give up his chemical weapons. On 23 June 2014, the OPCWDirector General Ahmet Üzümcü told reporters at a press conference that the last shipment of declared chemical weapons had left Syria on the Danish ship MV Ark Futura.

The entire chemical weapons stockpile was scheduled to be completely removed from the country by 6 February 2014, but fighting and the threat of attack by rebel groups severely delayed the removal process. Early on Wednesday 2 July 2014, Ark Futura arrived the port Gioia Tauro in southern Italy.

During the day, 78 containers with Syrias highest-priority chemicals were transported onto the U.S. cargo ship MV Cape Ray for destruction at sea. The transloading took place without incidents. On 7 July 2014, the destruction began at Cape Ray. It was expected to take about 60 days, and was completed long before schedule. On 19 August 2014, the OPCW Director General Ahmet Üzümcü confirmed that all chemical arms on board the

US ship Cape Ray was neutralized. Cape Ray will now sail to Germany and Finland where the effluent will be eliminated at industrial waste managementcompanies.

On 15 July 2014, Ark Futura arrived at Marchwood Military Port in the United Kingdom, where it offloaded the rest of Syria's Priority 1 chemicals for transportation to an destruction at Veolias hazardous waste facilities in Ellesmere Port. It then headed to Finland with some Priority 2 chemicals to be destroyed at a commercial facility at Riihimäki. The Norwegian vessel MV Taiko, has already delivered a consignment of Priority 2 chemicals to Finland for destruction at Riihimäki.

On 9 July 2014, Taiko arrived at Port Arthur in Texas, where the rest of the Priority 2 chemicals was offloaded and will be destroyed at a commercial facility there. Some military experts and observers suspect that the Syrian government may not have revealed the full extent of their stockpile and chemical capabilities. On 7 August 2014, the OPCW confirmed that 74.2% of Syria's CW stockpile has been destroyed so far.

Cluster Bombs

The Syrian army began using cluster bombs in September 2012. Steve Goose, director of the Arms division at Human Rights Watch said "Syria is expanding its relentless use of cluster munitions, a banned weapon, and civilians are paying the price with their lives and limbs," "The initial toll is only the beginning because cluster munitions often leave unexploded bomblets that kill and maim long afterward."

Scud Missile Attacks

In December 2012, the Syrian government began using Scud missiles on rebel-held towns, primarily targeting Aleppo. On 19 February, four Scud missiles were fired, three landed in Aleppo city and one on Tell Rifaat town, Aleppo governorate. Between December and February, at least 40 Scud missile landings were reported. Altogether, Scud missiles killed 141 people in the month of February. The United States condemned the Scud missile attacks. On 1 March, a Scud missile landed in Iraq. It is believed that the intention was to hit the Deir Ezzor governorate. On 29 March, a Scud missile landed on Hretan, Aleppo, killing 20 and injuring 50. On 28 April, a Scud missile landed on Tell Rifaat, killing four, two of them women and two of them children, SOHR reported. On 3 June, a surface to surface missile, not confirmed as a Scud, hit the village of Kafr Hamrah around midnight killing 26 people including six women and eight children according to SOHR.

Suicide Bombings

Rebel suicide bombings began in December 2011; the Al-Nusra Front has claimed responsibility for 57 out of 70 similar attacks through April 2013. The bombings have claimed numerous civilian casualties.

Barrel Bombs

A barrel bomb is a type of improvised explosive device used by the Syrian Air Force. Typically, a barrel is filled with a large amount of TNT, and possibly shrapnel (such as nails) and oil, and dropped from a helicopter. The resulting detonation can be devastating.

Thermobaric Weapons

Thermobaric weapons, also known as "fuel-air bombs," have been used by the government side during the Syrian civil war. Since 2012, rebels have said that the Syrian Air Force (government forces) is using thermobaric weapons against residential areas occupied by the rebel fighters, such as during the Battle of Aleppo and also in Kafr Batna. A panel of United Nations human rights investigators reported that the Syrian government used thermobaric bombs against the strategic town of Qusayr in March 2013. In August 2013, the BBC reported on the use of napalm-like incendiary bombs on a school in northern Syria.

SYRIAN CIVIL WAR

In March 2011, protests began in Syria against the Syrian government of Bashar al-Assad. In the following months, violence between demonstrators and security forces led to a gradual militarisation of the conflict. In August, al-Baghdadi began sending Syrian and Iraqi ISI members experienced in guerilla warfare across the border into Syria to establish an organisation there.

Led by a Syrian known as Abu Muhammad al-Julani, this group began to recruit fighters and establish cells throughout the country. In January 2012, the group announced its formation as *Jabhat al-Nusra li Ahl as-Sham*—Jabhat al-Nusra—more commonly known as al-Nusra Front. Al-Nusra grew rapidly into a capable fighting force, with popular support among Syrians opposed to the Assad government.

As *Islamic State of Iraq and the Levant,* 2013–14

On 8 April 2013, al-Baghdadi released an audio statement in which he announced that al-Nusra Front had been established, financed, and supported by the Islamic State of Iraq, and that the two groups were merging under the name "Islamic State of Iraq and Al-Sham".Al-Julani issued a statement denying the merger, and complaining that neither he nor anyone else in al-Nusra's leadership had been consulted about it.

In June 2013, Al Jazeera reported that it had obtained a letter written by al-Qaeda's leader Ayman al-Zawahiri, addressed to both leaders, in which he ruled against the merger, and appointed an emissary to oversee relations between them to put an end to tensions.

That same month, al-Baghdadi released an audio message rejecting al-Zawahiri's ruling and declaring that the merger was going ahead. Meanwhile, the ISIL campaign to free imprisoned ISIL members culminated in July 2013, with the group carrying out simultaneous raids on Taji and Abu Ghraib prisons, freeing more than 500 prisoners, many of them veterans of the Iraqi insurgency.In October 2013, al-Zawahiri ordered the disbanding of ISIL, putting al-Nusra Front in charge of jihadist efforts in Syria, but al-Baghdadi contested al-Zawahiri's ruling on the basis of Islamic jurisprudence, and his group continued to operate in Syria. In February 2014, after an eight-month power struggle, al-Qaeda disavowed any relations with ISIL.

According to journalist Sarah Birke, there are "significant differences" between al-Nusra Front and ISIL. While al-Nusra actively calls for the overthrow of the Assad government, ISIL "tends to be more focused on establishing its own rule on conquered territory". ISIL is "far more ruthless" in building an Islamic state, "carrying out sectarian attacks and imposing sharia law immediately". While al-Nusra has a "large contingent of foreign fighters", it is seen as a home-grown group by many Syrians; by contrast, ISIL fighters have been described as "foreign 'occupiers'" by many Syrian refugees. It has a strong presence in central and northern Syria, where it has instituted sharia in a number of towns. The group reportedly controlled the four border towns of Atmeh, al-Bab, Azaz and Jarablus, allowing it to control the entrance and exit from Syria into Turkey. Foreign fighters in Syria include Russian-speaking jihadists who were part of Jaish al-Muhajireen wal-Ansar (JMA). In November 2013, the JMA's Chechen leader Abu Omar al-Shishani swore an oath of allegiance to al-Baghdadi; the group then split between those who followed al-Shishani in joining ISIL and those who continued to operate independently in the JMA under new leadership.

In January 2014, rebels affiliated with the Islamic Front and the US-trained Free Syrian Army launched an offensive against ISIL militants in and around the city of Aleppo. In May 2014, Ayman al-Zawahiri ordered the al-Nusra Front to stop its attacks on its rival, ISIL. In June 2014, after continued fighting between the two groups, al-Nusra's branch in the Syrian town of Al-Bukamal pledged allegiance to ISIL. In mid-June 2014, ISIL captured the Trabil crossing on the Jordan–Iraq border, the only border crossing between the two countries. ISIL has received some public support in Jordan, albeit limited, partly owing to state repression there. ISIL has undertaken a recruitment drive in Saudi Arabia, where tribes in the north are linked to those in western Iraq and eastern Syria.

As *Islamic State,* 2014–present

On 29 June 2014, the organisation proclaimed itself to be a worldwide caliphate. Abu Bakr al-Baghdadi—known by his supporters asAmir al-Mu'minin, Caliph Ibrahim—was named its caliph, and the group renamed itself ad-Dawlah al-Islâmiyah. As a "Caliphate", it claims religious, political and military authority over all Muslims worldwide. The concept of it being a caliphate and the name "Islamic State" have been rejected by governments and Muslim leaders worldwide.

In June and July 2014, Jordan and Saudi Arabia moved troops to their borders with Iraq, after Iraq lost control of, or withdrew from, strategic crossing points that then came under the control of ISIL, or tribes that supported ISIL. There was speculation that Iraqi Prime Minister Nouri al-Maliki had ordered a withdrawal of troops from the Iraq–Saudi crossings in order "to increase pressure on Saudi Arabia and bring the threat of ISIS over-running its borders as well".

In July 2014, ISIL recruited more than 6,300 fighters, according to the Syrian Observatory for Human Rights, some of whom were thought to have previously fought for the Free Syrian Army. On 23 July 2014, Abu Sayyaf leader Isnilon Totoni Hapilon and some masked men swore loyalty to al-Baghdadi in a video, giving ISIL a presence in the Philippines. In September 2014, the group began kidnapping people for ransoming, in the name of ISIL.

On 3 August 2014, ISIL captured the cities of Zumar, Sinjar, and Wana in northern Iraq.Thousands of Yazidis fled up Mount Sinjar, fearful of the approaching hostile ISIL militants. The stranded Yazidis' need for food and water, the threat of genocide to them and to others announced by ISIL, along with the desire to protect US citizens in Iraq and support Iraq in its fight against ISIL, were all reasons for the 2014 American intervention in Iraq on 7 August and an aerial bombing campaign in Iraq which started on 8 August.

On 11 October 2014, it was reported that ISIL had dispatched 10,000 militants from Syria and Mosulto capture the Iraqi capital city of Baghdad, and Iraqi Army forces and Anbar tribesmen threatened to abandon their weapons if the US did not send in ground troops to halt ISIL's advance. On 13 October, ISIL fighters advanced to within 25 kilometres (16 mi) of Baghdad Airport.

At the end of October 2014, 800 radical militants gained partial control of the Libyan city of Derna and pledged their allegiance to Abu Bakr al-Baghdadi, thus making Derna the first city outside Syria and Iraq to be a part of the "Islamic State Caliphate". On 2 November 2014, according to the Associated Press, in response to the coalition airstrikes, representatives from Ahrar ash-Sham attended a meeting with al-Nusra Front, the Khorasan Group, ISIL, and Jund al-Aqsa, which sought to unite these hard-line groups against the US-led coalition and moderate Syrian rebel groups. However, by 14 November 2014, it was revealed that the negotiations had failed. On 10 November 2014, a major faction of the Egyptian militant group Ansar Bait al-Maqdis also pledged its allegiance to ISIL.

ISIL has often used water as a weapon of war. The closing of the gates of the smaller Nuaimiyah dam in Fallujah in April 2014, resulted in the flooding of surrounding regions, while water supply was cut to the Shia-dominated south. Around 12,000 families lost their homes and 200 km^2 of villages and fields were either flooded or dried up. The economy of the region also suffered with destruction of cropland and electricity shortages.

In mid-January 2015, a Yemeni official said that ISIL had "dozens" of members in Yemen, and that they were coming into direct competition with al-Qaeda in the Arabian Peninsula with their recruitment drive.

In January 2015, Afghan officials confirmed that ISIL had a military presence in Afghanistan, recruiting over 135 militants by late January. However, by the end of January 2015, 65 of the militants were either captured or killed by the Taliban, and ISIL's top Afghan recruiter, Mullah Abdul Rauf, was killed in a US drone strike in February 2015.

In late January 2015, it was reported that ISIL members had infiltrated the European Union and disguised themselves as civilian refugees who were emigrating from the war zones of Iraq and the Levant. An ISIL representative claimed that ISIL had successfully smuggled 4,000 fighters, and that the smuggled fighters were planning attacks in Europe in retaliation for the airstrikes carried out against ISIL targets in Iraq and Syria. However, experts believe that this claim was exaggerated to boost their stature and spread fear, although they acknowledged that some Western countries were aware of the smuggling. In early February 2015, ISIL militants in Libya managed to capture part of the countryside to the west of Sabha, and later, an area encompassing the cities of Sirte, Nofolia, and a military base to the south of both cities. In February 2015, it was reported that some Ansar al-Sharia in Yemen members had broken from al-Qaeda and pledged allegiance to ISIL.

On 16 February 2015, Egypt conducted airstrikes in Libya, in retaliation against ISIL's beheading of 21 Egyptian Christians. By the end of that day, 64 ISIL militants in Libya had been killed by the airstrikes, including 50 militants in Derna. However, by early March, ISIL had captured additional Libyan territory, including a city to the west of Derna, additional areas near Sirte, a stretch of land in southern Libya, some areas around Benghazi, and an area to the east of Tripoli.

On 7 March 2015, Boko Haram swore formal allegiance to ISIL, giving ISIL an official presence in Nigeria, Niger, Chad and Cameroon. On 13 March 2015, a group of militants from the Islamic Movement of Uzbekistan swore allegiance to ISIL; the group released another video on 31 July 2015 containing its spiritual leader also pledging allegiance. On 30 March 2015, the senior sharia official of Ansar al-Sharia in Libya, Abdullah Al-Libi, defected to ISIL.

From March through mid-April 2015, advances by Iraqi forces into ISIL-controlled territory were focused on Tikrit and the Saladin Governorate. In June 2015, the US Deputy Secretary of State announced that ISIL had lost more than 10,000 members in airstrikes over the preceding nine months.

In the same month, three simultaneous attacks occurred: two hotels were attacked by gunmen in Tunisia, a man was decapitated in France, and a bomb was detonated at a Shia mosque in Kuwait. ISIL claimed responsibility for the attacks in Kuwait and Tunisia. ISIL flags were present at the crime scene in France, but ISIL has not claimed responsibility for the attack. Responsibility for the November 2015 Paris attacks was also claimed by ISIL.

IRANIAN INVOLVEMENT IN THE SYRIAN CIVIL WAR

Iran and Syria are close strategic allies, and Iran has provided significant support for the Syrian Government in the Syrian Civil War, including logistical, technical and financial support, as well as training and some combat troops.

Iran sees the survival of the Syrian government as being crucial to its regional interests. Iran's supreme leader, Ali Khamenei, was reported in September 2011 to be vocally in favor of the Syrian government.

In the civil uprising phase of the Syrian civil war, Iran was said to be providing Syria with technical support based on Iran's capabilities developed following the 2009–2010 Iranian election protests. As the uprising developed into the Syrian civil war, there were increasing reports of Iranian military support, and of Iranian training of NDF (National Defence Forces) both in Syria, and in Iran. Iranian security and intelligence services are advising and assisting the Syrian military in order to preserve Bashar al-Assad's hold on power.

Those efforts include training, technical support, combat troops. By December 2013 Iran was thought to have approximately 10,000 operatives in Syria. But according to Jubin Goodarzi, assistant professor and researcher of Webster University, Iran aided the Assad regime with a limited number of deployed units and personnel, "at most in the hundreds ... and not in the thousands as opposition sources claimed". Lebanese Hezbollah fighters backed by Iran's government have taken direct combat roles since 2012. In the summer of 2013, Iran and Hezbollah provided important battlefield support for Assad, allowing it to make advances on the opposition.

In 2014, coinciding with the peace talks at Geneva II, Iran has stepped up support for Syrian President Assad. Syrian Opposition Interim Minister of Finance and Economy claimed that the "Iranian government has given more than 15 billion dollars" to Syria as of December 2013. According to the United Nations envoy to Syria, Staffan de Mistura, the Iranian government spends at least $6 billion annually on maintaining Assad's government. Nadim Shehadi, the director of the Fares Center for Eastern Mediterranean Studies at Tufts University, said that his research puts the actual number at $15 billion annually.

From January 2013 onward, the Iranian Revolutionary Guard Corps lost more than 1,100 troops in Syria. 360 of the deaths have been Iranian nationals, mostly officers, including several brigadier generals. The remaining deaths consist of auxiliaries recruited from Afghan and Pakistani immigrants inside Iran, who joined the IRGC in exchange for salaries and citizenship, in an arrangement similar to a Foreign Legion. The Afghans are recruited largely from refugees inside Iran, and usually had combat experience before joining the IRGC; their status as members of the Iranian military is only vaguely acknowledged and sometimes denied, despite the troops being uniformed fighters led by IRGC officers, trained and equipped in Iran, with state funerals involving uniformed IRGC personnel. Among the dead are 715+ Afghans and at least 66 Pakistanis. Officially, the Afghan auxiliaries are part of the independent Liwa Fatemiyoun group, though news media outside of Iran often simply refers to this organization as the "Fatemiyoun Brigade" or "Fatemiyoun Division" of the IRGC, while the Pakistanis are part of the "Zaynabiyun Brigade".

Background

Iran sees the survival of the Syrian government as being crucial to its interest. Its only consistent ally since the 1979 Islamic revolution, Syria provides a crucial thoroughfare to Hezbollah in Lebanon. Iranian leaders have cited Syria as being Iran's "35th province", with President Bashar al-Assad's Alawite minority led government being a crucial buffer against the influence of Saudi Arabia and the United States.

The Syrian city of Zabadani is vitally important to Assad and to Iran because, at least as late as June 2011, the city served as the Iranian Revolutionary Guard Corps's logistical hub for supplying Hezbollah. Prior to the Syrian war, Iran had between 2,000 and 3,000 IRGC officers stationed in Syria, helping to train local troops and managing supply routes of arms and money to neighboring Lebanon. In April 2014, Hossein Amir-Abdolahian, Iranian deputy foreign minister said *We aren't seeking to have Bashar Assad remain president for life. But we do not subscribe to the idea of using extremist forces and terrorism to topple Assad and the Syrian government.*

2011

In the civil uprising phase of the Syrian civil war, Iran was said to be providing Syria with technical support based on Iran's capabilities developed following the 2009–2010 Iranian election protests.

In April 2011 U.S. President Barack Obama and U.S. Ambassador to the United Nations Susan Rice accused Iran of secretly aiding Assad in his efforts to quell the protests, and there were reports of Syrian protesters hearing security-force members speaking Persian.

The Guardian reported in May 2011 that the Iranian government was assisting the Syrian government with riot control equipment and intelligence monitoring techniques. According to US journalist Geneive Abdo writing in September 2011, the Iranian government provided the Syrian government with technology to monitor e-mail, cell phones and social media. Iran developed these capabilities in the wake of the 2009 protests and spent millions of dollars establishing a "cyber army" to track down dissidents online. Iran's monitoring technology is believed to be among the most sophisticated in the world, perhaps only second to China.

2012

In May 2012, in an interview with the Iranian Students News Agency which was later removed from its website, the deputy head of Iran's Quds Force said that it had provided combat troops to support Syrian military operations. It was alleged by the Western media that Iran also trained fighters from Hezbollah, a Shia militant group based in Lebanon. Iraq, located between Syria and Iran, was criticized by the U.S. for allowing Iran to ship military supplies to Assad over Iraqi airspace. *The Economist* said that Iran had, by February 2012, sent the Syrian government $9 billion to help it withstand Western sanctions. It has also shipped fuel to the country and sent two warships to a Syrian port in a display of power and support.

In March 2012, anonymous U.S. intelligence officials claimed a spike in Iranian-supplied arms and other aid for the Syrian government. Iranian security officials also allegedly traveled to Damascus to help deliver this assistance. A second senior U.S. official said members of Iran's main intelligence service, the Ministry of Intelligence and Security, were assisting Syrian counterparts in charge of the crackdown.

According to a U.N. panel in May 2012, Iran supplied the Syrian government with arms during the previous year despite a ban on weapons exports by the Islamic Republic. Turkish authorities captured crates and a truck in February 2012, including assault rifles, machine guns, explosives, detonators, 60mm and 120mm mortar shells as well as other items on its border. It was believed these were destined for the Syrian government. The confidential report leaked just hours after an article appeared in *The Washington Post* revealing how Syrian opposition fighters started to receive more, and better, weapons in an effort paid for by Persian Gulf Arab states and co-ordinated partly by the US. The report investigated three large illegal shipments of Iranian weapons over the past year and stated "Iran has continued to defy the international community through illegal arms shipments. Two of these cases involved [Syria], as were the majority of cases inspected by the Panel during its previous mandate, underscoring that Syria continues to be the central party to illicit Iranian arms transfers."More anonymous sources were cited by the UN in May 2012, as it claimed arms were moving both ways between Lebanon and Syria, and alleged weapons brought in from Lebanon were being used to arm the opposition. The alleged spike in Iranian arms was likely a response to a looming influx of weapons and ammunition to the rebels from Gulf states that had been reported shortly before. On 24 July 2012, Iranian Revolutionary Guards Corp commander Massoud

Jazayeri said Iranians would not allow enemy plans to change Syria's political system to succeed.

In August 2012 Leon Panetta accused Iran of setting up a pro-Government militia to fight in Syria, and chairman of the joint chiefs of staff General Martin Dempsey compared it to the Mahdi Army of Iraqi Shia leader Muqtada al-Sadr. Panetta said that there was evidence that the Iranian Revolutionary Guards were attempting to "train a militia within Syria to be able to fight on behalf of the regime". 48 Iranians were captured by the FSA in Damascus, and U.S. officials said that the men who were captured were "active-duty Iranian Revolutionary Guard members".

In September 2012, Western intelligence officials stated that Iran had sent 150 senior members of the Iranian Revolutionary Guards to preserve the Assad government, and had also sent hundreds of tons of military equipment (among them guns, rockets, and shells) to the Assad government via an air corridor that Syria and Iran jointly established. These officials believed that the intensification of Iranian support had led to increased effectiveness against the Free Syrian Army by the Assad government.

According to rebel soldiers speaking in October 2012, Iranian Unmanned aerial vehicles had been used to guide Syrian military planes and gunners to bombard rebel positions. CNN reported that the UAV or drones—which the rebels refer to as "wizwayzi" were "easily visible from the ground and seen in video shot by rebel fighters".

Rebels have displayed captured aircraft they describe as Iranian-built drones — brightly colored, pilotless jets. They're accompanied by training manuals emblazoned with the image of Iran's revolutionary leader, the lateAyatollah Ruhollah Khomeini.

2013

In January 2013, a prisoner swap took place between the Syrian Rebels and the Syrian Government authorities. According to reports, 48 Iranians were released by the Rebels in exchange for nearly 2,130 prisoners held by the Syrian Government. Rebels claimed the captives were linked to the Iranian Revolutionary

Guard.US State Department spokeswoman Victoria Nuland described the Iranians as "members of the Iranian Revolutionary Guard," calling it "just another example of how Iran continues to provide guidance, expertise, personnel, technical capabilities to the Syrian regime."

Iran reportedly decided in June 2013 to send 4,000 troops to aid the Syrian government forces, described as a "first contingent" by writer/reporter Robert Fisk of *The Independent*, who added that the move underscores a Sunni vs. Shiite alignment in the Middle East. Iran was also reported to have proposed to open a new Syrian front against Israel in the Golan Heights, this coming a day after Egyptian President cut off diplomatic relations with Syria and demanded that Iran support for the pro Syrian-government Hezbollah end. A Syrian official called the severing of relations by Morsi "irresponsible" and said it was part of a move by the U.S. and Israel to exacerbate divisions in the region.

According to American officials questioned by journalist Dexter Filkins, officers from the Quds force have "coordinated attacks, trained militias, and set up an elaborate system to monitor rebel communications" in Syria from late 2012 to 2013. With help from the Hezbollah, and under the leadership of Quds Force general Qassem Soleimani, the al-Assad government has won back strategic territory from rebels in 2013, in particular an important supply route during the Al-Qusayr offensive in April and May.

In the fall of 2013 Iranian Brigadier General Mohammad Jamali-Paqaleh of the Revolutionary Guards was killed in Syria, reportedly while volunteering to defend a Shia shrine. In February, General Hassan Shateri, also of the Revolutionary Guards, had been killed while travelling from Beirut to Damascus.

2014

Iran has stepped up support on the ground for Syrian President Assad, providing hundreds more military specialists to gather intelligence and train troops. This further backing from Tehran, along with deliveries of munitions and equipment from Moscow, is helping to keep Assad in power. This surge of support was in part a decision strongly promoted by Qasem Soleimani, the head of the Quds force, to exploit the outbreak of infighting between rebel fighters and the al-Qaeda inspiredIslamic State of Iraq and Sham (ISIS). Former Iranian Revolutionary Guard commander said Iranian forces, said that "top Quds force commanders were tasked with advising and training Assad's military and his commanders", adding that "Revolutionary Guards directed the fighting on the instructions of the Quds Force commanders". In addition there are thousands of Iranian paramilitary Basij volunteer fighters as well as Shi'ites from Iraq. Former Iranian official and a Syrian opposition source also put the count of those auxiliary forces in the thousands.

A Syrian opposition source said in recent months Iranian led forces had begun operating in coastal areas including Tartous and Latakia. They have local ID cards, wear Syrian military fatigues and work with the elite Syrian air force intelligence unit.

2015

Citing two Lebanese sources, Reuters reported on October 1, 2015 that hundreds of Iranian troops arrived in Syria over the previous 10 days and would soon join Syrian government forces and their Lebanese Hezbollah allies in a major ground offensive backed by Russian air strikes. The *Wall Street Journal* reported on October 2, 2015 that Iran's Revolutionary Guard (the IRGC) has had some 7,000 IRGC members and Iranian paramilitary volunteers operating in Iran and was planning to expand its presence in the country through local fighters and proxies. The *Journal* also reported that some experts estimate 20,000 Shiite foreign fighters are on the ground, backed by both Shiite Iran and Hezbollah.

At least 121 IRGC troops, including several commanders, have been killed in the Syrian Civil War since it began.

Key victories were achieved with substantial support provided by the Quds force, namely the al-Ghab plains battles, Aleppooffensives, Dara'aya offensives of 2015 and the al-Qusayr offensives which established government and Hezbollah control over the northern Qalamoun region and the border crossings from Lebanon to Syria. In June 2015, some reports suggested that the Iranian military were effectively in charge of the Syrian government troops on the battlefield.

After the loss of Idlib province to a rebel offensive in the first half of 2015, the situation was judged to have become critical for Assad's survival. High level talks were held between Moscow and Tehran in the first half of 2015 and a political agreement was achieved. On 24 July General Qasem Soleimani visited Moscow to devise the details of the plan forcoordinated military action in Syria.

In mid-September 2015, the first reports of new detachments from the Iranian revolutionary guards arriving in Tartus and Latakia in west Syria were made. With much of the Syrian Arab Army and National Defence Forces units deployed to more volatile fronts, the Russian Marines and Iranian Revolutionary Guard (IRG) have relieved their positions by installing military checkpoints inside the cities of Slunfeh (east Latakia Governorate), Masyaf (East Tartus Governorate) and Ras al-Bassit(Latakia coastal city). There were also further reports of new Iranian contingents being deployed to Syria in early October 2015.

On 1 October 2015, citing two Lebanese sources, Reuters reported that hundreds of Iranian troops had arrived in Syria over the previous 10 days to join Syrian government forces and their Lebanese Hezbollah allies in a major ground offensive backed by Russian air strikes that started on 30 September 2015 and were welcomed as vital by Bashar Assad.

On 8 October 2015, brigadier general Hossein Hamadani, the deputy to General Qasem Soleimani in Syria was killed. On 12 October, two more senior commanders of the Iranian Revolutionary Guard Corps, Hamid Mokhtarband and Farshad Hassounizadeh, were reported by Iranian media to have been killed in Syria.

At the end of October 2015, Iran agreed to take part in the Syria peace talks in Vienna. The talks for the first time brought Iran to the negotiating table with Saudi Arabia, which are said to be engaged in a proxy war in Syria. The talks however were promptly followed by an exchange of sharp rebukes between Iran's and Saudi Arabia's top officials that cast doubt on Iran's future participation in those.

PUTIN'S AMBITIONS FOR THE WAR AGAINST ISIS

Vladimir Putin admitted what had been known to Western intelligence services (and, surely, Russian ones, too) for some time: a bomb, likely planted by terrorists with connections to ISIS, brought down a passenger plane flying from Sharm el-Sheikh, Egypt, to St. Petersburg, Russia, on October 31st, killing all two hundred and twenty-four people on board. At a meeting of security officials at the Kremlin—the sort of event that is more a show for the Russian state media than a substantive policy session—Alexander Bortnikov, the head of the Federal Security Service (F.S.B.), told Putin that an improvised explosive device equivalent to a kilogram of T.N.T. was to blame. Putin, who appeared genuinely moved by the attack and its implications, called for a moment of silence, and then said of those responsible, "We will find them anywhere on the planet and punish them." Russian military operations, he added, will prove that "vengeance is inevitable."

In the days after the tragedy, the Kremlin downplayed talk of terrorism. The minister of transport said that claims by an ISISaffiliate in Egypt to have bombed the plane "can't be considered accurate." Earlier this month, when British officials said they had evidence that an explosive had been planted on board and cancelled direct flights from Sharm el-Sheikh, Konstantin Kosachyov, a Russian parliamentarian, claimed that Britain's real intention was to put "psychological pressure" on Russia. "There are plenty in the world who would prefer to knowingly and without the necessary grounds write off this catastrophe as jihadists' response to Russia," he said. That argument showed some strain two weeks ago, when Russia, too, decided to suspend all flights from Egypt. Still, Putin's spokesman insisted that the cancellation of Egypt flights did "not mean that a terrorist attack is the main suspected cause of the catastrophe."

Why the lag in announcing what seemed increasingly certain? Most likely, Putin and his advisers simply didn't know how to react—and when Putin doesn't like his options he tends to stall for time. (That is one advantage of an authoritarian system: there is no legislature or opposition party, and little pressure from the media, to force a decision.)

Had the Kremlin acknowledged that the plane was blown up by ISIS, as an affiliate of the group claimed in the days after the disaster, it would have demonstrated exactly the sort of cause-and-effect it has been trying to avoid in its Syria war. State television has serialized the Russian bombing campaign in the high American style, with splashy news footage provided by military satellites and cameras mounted on warheads, speaking to Russians' buried yearnings for geopolitical greatness: public support for Russia's intervention grew from thirty-nine percent in September to fifty-five percent in October, according to the Levada Center, an independent polling agency.

Yet Putin and his advisers seem to have considered this mood potentially fragile, the euphoria of a media-friendly bombing campaign that appeared to cost little and risk nothing. The grim news of two hundred and twenty-four dead countrymen could make a distant war seem awfully close—not only leading to questions about the virtue of Russian policy but also requiring Putin do something in response.

Then came Paris, where terrorists with connections to ISIS killed a hundred and twenty-nine people last Friday. The scenes of carnage changed thinking in world capitals, not least Moscow. Gleb Pavlovsky, a former Putin adviser turned critic, told the Ekho Moskvy radio station that the Kremlin has known for some time the true cause of the crash but chose to stay silent. A terrorist act "would certainly have been perceived by public opinion as a punishment for the invasion of Syria. And that would be a painful thing to deal with," he said. But then, he went on, "The terrible events in Paris solved this problem." After Paris, the notion of an ISIS bomb on a Russian plane no longer served as an unwelcome reminder of a faraway war's potential costs at home. Rather, it proved that Russia and the West faced a single enemy, and that there could be no doubt that the world's powers would need to unite against an evil so horrible.

Putin's argument to the rest of the world is similar to the one he is making to his own people. In his telling, Russia tried to cooperate with the United States and others in fightingISIS—an offer the West rejected. (He neglects to mention that Russia has prioritized targets other than ISIS in Syria, choosing instead to hit other groups that threaten the Assad regime.) "It seems to me that that now, finally, the realization is coming to everyone that only all of us together can fight effectively," Putin said at the G-20 Summit, in Antalya. He is a adherent of Yalta-era geopolitics, in which states achieve victory together and then sit down to carve up the world. And he wants today's global powers to form an alliance similar to the one that defeated Nazism.

The Paris attacks, and the prospect that this was not ISIS's last attack in Europe, seem to be nudging Western powers in this direction. Putin badly wants them to reconsider his pariah status and forgive his meddling in Ukraine. What he may get, if anything, is a tactical alliance to fight ISIS without the lifting of sanctions or the end of Russia's broader diplomatic isolation. Yet it will be hard for the West to maintain that sort of discipline. If last year's G-20 summit, held in the wake of Russia's annexation of Crimea, represented the apex in the public shunning of Putin—so much so that he went home early—then this year's summit marked his return, for now, to the club of respectable statesmen.

President Obama and Putin had a one-on-one meeting that lasted nearly an hour, thus continuing the thaw of the diplomatic deep freeze in which the Obama Administration had once wanted to plunge him. British Prime Minister David Cameron also met with Putin in private. But no public statement was stronger than that of French President François Hollande, who, staying back in Paris, declared that a "single coalition"—including Russia—was needed to fight ISIS.

Questions about the utility of such an alliance come down to what Putin really wants to achieve in Syria, and how much Russian policy overlaps with the interests of the current U.S.-led coalition. Until now, Russia's bombing campaign has focused not on ISIS targets but on the other rebel groups fighting Bashar al-Assad, serving as the air force to a combined Syrian-Iranian push to recapture territory lost to the rebels. On Wednesday, a military source told reporters at *Vedomosti*that Russian artillery was providing "covering fire" to Syrian troops in the Homs region. The campaign recalls Russia's insertion of its soldiers into Ukraine at key moments in the war there: a jolt of military force to give its proxy a battlefield advantage before a likely round of diplomatic negotiations. A Russian draft proposal, obtained by Reuters last week, calls for a constitutional reform lasting up to eighteen months and then early presidential elections.

Assad himself has never been a sacred figure for Russia. The Kremlin would like him to stay—and, particularly after watching the catastrophic overthrow of Muammar Qaddafi, in Libya, certainly prefers that outcome to anything that resembles externally imposed regime change—but he could just as easily be sacrificed. But Putin's Syria policy was always only partially about Syria. It was also about Ukraine, where Putin is loath to give up his ability to dial tensions down or up at will to get what he wants from Kiev and its Western backers.

He presumably would like to keep that instrument without having to pay for it. Five Ukrainian soldiers were killed on November 14th, the highest toll in two months, and the deaths will continue as long as Ukrainian President Petro Poroshenko does not implement his part of a political deal with rebel-held areas to Putin's liking. Above all, in Syria, Putin seeks to extend Russia's influence, both in the Middle East and globally, with his country granted the kind of superpower status that he sees as its birthright.

The sight, on Tuesday, of dozens of cruise missiles launched from Russia's strategic bomber fleet of propeller-driven Tu-95s and gargantuan Tu-160s—the first use of such aircraft in combat since the Soviet war in Afghanistan—was meant to make the point in unsubtle terms.

Stalin and Churchill may have been rivals, but they were equals of a sort, leaders of storied nations with their own undeniable national interests and prerogatives, joined together in an alliance of necessity. This is what Putin means when he told a Russian naval commander, on Tuesday, to work with French ships "as allies." It may sound like wishful thinking, for now, on Putin's part—but no one else has come up with anything better.

6

Peace Process between India and Pakistan

HURDLES TO PEACE

EVEN as positive signs were emerging on the resumption of official-level talks between India and Pakistan, trouble once again erupted on the Line of Control (LoC) following the killing of five Indian soldiers on August 6. The Indian Army was quick to blame its Pakistani counterpart for the killings, and the charge was denied strenuously by both the Pakistan Army and the government in Islamabad.

The flare-up came right on the heels of statements made by the newly elected Pakistani political leadership for a quick resumption of the dialogue process at the highest levels. The Prime Ministers of India and Pakistan, Manmohan Singh and Nawaz Sharif, are scheduled to meet on the sidelines of the United Nations General Assembly session in September.

Sharif was quick to express his condolences for the loss of five "precious lives" and once again emphasised his desire for an improvement in the ties between the two countries. Since returning to power, Sharif has been saying that the two countries should give priority to increasing their trade and economic ties.

Currently, India accounts for just 1.2 per cent of Pakistan's exports, and only 0.9 per cent of India's exports go to Pakistan. Sharif holds the overall charge of the Defence and Foreign

Ministries. He reiterated that the two countries "need more dialogue" to address the frequent flare-ups along the LoC. "Both countries need more robust rules of engagement to build on and to ensure adherence to the 2003 ceasefire agreement," he said.

Indian reaction

India's Defence Minister A.K. Antony had suggested initially that the killing of the soldiers was the handiwork of non-military actors. But he was forced to backtrack on his statement on the floor of Parliament under pressure from the opposition and the Prime Minister's Office (PMO), and he stated that Pakistani forces were indeed complicit in the killings.

It was claimed that the Minister had not originally reflected the Army's view that the regular Pakistan Army forces deployed along the LoC were responsible for the intrusion and the killings. The Directors General of Military Operations (DGMOs) of both the armies spoke on the hotline the day after the incident and no breaches of the ceasefire agreement were reported.

The Indian electronic and print media had by that time gone on an overdrive, claiming that there was sufficient proof of the Pakistan Army's involvement, and demanded an immediate military riposte from the Indian side to avenge the killings.

With the country's politics already gripped by election fever, all the parties, including the Congress, which heads the United Progressive Alliance (UPA) coalition government at the Centre, jumped onto the "revenge" bandwagon. The "Youth Congress" tried to outdo the activists of the Bharatiya Janata Party (BJP) in their exhibition of patriotic fervour. Noisy demonstrations were held in front of the Pakistan High Commission, and the Pakistan International Airlines' office in New Delhi was vandalised.

The August 6 incident could have been triggered by an event that went largely unreported in the Indian media. The Pakistani media reported that five villagers from the Pakistani side of the LoC were kidnapped by Indian soldiers on July 28.

There was also speculation that the ambush of the five Indian soldiers was a response to the killing of five militants in Kupwara in Kashmir by the Indian security forces in late July. Militant groups in Kashmir and those supporting them in Pakistan had sworn revenge.

Firing from the Indian side has resulted in the death of a few Pakistani soldiers in the last couple of months. In June this year, one Indian soldier was killed on the LoC, just after Sharif rode back to power. The Indian Army said that he had fallen victim to unprovoked firing from the other side. But the incident was played down by both the Indian government and the media. Sadly, this time New Delhi chose to succumb to jingoistic pressures and electoral compulsions.

INDIA - PAKISTAN LOOK FOR BILATERAL SOLUTIONS SANS OUTSIDERS

There is a shifting discourse on India – Pakistan relations in the West holding rivalry between two nuclear armed neighbours as the root cause of current impasse in Afghanistan. The discourse runs on the lines that India – Pakistan are reaching a negative crest in their relationship underscored by growing economic and military asymmetry. This according to western analysts is enhancing the Pakistani insecurities that has resulted in three negative movements in Pakistani security discourse.

First is Pakistan's attempt to increase its nuclear arsenal both qualitatively and quantitative, making it the fastest growing arsenal in the world. Second and even more destabilising is development of battle field nuclear weapons by mounting them on short range and cruise missiles. What is most dangerous and destabilising is the attempt to link these tactical weapons with their conventional warfare doctrine in an attempt to deny India so called space for conventional war "under nuclear overhang".

The second perspective is the growing India – Pakistan rivalry and jockeying for strategic space in Afghanistan in a clear attempt to hyphen India once again. This perception is fuelled by nervous Pakistani military establishment which feels the future political discourse in Afghanistan including the Quetta Shura led Taliban may not be as favourable to them as indeed they have been able to perpetuate under the veneer of "TINA" factor and salience of Pakistan as logistic support hub. This is changing as the American and NATO forces begin their pull out and logistic route through Pakistan loses its relevance. What is more worrisome for Pakistani establishment is the fact even the Taliban in whatever form of reintegration it joins the political process they will also realise that for the future economic development and meting aspirational needs of "emirate" need to have good relations both with West and other major donor countries that puts India right in front.

So Pakistan is attempting to use its current leverages by creating post 2014 horror scenarios and draw on the shaken sensibilities of the west and cut a deal that ensures its post pull out relevance and curry favour with Taliban as an honest broker. In this melting pot they throw in the Haqqani group to provide further credibility to its strategic depth story.

However there is a change in the attitude of Pakistani interlocutors (Track II) over the past six months or so. Earlier they were dismissive about the West's ability to hold fast in Afghanistan leading to hasty pull out following which the afghan Army they believed was sure to collapse.

The import of both post 2014 scenario in terms of relative credibility of ANA seen in recent operational performance and feasibility of substantial presence of Western forces at least of counter insurgency and combat support operations including cross border drone attacks have made them to rethink their own position based on spoilers role?

So the attempt now is to use its current but fast diminishing leverages to create a space in post 2014 scenario that ensures Pakistan's interests are not harmed and use that as a base to leverage its position from thereon.

Third and last issue is improvement of relations with India and providing great publicity to these moves as a means to put pressure on India to help gain give both political and economic bargains as part of grand reconciliation brokered by the west.

The current discourse of India – Pakistan rivalry being central to the deteriorating situation in Afghanistan is part of this. Pakistani military establishment believes that as long as it can leverage both the cross border terrorism as also the conventional asymmetry through use of nuclear card it has little problem in managing relations with India. In fact Pakistan wants to use "regional stability" and "building bridges" with India card to extract maximum mileage in bilateral relations through Western pressure concerned with situation in Pakistan.

This is not the only game plan, it realises that there are enough constituencies in India that are keen to normalise relations with Pakistan at any costs, secure in the belief that the three aspects highlighted particularly the nuclear and growing internal instability in Pakistan will force Indian elites to seek early dialogue and concessions.

The Pakistani perspective needs to be seen from larger geo strategic perspective wherein cornered international forces are willing to make any compromises, accommodation and even arm twisting to ensure early and somewhat credible exit. It is this fear of pre pull out instability that Pakistan is attempting to leverage.

India, which wants stability on its Western borders with Pakistan and also in Afghanistan, is caught in a bind. What are the options? Will attempt to flag three possible courses;

- Clear message to Pakistan and international community that India reserves the right of acting in self defence and restoring deterrence credibility if another Mumbai 26/11 attack was to take place. As such an attack will cross the threshold of Indian tolerance leaving no option for Indian establishment to act.
- Second, India must look at its engagement in Afghanistan from the cold prism of national self interest. If these demand training of national security forces for security of national sovereignty or fight against subversive forces from within than it must support the Government of Afghanistan including developmental assistance as it has been doing all these years.
- Lastly any dialogue with Pakistan must be based on clear cut objectives. We must engage with Pakistan but must

make clear both terms and redlines. Pakistan must address three important India concerns, stop cross border terror. The insidious comments such as no guarantees on Kashmir being disputed territory will not work. Second it must address the issue of bringing to quick justice perpetrators of 26/11 including Hafiz Saeed. The proposed dialogue with radical groups must address this issue with clear commitment of Army being on board in this political move.

Next Pakistan must move forward on normalising economic relations with India. This must be on reciprocal basis with India certainly offering greater concession provided Pakistan shows positive intent that could include, MFN and transit rights for India.

Given the right atmospherics two suggestions can be considered. One rethink on IPI pipeline and second a Free Trade Zone around Lahore where large number of industries can participate and use Pakistani super highways as export routes from either Karachi or Gwadar. Despite US and other concerns both can be win-win options.

It is important that both India and Pakistan must remain committed in bilateral discourse sans external leverages. There is a need to try and shed baggage of the past and look for innovative solutions.

What should be clear to Pakistani is the fact that India does not conflict but improved relations, having said that there can be no question of allowing Pakistan to exploit geo political scenario at India's behest. In the post 2014 scenario it will be better that both learn to sink their differences and move forward in resolving bilateral issues.

It is however important for Pakistan to understand that Indian state is resilient enough not to be undermined by cross border terrorism which must be discarded as instrument of state policy. Simultaneously India would like it to be internally strong to deal with its own challenges posed by radical and extremist ideologies.

KASHMIR: STANCES OF PAKISTAN AND INDIA

The checkered history of Pak-India relations is mired by suspicion and covert as well as open wars. Kashmir, according to the Partition formula, was likely to be part of Pakistan but the Indian government acted otherwise and occupied a large part of the state by military action. The people of Kashmir have invariably been challenging this occupation, initially through peaceful means and subsequently by armed resistance. Islamabad holds that the people of Kashmir should have the right to decide their destiny in a fair and free plebiscite under the relevant United Nations Security Council (UNSC) resolutions. Traditionally, Pakistan's Kashmir policy has revolved around this historical stance. The country has always claimed that the people of Jammu and Kashmir (J&K) are suffering under Indian rule and seek its help. Thus, the government and the people of Pakistan have always been on the forefront of the Kashmir cause, despite the huge cost involved.

However, notwithstanding its traditional stand on Kashmir, Islamabad has never hesitated to try fresh approaches for settling this vexed problem. Pakistan's first military ruler, General Muhammad Ayub Khan (1907-74) engaged with India in pursuit of mutually acceptable solution in which the United States and United Kingdom played an arbitrary role during 1962-63. However, New Delhi was not willing to concede any meaningful concession, apart from handing over a 3,500-square-mile slice of border area adjacent to Muzaffarabad. In return, it demanded a final settlement on the basis of the status quo. Subsequently, India took advantage of the political turmoil in East Pakistan and invaded it. After a brief war, East Pakistan became the independent state of Bangladesh. This had a huge psychological impact on Pakistan's security establishment and on the psyche of the nation.

To mend ties, Indian Prime Minster Indira Gandhi and her Pakistani counterpart Zulfikar Ali Bhutto reached an agreement at Simla to settle the Kashmir dispute through peaceful means. However, this agreement did not materialize as both countries later offered different interpretations of the draft agreement and to the verbal understanding that had been reached between the two heads of state, which had not been properly documented.During 1973-1989, considerable time was given to bilateralism to settle this dispute but, due to various pretexts, this opportunity too was lost.

Ironically, it was New Delhi that had taken the Kashmir issue to the United Nations in 1948 and accepted its resolutions, which basically upheld the Kashmiri people's right to self-determination. But India never prepared to implement these resolutions.

A recent revelation confirms that Jawaharlal Nehru, who was India's Prime Minister in 1948, had made commitments on the UN resolutions merely to buy time and was not serious about implementing them in any way. To strengthen its rule over Kashmir, India gradually clipped the state government's powers and declared it an integral part of India.

Despite two open wars, one nearly full-scale war (i.e. the Kargil confrontation in 1999) over Kashmir, and the Tashkent and Simla agreements between Pakistan and India, the Kashmir dispute remains unresolved. Meanwhile, an armed resistance movement continues inside Indian held Kashmir (IHK) and the masses have rendered huge sacrifices to obtain the right of self-determination. Until 9/11, both countries had been engaged in periodic negotiations. The Indian Prime Minster Atal Behari Vajpayee visited Lahore in February 1999 and Pakistan's President General Pervez Musharraf went to Agra in 2001 to meet the Indian leadership to find a solution to all the intractable problems, particularly the Kashmir problem. But the two countries failed to narrow down their divergent views. Thus both these summits, despite the initial fervor, proved futile and added to despair among the people and leaders on both sides.

HUMAN RIGHTS ABUSES IN KASHMIR

Human rights abuses in all the administered areas areas of Kashmir have been reported by non governmental agency's such as Human Rights Watch

Jammu and Kashmir

Human rights abuses in Jammu and Kashmir, a disputed territory administered by India, are an ongoing issue, ranging from mass killings, forced disappearances, rape, encounter killings, torture and the use of child soldiers by insurgents to political repression and suppression of freedom of speech. The Indian central reserve police force and border security personal and variousparamilitary groups have been accused, of committing systematic human rights abuses against the Muslim majority and Hindu minority population.

Paramilitary Groups

During the eruption of armed rebellion the Islamic insurgency has claimed to have specifically targeted the Hindu Kashmiri Pandits minority and violated their human rights. Reports by Indian government state 219 Kashmiri pandits were killed and around 1,40,000 migrated due to millitancy while over 3000 stayed in the valley. Reports from Amnesty International, Human Rights Watch and the International Commission of Jurists confirmed Indian reports of systematic human rights violations by Pakistan-backed militants.

According to a resolution passed by the United States Congress in 2006, Islamic terrorists infiltrated the region in 1989 and since then nearly 400,000 Pandits were either murdered or forced to leave their ancestral homes.

These groups which received weapons and other support from Pakistan targeted the Hindus in the Kashmir valley forcing an estimated 100,000 to flee and an estimated 350,000 are displaced since 1990.

The Hizb-ul-Mujahideen which was founded in 1980's as a militant wing of Jamaat-e-Islami in conjunction with Lashkar-e-Tayyiba carried out a massacre of 23 people including women and children in Wandhamaforces and two years later in another joint operation they massacred 35 Sikh men in Chattisinghpora.

Pakistan-backed paramilitary groups have also been accuse of using children as young as 10 to act as messengers and spies.

They have also use children to throw grenades at security forces and to plant explosive devices. Militant groups have also kidnapped journalists, tortured and killed them and have intimidated newspapers into not publishing story's on human rights abuses.

Indian Security Forces

In July 1990 Indian military was given special powers under Armed Forces (Special Powers) Act, 1958(AFSPA), which human rights groups claim gives the security force virtual immunity for crimes committed. On the 26 of February 2009 the chief minister stated the act should be repealed, the security forces however said that revoking the act would be detrimental to security and help terrorist moral.

In 1992 the International Labour Organization has described the abuses carried out as having "reached a staggering proportion" and that they were "unprecedented in it's brutality". International NGO's as well as the US state department have documented human rights abuses carried out during India's counter terrorism operations, disappearances, torture and arbitrary executions have all been carried out with impunity.

Human rights watch has also accused the Indian security forces of using children as spies and messengers, although the Indian government denies this allegation. India has also created auxiliaries made up from captured or surrendered militants. These groups have targeted reporters and human rights activists, they have also been accused of committing over 200 rapes in an attempt to intimidate the local population.

The security forces have also recruited ex service personal to set up village defense committees, these groups have carried out extra judicial killings, assaults and other human rights violations.

An investigation by the Jammu and Kashmir state human rights commission has found 2730 bodies in unmarked graves at 38 sites in northern Kashmir. At least 574 of these were identified as being local people, though the government had previously stated the graves held only militants they had been unable to identify and that most had been Pakistani.

HUMAN RIGHTS ABUSES IN JAMMU AND KASHMIR

Human rights abuses in Jammu and Kashmir, a disputed territory administered by India, are an ongoing issue. The abuses range from mass killings, forced disappearances, torture, rape and sexual abuse7to political repression and suppression of freedom of speech. The Indian central reserve police force, border security personnel and various militant groups have been accused and held accountable for committing severe human rights abuses against Kashmiri civilians. A WikiLeaks issue accused India of systemic human rights abuses, it stated that US diplomats possessed evidence of the apparent wide spread use of torture by Indian police and security forces.

Terrorist violence led by Jammu Kashmir Liberation front has caused ethnic cleansing of several hundred thousand Kashmiri Hindu Pandits, who comprises an estimated 3% of the Kashmir valley's population.

According to Asia Watch, the militant organizations forced the Hindus residing in the Kashmir valley to flee and become refugees in Delhi and Jammu. Although there is controversy regarding whether or not all pandits left due to fear of violence or were they encouraged by government to leave in order to undermine the support for millitant movements. Reportedly, "Kashmiri militants could perpetrate such crime because of the aide and patronization it received from Pakistan's Inter-Services Intelligence (ISI). The chief perpetrators were the Jammu & Kashmir Liberation Frontand the Hizbul Mujahideen. They got "trained and armed" by the ISI. Ethnic cleansing continued till a vast majority of the Kashmiri Pandits were evicted out of the valley after having suffered many acts of violence, e.g. sexual assault on women, arson, torture, extortion of property etc. Some of the separatist leaders in Kashmir reject these allegations. The Indian government is endeavouring to reinstate the displaced Pandits in Kashmir. The remnants of Kashmiri Pandits have been living in the squalors in Jammu, but the most of them believe that, until this violence ceases to exist, returning to Kashmir is not an option.

A US state government finding reports that the Indian army in Jammu and Kashmir, has carried out extrajudicial killings of innocent civilians and suspected insurgents, however the report has also mentioned killings and abuse being carried out by insurgents and separatists. In 2010, statistics presented to the Indian government's Cabinet Committee on Security showed that for the first time since the 1980s, the number of civilian deaths attributed to the Indian forces was higher than those attributed to terrorist actions. In a 1993 report, Human Rights Watch claimed that militant organizations have targeted civilians. The official stance of the Indian Army was that 97% of the reports about the human rights abuse have been found to be "fake or motivated" based on the investigation performed by the Army.

Kashmiri Insurgents

Kashmiri insurgents are also called as "freedom fighters", fighting against the rule of India in Kashmir. According to a Time Magazine's article, in August 2008 half a million Kashmiri protesters at Srinagar crying "*Azadi*" (freedom) and waving Pakistani flags. Reports from Amnesty International, Human Rights Watch and the International Commission of Jurists have confirmed Indian reports of systematic human rights violations by militants which claim Jammu and Kashmir to be part of Pakistan. The Jammu Kashmir Liberation Front (JKLF) has also been blamed of carrying out human rights violations, ranging from kidnapping to ethnic cleansing of several hundred thousand Hindu Kashmiri Pandits. A 2010 US state departmnet report blamed separatist insurgents in Kashmir and other parts of the country of committing several serious abuses, including the killing of security personnel as well as civilians, and of engaging in widespread torture, rape, beheadings, kidnapping, and extortion.

In August 2000, militant groups killed 30 Hindu pilgrims in what became known as the 2000 Amarnath pilgrimage massacre. The Indian government blamed the Lashkar-e-Taiba for the killings. The *BBC* writes that "hundreds of Hindu labourers ha[d] been leaving the Kashmir Valley" in August 2000 due to targeted killings against Hindu workers.

Ethnic Cleansing of Hindus and Sikhs

The Hindu Kashmiri Pandits, a small but prominent group, who had stably constituted approximately 4 to 5 per cent of the population of the Kashmir valley during Dogra rule (1846–1947), and 20 per cent of whom had left the Kashmir valley by 1950, began to leave in much greater numbers in the 1990s. According to a number of authors, approximately 100,000 of the total Kashmiri Pandit population of 140,000 left the valley during that decade. Other authors have suggested a higher figure for the exodus, ranging from the entire population of over 150,000, to 190,000 of a total Pandit population of 200,000, to a number as high as 253,000. The US government has reported on the terrorist threat to Pandits still living in the Kashmir region. Hindu women suffered heinous torture in Kashmir. In the words of one of the best-known Indian psychoanalysts Sudhir Kakar, "*slogans of "Long Live Pakistan" were carved with red-hot iron rods on the thighs of [the] Hindu daughters*"

During the eruption of armed rebellion the Islamic insurgency has claimed to have specifically targeted the Pandits and violated their human rights. Reports by Indian government state 219 Kashmiri pandits were killed and around 1,40,000 migrated due to millitancy while over 3000 stayed in the valley The local organisation of pandits in Kashmir, Kashmir Pandit Sangharsh Samiti claimed that 399 Kashmiri Pandit were killed by insurgents.

The violence was condemned and labeled as ethnic cleansing in a 2006 resolution passed by the United States Congress. It stated that the Islamic terrorists infiltrated the region in 1989 and began an ethnic cleansing campaign to convert Kashmir to a Muslim state. According to the same, since then nearly 400,000 Pandits were either murdered or forced to leave their ancestral homes. According to Hindu American Foundation report, the rights and religious freedom of Kashmiri Hindus have been severely curtailed since 1989, when there was an organized and systematic campaign by Islamist militants to cleanse Hindus from Kashmir. Less than 4,000 Kashmiri Hindus remain in the valley, reportedly living with daily threats of violence and terrorism. The CIA has reported nearly 506,000 people, about half of which are Pandit Hindus are displaced due to the insurgency. The United Nations Commission on Human Rights reports that there are roughly 1.5 million refugees from Indian-administered Kashmir, bulk of whom arrived in Pakistan-administered Kashmir and in Pakistan after the situation on the Indian side worsened in 1989 insurgency.

Post-1989, Kashmiri Pandits and other minority groups in Jammu and Kashmir have been targets of ethnic cleansing by Jihadi elements which India alleges and blames on the Inter-Services Intelligence. The Kashmiri Pandits, a community of Hindu Brahmins, then comprising 5% of the population of the state were the primary targets of Islamic militants, who also sought to also eliminate Kashmir's record of 5000 years of Hindu Sanskrit culture and scholarship as well as the tolerant indigenous multiculturalism referred to as *Kashmiriat*. As many as 400,000 Kashmiri Pandits fled the state and ethnic violence is considered to have killed 30,000 people. Muslim paramilitaries raped, tortured and killed thousands of Kashmiri Pandits, burnt their temples, idols and holy books.

According to Bhatt a United Nations adviser, the houses of Kashmir Pandits have been burnt, many killed, and that there has been "an almost total ethnic cleansing of Kashmir Pandits from Kashmir by fundamentalist forces of terrorism organised and supported from Pakistan".

Other minorities such as Kashmiri Sikhs were also targeted. According to Chitkara the killing of Sikhs near Anantnag in 2001, by the *Jehadis* was aimed at ethnic cleansing. Hindus have migrated from most of the Kashmir valley, Sikhs who form a very small percentage could be forced to migrate in the wake of such killings. The Indian agencies are also blamed for the massacre of Sikhs at Chattisingpora, which killed 37 Siks at the time of Clinton's visit to India.

Indian Armed Forces

Thousands of Kashmiris have reported to be killed by Indian security forces in custody, extradjudicial executions and enforced disappearances and these human right violations are said to be carried out by Indian security forces under total impunity. Civilians including women and children have been killed in "reprisal" attacks by Indian security forces and as a "collective punishment" villages and neighbourhoods have been burn down and women raped. International NGO's as well as the US State Department have documented human rights abuses including disappearances, torture and arbitrary executions carried out during India's counter terrorism operations United Nations has expressed serious concerns over large number of killings by Indian security forces. Human Rights Watch has also accused the Indian security forces of using children as spies and messengers, although the Indian government denies this allegation. Torture, widely used by Indian security, the severity described as beyond comprehension by amnesty international has been responsible for the huge number of deaths in custody The Telegraph, citing a WikiLeaks report quotes the International Committee of the Red Cross (ICRC) that Indian security forces were physically abusing detainees by beatings, electrocutions and sexual interference. These detainees weren't Islamic insurgents or Pakistani-backed insurgents but civilians, in contrast to India's continual allegations of Pakistani involvement. The detainees were "connected to or believed to have information about the insurgents". According to ICRC, 681 of the 1296 detainees whom it interviewed claimed torture. US officials have been quoted reporting "terrorism investigations and court cases tend to rely upon confessions, many of which are obtained under duress if not beatings, threats, or in some cases torture." Amnesty International accused security forces of exploiting the Armed Forces Special Powers Act that enables them to "hold prisoners without trial". The group argues that the law, which allows security to detain individuals for as many as two years "without presenting charges, violating prisoners' human rights".

Indian Army

The soldiers of the 4th Rajputana Rifles of the Indian Army on 23 February 1991 launched a search operation in a village Kunan Poshpora, in the Kupwara district of Jammu and Kashmir and allegedly gang raped 53 women of all ages. Nevertheless, the committee that led a thorough investigation concluded that the allegations were "grossly exaggerated" and the incident was "*a massive hoax orchestrated by militant groups and their sympathizers and mentors in Kashmir and abroad as a part of sustained and cleverly contrived strategy of psychological warfare and as an entry point for reinscribing Kashmir on the International Agenda as a Human rights issue.*" However, Human Rights organizations including Human Rights Watch have reported that the number of raped women could be as high as 100. The Indian Army is also accused of many massacres such as Bomai Killing, 2009, Gawakadal massacre, 2006 Kulgam massacre, Zakoora And Tengpora Massacre, 1990, Sopore massacre. They also didn't speared the health care system of the valley. The major hospitals witnessed the crackdowns and army men even entered the operation theaters in search of terrorist patients.

Border Security Force

On 22 October 1993, the 13th Battalion of the Border Security Forces was accused of arbitrarily firing on a crowd and killing 37 civilians in Bijbehara The number of reported dead and wounded vary by source. Amnesty International reported that at least 51 people died and 200 were wounded on that day.

The Indian government conducted two official enquiries and the National Human Rights Commission of India (NHRC) conducted a third. In March 1994 the government indicted the Border Security Force (BSF) for firing into the crowd "without provocation" and charged 13 BSF officers with murder. In another incident which took place at Handwara on 25 January 1990, 9 protesters where killed by the same unit.

Central Reserve Police Force

During the Amarnath land transfer controversy more than 40 unarmed protesters were killed by the personnels of Central Reserve Police Force. At least 300 were detained under Public Safety Act, including teenagers. The same practice was again repeated by the personnels of the Central Reserve Police Force, during the 2010 Kashmir Unrest, which resulted in 112 deaths, including many teenager protesters at various incidents.

Special Operations Group

The Special Operations Group was raised in 1994 for counter terrorism. A volunteer force, mainly came for promotions and cash rewards, comprising police officers and policemen from the Jammu and Kashmir Police. The group is accused of torture and costodial killings. A Senior Superintendent of this group and his deputy are among the 11 personnels, who were convicted for a fake encounter, which killed a local carpenter, and was labelled as a millitant to get the promotions and rewards.

Armed Forces (Special Powers) Act, 1958

In July 1990 Indian Armed Forces were given special powers under the Armed Forces (Special Powers) Act, 1958 (AFSPA) that gives protection to Indian Armed Forces personnel from being prosecuted. The law provides them a shield, when committing human rights violations and has been criticized by Human Rights Watch as being wrongly used by the forces. This law is widely condemned by human rights groups. United Nations High Commissioner for Human Rights Navanethem Pillay has urged India to repeal AFSPA and to investigate the disappearances in Kashmir.

"All three special laws in force in the state assist the government in shielding the perpetrators of human rights violations from prosecution, and encourage them to act with impunity. Provisions of the Armed Forces (Jammu and Kashmir) Special Powers Act clearly contravene international human rights standards laid down in the International Covenant on Civil and Political Rights, as members of the UN Human Rights Committee have pointed out. One Committee member felt that provisions of the act — including imunity from prosecution — were highly dangerous and encouraged violations of the right to life".

—A clipping from a report published by the Amnesty International, 1995.

According to the Armed Forces Special Powers Act (AFSPA), in an area that is proclaimed as "disturbed", an officer of the armed forces has powers to:

- Fire upon or use other kinds of force even if it causes death, against the person who is acting against law or order in the disturbed area for the maintenance of public order, after giving such due warning.
- Destroy any arms dump, prepared or fortified position or shelter or training camp from which armed attacks are made by the armed volunteers or armed gangs or absconders wanted for any offence
- To arrest without a warrant anyone who has committed cognizable offences or is reasonably suspected of having done so and may use force if needed for the arrest.
- To enter and search any premise in order to make such arrests, or to recover any person wrongfully restrained or any arms, ammunition or explosive substances and seize it.
- Stop and search any vehicle or vessel reasonably suspected to be carrying such person or weapons.
- Any person arrested and taken into custody under this Act shall be made over to the officer in charge of the nearest police station with the least possible delay, together with a report of the circumstances occasioning the arrest.
- Army officers have legal immunity for their actions. There can be no prosecution, suit or any other legal proceeding against anyone acting under that law. Nor is the government's judgment on why an area is found to be disturbed subject to judicial review.
- Protection of persons acting in good faith under this Act from prosecution, suit or other legal proceedings, except with the sanction of the Central Government, in exercise of the powers conferred by this Act.

Fake Encounters

According to the Srinagar-based Association of Parents of Displaced Persons (APDP), a minimum of 8,000 people have disappeared since the insurgency began. In February 2003, the government of India-administered Kashmir, led by Mufti Mohammad Sayeed, told the state legislative assembly that 3,744 people were missing and that many of those reported missing since 1990 were actually in Pakistan, where they had signed up to be trained as militants. Hundreds of civilian's including women and children have been reported to be extrajudicially executed by Indian security forces and killings concealed as fake encounters. Despite government denial, Indian security officials have reportedly confessed to human right watch of widespread occurrence of fake encounters and its encouragement for awards and promotions According to a BBC interview with an anonymous security person, 'fake encounter' killings are those in which security personnel kill someone in cold blood while claiming that the casualty occurred in a gun battle.

It also asserts that the security personnel are Kashmiris and "even surrendered militants". In 2010 three men were reported missing proceeding these missing reports 3 men claimed to be militants were killed in a staged gun battle the army also claimed they had found Pakistani currency among the dead. The major was subsequently suspended and a senior soldier transferred from his post. In 2011, a Special Police Officer and an Indian Army Jawan were charged by the Kashmir police for murder of a civilian whom the duo had killed in an encounter claiming that he was a top Lashkar-e-Taiba militant.

Disappearances

Indian security forces have been implicated in many reports for enforced disappearances of thousands of Kashmiris where the security forces deny having their information and/or custody. This is often in association with torture or extrajudicial killing. The number of men disappeared have been so many to have a new term "half-widows" for their wives who end up impoverished. Human right activists estimate the number of disappeared over eight thousand, last seen in government detention. These are believed to be dumped in thousands of mass graves across Kashmir

Mass Graves

Mass graves have been identified all over Kashmir by human right activists believed to contain bodies of thousands of Kashmiris of enforced disappearances. A state human rights commission inquiry confirmed there are thousands of bullet-ridden bodies buried in unmarked graves in Jammu and Kashmir. Of the 2730 bodies uncovered in 4 of the 14 districts, 574 bodies were identified as missing locals in contrast to the Indian governments insistence that all the graves belong to foreign militants According to a new deposition submitted by Parvez Imroz and his field workers asserted that the total number of unmarked graves were about 6,000. The British parliament commented on the recent discovery and expressed its sadness and regret of over 6,000 unmarked graves. Christof Heyns, a special rapporteur on extrajudicial executions, has warned India that "all of these draconian laws had no place in a functioning democracy and should be scrapped."

Extrajudicial Killings by Security Personnel

In a 1994 report, Human Rights Watch described summary executions of detainees as a "hallmark" of counter-insurgency operations by Indian security forces in Kashmir. The report further stated that such extrajudicial killings were often administered within hours of arrest, and were carried out not as aberrations but as a "matter of policy". In a 1995 report, Amnesty International stated that hundred of civilians had been victims of such killings, which were often claimed by officers as occurring during "encounters" or "cross-fire". A 2010 US state department report cited extrajudicial killings by security forces in areas of conflict such as Kashmir as a major human rights problem in India.

Suicide

According to a report, 17,000 people mostly women have committed suicide during the last 20 years in the Valley. According to a study by the Medecins Sans Frontieres,

"Women in Kashmir have suffered enormously since the separatist struggle became violent in 1989-90. Like the women in other conflict zones, they have been raped, tortured, maimed and killed. A few of them were even jailed for years together. Kashmiri women are among the worst sufferers of sexual violence in the world. 'Sexual violence has been routinely perpetrated on

Kashmiri women, with 11.6% of respondents saying they were victims of sexual abuse'," At the beginning of the insurgency there were 1200 patients in the valley's sole mental hospital. The hospital is now overcrowded with more than 100,000 patients.

ADDING NEW HURDLES TO A DETERIORATING PEACE PROCESS

We regret the two countries have missed an opportunity to make a new beginning along the path of dialogue and negotiation. When Prime Minister Narendra Modi and Prime Minister Sharif announced in Ufa that they would resume a process of dialogue and engagement, we wholeheartedly and publicly welcomed it. We appreciated that the two Prime Ministers had agreed that "India and Pakistan have a collective responsibility to ensure peace and promote development" and, for this, they were "prepared to discuss all outstanding issues." A peaceful solution to the Kashmir issue is obviously central to this and is the key to positively transforming relationships and to unlocking a new future of lasting peace, stability and prosperity for the entire South Asian region.

The fact that the two Prime Ministers agreed to start a process of talks, which could perhaps include high-level backchannel talks away from the media glare, was a very positive development in our view. We saw this as a possible sign that reason was emerging over illusion. We expected that the opening of a process could lead to a situation where tensions might be ratcheted down and a measure of trust could be rebuilt. We hoped that a full-fledged and inclusive peace process could eventually begin in which the leaderships of the two countries and the people of Jammu & Kashmir could all start focusing on the arduous task of resolving conflicts. In hope of such a peace process, we offered our support and we were prepared to offer our patience to the process. We understand that fresh starts require encouragement and also take time to be built on.

The cancellation of the talks we are deeply concerned that the dangerous trajectory that the region has been heading along is being reinforced following this breakdown. It is highly alarming that the Government of India opted to make the discussions on the Kashmir issue and the role of the Hurriyat subjects of new, narrowly drawn "red lines", new positions that impose a straightjacket on the future prospects for any meaningful peace process. This is what the stand laid out by Sushma Swaraj on the Kashmir Issue and Hurriyat essentially amounted to. Such a doctrine based on narrow-mindedness rather than enlightenment will get us nowhere.

The imposition of a so-called "red line" against meeting us raises serious questions as to whether there is really any intent on the part of the Modi Government to strive and work towards a resolution of the Kashmir conflict and the achievement of a lasting peace. When hurdles actually needed to be removed by both sides, why is the Government of India erecting a set of new barriers in the way of initiating a process of dialogue? Why this sudden injection of an entirely new level of inflexibility regarding the dialogue process?

Sadly, what we have seen in the last year or so from Prime Minister Modi's government, is a hardening and narrowing of mindsets and an approach that is based more on machismo rather than a commitment to dialogue and a willingness to engage in serious problem-solving. In the last year, while the path of dialogue was being shunned and the situation in Kashmir became more tense and polarised, we have witnessed a litany of made-for-TV chest-thumping statements coming from the highest levels in New Delhi.

Appallingly, when ceasefire violations and tensions were rising dangerously at the LoC and innocent civilians were being killed in Jammu & Kashmir, we even had to listen to Prime Minister Modi himself giving bellicose statements, such as "[it's] not the time for boli (talk) but for goli (bullets)." While we hold out a lingering hope that these were aberrations, if the kind of thinking on Kashmir we have seen over the last year and especially over the last few days has become the new norm in New Delhi, then I am very sorry to say that it will be a recipe for disaster. It can hardly offer a way forward towards renewed efforts at dialogue and peace in the region.

As he himself promised during his election campaign, We had hoped that Prime Minister Modi, as promised in his election campaign, would continue forward with the vision of peace and dialogue that former Prime Minister Atal Bihari Vajpayee espoused. Mr Vajpayee, had declared from the base of the Minar-e-Pakistan in Lahore that it was his dream and wish to resolve the Kashmir issue. He had affirmed the need for unconditional talks, reaching out to us as well as Pakistan and asked for talks to be held under the ambit of "insaniyat" [humanity]. He believed in complementary processes of dialogue, including the Delhi-Islamabad, Srinagar-Delhi, Srinagar-Muzzafarabad and Srinagar-Islamabad tracks. Mr Vajpayee had the wisdom to realise that the Kashmiri leadership could be a partner for peace and a bridge between India and Pakistan. He facilitated our interactions and even our visit to Pakistan to meet President Pervez Musharaf so that we could help push the process forward. While a break through on Kashmir eventually proved elusive, the steps Vajpayee took at least created the necessary space and context for all the parties to begin to engage in a process that was aimed at finding solutions.

The basic point here is that it is possible to initiate a peace process. India and Pakistan have found ways in the past to move forward while involving Kashmiris in the effort. Indeed, some useful progress was achieved in terms of reducing war risks and allowing people-to-people interaction across the LoC. Even some potentially workable ideas on a possible way forward towards a Kashmir settlement were developed. Those ideas could serve as a starting point for discussions even today.

The lessons here are clear. Moving forward and achieving progress requires an open mind, the courage to cooperate and accommodate, the willingness and maturity to be flexible, and the boldness to break out of old patterns and failed approaches. It took tremendous courage and a big heart for Mr. Vajpayee to take the stepswithout the solid parliamentary majority that the present BJP enjoys.

Involving and creating space for Kashmiris to be included in the process demonstrated an understanding on the part of Mr. Vajpayee that the road to peace runs through Kashmir and that, at its core, Kashmir is a human issue requiring a political solution. Indeed, only by humanising the issue of Kashmir and listening to the people of Jammu & Kashmir is it possible for the two countries to start finding a workable solution.

Sadly, in the stand that was put forward by Sushma Swaraj on Saturday, we see a marked departure from the type of statesmanship and courage that Prime Minister Vajpayee once demonstrated. Where is the "insaniyat" in insisting that others can not meet us, in arresting us and in the attempt to silence us? By seeking to completely quarantine us are we not being dehumanised? Doesn't the attempt to impose a new doctrine of narrow bilateralism, which asserts that Kashmiris are not even a party to the Kashmir issue, amount to dehumanising it? For Kashmiris who have been watching all of this unfold, there are real concerns about whether more repressive, undemocratic and militaristic approaches are to be expected in future.

At another level, the inflexibility that prevented the NSA-level talks from going forward bordered on the absurd. The type of "red lines" which have been drawn by New Delhi on Kashmir makes one recall that anecdote described in Jonathan Swift's satire "Gulliver's Travels", where runaway narrow-mindedness leads to a situation where two countries got hopelessly embroiled in unending cycles of war over the correct way to break an egg — at the little end or the big end.

The bigger picture was forgotten in all the media frenzy. Whether it is addressed head-on or as part of a broader Indo-Pak peace process that has seven baskets of issues or ten baskets of issues, whether you call it "composite" or "resumed" or "structured, whether X meets Y before or after Z or at a later stage, whether the issue is approached at the little end or the big end, whatever the procedures and steps involved, at the end of the day the Kashmir egg has to be cracked. Inevitably, a solution to Kashmir has to be found through a process that includes the people of Jammu & Kashmir. At the end of the day the goal is to achieve lasting peace in South Asia. How can "redlines" on dialogue possibly serve that purpose? Suffice it to say that, except for a few vested interests, right now everybody is a loser as a result of the failure of leadership and imagination that was witnessed over the weekend. Indeed, the common people of Jammu & Kashmir, India and Pakistan all lose as long as this intransigence persists and this deadlock continues.

Two possibilities

Prime Minister Modi needs to have a serious rethink on his government's Kashmir policy. There are two possibilities. Prime Minister Modi can choose to adopt the same old default policy approach that has allowed the Kashmir issue to linger on for more than six decades. Or he can adopt a visionary detour and pursue a serious political and diplomatic effort to resolve the Kashmir issue once and for all. Rather than narrowing the space for dialogue, Prime Minister Modi needs to focus on his responsibility to lead the region out of deadlock and away from the risks of dangerous escalation and confrontation. Instead of thinking about the next cycle of state elections, he needs to think about the future generations of South Asia. Ultimately, leadership is about finding solutions not evading them.

As for us, we support the way of dialogue. We are firm in the view that there is no military solution and negotiation is the way. This is why we welcomed Prime Minister Modi's initial gesture to invite Prime Minister Sharif to his inauguration and this is why we hailed Prime Minister Sharif for having the courage to accept the invitation to come to New Delhi. This is also why we openly welcomed the decision of the two Prime Ministers in Ufa to make another attempt at a dialogue. It is because of our belief in the path of dialogue that we expressed our dismay at the collapse of talks in August 2014 and we do so now again in August 2015. These setbacks are all the more concerning to us because the Government of India has unnecessarily made us — the Hurriyat — the reason (and perhaps excuse?) for avoiding serious dialogue.

"The type of 'red lines' drawn by New Delhi on Kashmir recalls Jonathan Swift's satire Gulliver's Travels, where runaway narrow-mindedness locks two countries in unending cycles of war over the correct way to break an egg. "

There is consensus on the need for an unconditional process of dialogue in Jammu & Kashmir. Even the pro-India political parties, the Peoples Democratic Party and National Conference want New Delhi to initiate such a process with Pakistan and with us. All Kashmiris believe in an inclusive peace process and believe that any negotiated solution should represent the will of all the people of Jammu & Kashmir, including all five regions of the state on both sides of the LoC.

We believe that the time is ripe for a bold move forward. If something is not done now — during relatively quieter times — to initiate a process of dialogue, it will become near impossible later if there is further escalation or a crisis. From our point of view, there must be a serious, result-oriented and time-bound process of dialogue between the leadership of India and Pakistan, and of Jammu and Kashmir. Let this process start sooner rather than later. Perhaps the best thing all the parties could do right now is to try to keep the media out of it. If we are all serious then all the parties should start engaging quietly away from the cameras. Let all of the parties engage actively with one another to at least exchange their views. Let the dialogue be unofficial and without conditions, but let each party seriously introspect as to whether they can be partners for peace and explore whether they can find partners in others to end this horrible conflict once and for all. We must all try our best and exhaust the possibilities to seek a peaceful solution. Perhaps together we will be able to find some way to take a historic step forward towards a real peace process.

POST-9/11 DEVELOPMENTS

After 9/11, new international game rules were set by the United States. The newly coined 9/11 terminology helped New Delhi to bracket Pakistan with Taliban, a hub of terrorism, and project India as a victim of terrorism. Besides, the situation also offered India and Pakistan a watershed opportunity to transform their diplomatic relations with the USA. New Delhi immediately extended all-out support to Washington's War on Terror, presenting its war-related facilities for use against the Taliban regime. Meanwhile, Islamabad lost no time in jumping on to the US bandwagon and becoming, once again, a frontline state for the USA. Pakistan feared that India might snatch the opportunity to forge an anti-Pakistan alliance with the US. It quickly disappointed New Delhi and created a sense of despair both in the corridors of the Indian establishment and the public.

During this period, a number of events occurred that favored New Delhi; for instance, the UN Resolution 1373 (2001) adopted by the Security Council at its meeting on September 28, 2001, clearly ignored the distinction between the freedom movement and terrorism, whereas the US dubbed all resistance movements for the right to self-determination as terrorist campaigns. Besides a few exceptions, the entire world community accepted this flaw in interpretation.

Kashmir was among the first casualties of these new game rules. Soon after, the traditional sympathy towards oppressed people disappeared and the world media and big countries started to call freedom fighters terrorists. India cashed in on this trend and portrayed itself as a victim of terrorism, not a brutal oppressor confronting the freedom struggle of the Kashmiris.

Just three months after the September 11 events, the Indian parliament was attacked. The episode invited condemnation from all over the world and sympathy towards India, while Pakistan was pressurized to rein in militants active inside IHK.

Indian Prime Minister Atal Behari Vajpayee, according to renowned writer Arundhati Roy, seized the opportunity to compare this attack with the 9/11 attacks. India snapped diplomatic relations and all communication links with Pakistan and manned its border with Pakistan with half a million soldiers, challenging Pakistan to change its Kashmir policy or face dire consequences.

Responding in the same coin, Pakistan also mobilized it forces. The standoff created a war-like situation in the region and alarmed the US, which was heavily dependent on Pakistan for its crucial logistic support in the US war in Afghanistan. It was untenable for the US to allow Pakistan to shift its focus from the Afghan border to the eastern one.

PAKISTAN'S POLICY IN THE CHANGING SCENARIO

The events of 9/11, the attack on the Indian parliament, and the following war-like situation between India and Pakistan not only greatly impacted the Kashmiri resistance movement but also compelled Islamabad to change its track on Kashmir. Moreover, the unfriendly international environment and Pakistan's deep involvement in Afghanistan forced Islamabad to rethink its relations with India and its Kashmir policy. The decision of General Pervez Musharraf to join the US-led War on Terror was also a factor in changing Islamabad's strategic position on Kashmir, particularly in terms of its ideological foundation. The economic condition of the country, unrest in the tribal areas, and — allegedly externally sponsored — violence in some parts of Balochistan, and the growing engagement along the Afghan border also played an instrumental role in bringing about a paradigm shift in Islamabad's thinking towards India. It is also said that Pakistan's trusted friends, like China and Saudi Arabia, advised it to seek an unconventional way out for a lasting deal with India over the Kashmir issue and bilateral relations; besides, constant persuasion from the United States also continued.

Pakistan's capacity to protract the low cost conflict in Kashmir is beyond any doubt. Although the likely spillover effects of this on Pakistan's polity are obvious, they will be, to a great degree, manageable. On the other hand, despite its conventional military superiority and strong diplomatic backing from the world, India could not subdue the resolve of Pakistan to support Kashmir's right to self-determination and its demand for sovereign equality with India. Pakistan's ties with the United States, and its role as an ally of the West, are considered advantageous for seeking a settlement of the Kashmir issue. As the country's former Foreign Secretary Shamshad Ahmad observed:

> We cannot deny the post-9/11 reality that our "friends," the Americans, now have deeper than ever stakes in India-Pakistan rapprochement as a factor of stability for regional and global peace.

The 'covert' US engagement with Islamabad, Delhi and Kashmiris is no longer a secret. Washington has expressed its desire at a number of times to help settle the Kashmir issue within the existing territorial parameters but with minor realignment. It views India as a potential rival to China, not only in the region but also in global affairs. Siddharth Srivastava, a New Delhi-based journalist, observes:

The US is striving to build India as a strategic counterweight to China, along with Japan and Australia.

Termed as naïve by critics, Pakistan's calculations of the ground realities are optimistic, being based on the belief that India will never be able to bring normalcy into Kashmir because Kashmiris are highly skeptical towards it, and that India will need Pakistan's support and will ultimately make tangible transformations in its current stance over Kashmir. The majority of Kashmiris do not trust the Indian government and, ever since the eruption of the resistance, their aspiration for the right of self-determination has multiplied manifold and now cuts across even the hardcore pro-India circles in the Kashmir Valley. India's carrot and stick tactics and the brutalities of its forces have alienated the local population and invoked armed resistance, which may not die down easily. It is this assessment of the situation that emboldened Islamabad to make tangible concessions on Kashmir and bring India to the table for talks. Some also believe that the personal ambition of the President Musharraf — his wish to be regarded in history as a statesman who settled one of the world's most complicated disputes — is a driving factor that has brought essential changes in Islamabad's policies.

Besides various other factors that caused India and Pakistan to change their policies on the Kashmir issue, back channel diplomacy led by the US played a major role in alleviating the crisis and creating a viable atmosphere for initiatives towards a comprehensive normalization process.

Change in India's Approach

For a long time, India's approach for dealing with Pakistan had revolved mainly around zero tolerance in any concerns related to India's security or political ideology. However, its inability to 'punish' Pakistan and to break its back economically (by creating a war-like environment in the region) had a sobering impact on the Indian mindset and led New Delhi to conclude that its conventional policies vis-à-vis Pakistan and Kashmir were getting nowhere. In the past, New Delhi had publicly pronounced several times that it would take punitive action and destroy what it alleged were militant training camps inside Azad Jammu and Kashmir (AJK) by air strikes. However, its hostile attitude did not yield the desired results and Islamabad did not succumb to its pressure.

At the same time, economic tycoons and multinational companies were pressuring the Indian government to normalize relations with Islamabad as hostile relations between the two neighbors and the constant fear of war had a negative impact on business activity and international investment. New Delhi needed peace in the region and internal stability to continue its current annual growth rate of 8-10 percent and obtain further foreign investment. As one researcher on the peace process put it:

> Improved relations would lead to improved trade: there was money to be made, and this had become a strategic objective for both Islamabad and New Delhi.

India realized that its successful economic journey would cease if it did not settle disputes with Pakistan. It had to think about the immense potential in bilateral trade and in trade with landlocked Afghanistan and Central Asia via Pakistan. Besides, India aspires for a permanent seat in the UN Security Council for which it had to ensure friendly relations with neighbors and settle the Kashmir issue in the context of which India is regarded among those countries that did not comply with the UNSC resolutions. Moreover, the Kashmir resistance poses a huge financial burden on the Indian treasury. It is also acknowledged that the Indian security forces do not have the capacity to fix the problem; rather, they invite anger by frequently committing severe human rights violations that aggravate the already complex situation.

After the withdrawal of Indian forces from the Pakistani borders, Pakistan made a chain of unilateral concessions pronounced by President General Musharraf himself. It began with a unilateral ceasefire on LoC announced by Prime Minister Zaffarullah Khan Jamali in November 2003. In the following month, speaking to *Reuters*, General Musharraf said he had "left aside" the 55-year-old demand for a UN mandated plebiscite on Kashmir and wished to meet India "halfway" in a bid for peace in the subcontinent.

These multiple pulls created a sense of obligation among the Indian ruling elite to at least take some measures to show that they were serious about settling the problems. Eventually, the Indian Prime Minister Atal Behari Vajpayee went to Kupwara in the south of the Kashmir Valley and offered a hand of friendship to Pakistan in April 2004. This was regarded a departure from the conventional Indian thinking on Kashmir and Pakistan, and paved the way for further initiatives on Kashmir. It also created a palatable environment for Vajpayee to visit Islamabad to attend the South Asian Association for Regional Cooperation (SAARC) summit.

Musharraf's 'Out of the Box' Thinking

Islamabad has consistently said that it supports the resistance in IHK diplomatically and politically, and has nothing to do with the armed struggle. It has also invariably linked talks with India with progress on the Kashmir settlement. But it relinquished both of these stands in the quest to find a compromised solution. Pakistan accepted the responsibility to rein in militants operating from areas under its control. It also pledged to stop all kinds of cross-border activities from Azad Kashmir. Pakistan had never acknowledged the armed resistance in IHK as terrorism, but astonishingly, it ceded even this stance and conceded to the Indian interpretation of the movement. As a retired former Ambassador aptly commented:

This amounted to an admission of its guilt and was unprecedented in that Pakistan unilaterally took on a responsibility that was not only almost impossible to honor, but even more importantly, it was given without any reciprocal obligation by the other side.

To further the shift in policy, the Pakistani President articulated his ideas on Kashmir for the first time while speaking to journalists during an *iftar*dinner held in Islamabad in October 2004. Although he said these were "off the cuff" ideas, the nature of the proposals on the Kashmir settlement that he forwarded suggests that he had in mind a well-conceived and thought-out plan, on which he was gauging feedback. The crux of the proposals is outlined below:

- Identify seven regions, demilitarize them, and change their status before looking for possible options to resolve the dispute.
- The status quo in Kashmir is unacceptable and the LoC cannot be a solution to the lingering dispute.
- As a starting point for a step-by-step approach on the option of demilitarization, the regions on both sides of the LoC need to be analyzed for local culture and demographic composition. After identifying these regions, there could be gradual demilitarization, following which the two sides could discuss who should control these areas.
- Pakistan and India could also have joint control of these areas or the United Nations could be asked to play a role.

Later, Musharraf dilated upon his ideas with the *CNBC* anchorperson, Karan Thapar, on January 8, 2006. He suggested the concept of self-governance and joint management of the entire Kashmir area. In his words, "self-governance is more than autonomy but less than independence. In other words, both India and Pakistan will keep the parts of Kashmir they control but under their joint management. Self-governance is devolved to the Kashmiris, independence being firmly ruled out."

The interviewer, Karan Thapar, afterwards elaborated this concept in his article, saying, "...The self-governance would apply to the full state of Jammu and Kashmir as it existed in 1947. This means it would be implemented in Northern Areas (Gilgit Baltistan). Additionally, the border within old Kashmir state would be open and thus irrelevant."

Subsequently, Musharraf had a comprehensive discussion on his proposals with the noted Indian lawyer and journalist, A. G. Noorani, who published it in the Indian magazine *Frontline* on August 12-25, 2006. Later on, President Musharraf also spoke to *NDTV* on similar ideas, going further to clearly articulate his position as follows:

- Kashmir will have the same borders but people will be allowed to move freely back and forth in the region;
- The region will have self-governance or autonomy, but not independence;
- Troops will be withdrawn from the region in a phased manner
- A joint supervision mechanism will be set up with India, Pakistan and Kashmir represented in it.

The proposals offered by Musharraf sent clear signals that: a) Islamabad was ready to compromise its traditional stance that the people of Kashmir will decide their destiny through free and fair plebiscite; b) Indian and Pakistani sovereignty would remain as it currently was at the end of the day; c) The LoC would be irrelevant, except as a line on a map to demarcate both parts of the state; d) Self-governance or self rule would be granted to both parts of Kashmir and joint management established.

Pakistan's proposals paved the way to move forward on a slightly faster track as India did not view them as being against its strategic or political interests. Previously, Pakistan had banked on the UNSC resolutions that guaranteed the right of self-determination to the Kashmiris, besides recognizing Pakistan as a principal party to the dispute. Musharraf relinquished these positions unilaterally without seeking any quid pro quo. In other words, he came close to almost acknowledging the Indian claim that Kashmir could not be receded from the Union. India also tactfully rephrased its traditional stance that "J&K is its integral part" in more acceptable language, now asserting that "Borders cannot be redrawn but any kind of solution could be acceptable to India." Musharraf agreed to this proposition while rejecting the status quo and showed willingness to embrace some kind of joint management of the state.

Moreover, Pakistan accepted the pro-Indian Kashmiri leadership's role in the future dispensation and changed its position that only the All Parties Hurriyat Conference (APHC) should be the representative of Kashmiri people in the negotiation process. President Musharraf said that the President of the National Conference, Omer Abdullah, and Mahbooba Mufti had a role to play in the Kashmir political landscape. This gesture comforted the Indian establishment as Pakistan's demands were in line with their own views and interests. These major departures from the traditional stance made Musharraf a good bet for India to deal with Pakistan on Kashmir and settle other issues broadly allied to Pak-India trade and access to markets in Central Asia and Afghanistan.

A Review of the Composite Dialogue

The dialogue process between Islamabad and New Delhi is slowly progressing despite several ups and downs. It is often said that the continuation of the process is in itself a success because, in the past, the two countries have been unable to remain engaged in a sustainable dialogue. However, the substance of the process and prospects of its success need to be analyzed.

Until February 1994, India and Pakistan were engaged in sporadic dialogues that always ended with zero progress. This is why both countries formally suspended dialogue in 1994. Islamabad's approach was to settle the Kashmir issue first, after which the other problems would get settled almost automatically, whereas India was interested in dilating first on other issues, such as trade and travel. Eventually, to bridge the gap between the two positions, both governments agreed to address all political and territorial issues simultaneously, including Jammu and Kashmir. Consequently, the foreign secretaries of the two countries met in Islamabad and resumed the stalled dialogue process in June 1997. They institutionalized the process by identifying eight areas to deliberate upon and established working groups to make progress on each issue separately but simultaneously.

This entire process was called off when the Kargil confrontation occurred. As discussed earlier, post-9/11 events also contributed in the stalemate between the two countries. Later, in 2004, India and Pakistan launched a renewed peace process aimed at resolving all their longstanding disputes. However, the Kashmir dispute still dominates over other issues. Even after voicing his new approaches, President Musharraf said that if progress on Kashmir could not make headway, the entire process would be back to square one. Recently, Prime Minister Shaukat Aziz has underscored the settlement of Kashmir as a precondition for further progress on other related disputes as well as for offering trade and business opportunities to India.

Since January 2004, both neighbors have been engaged on two different levels. The first is the official level, at which concerned officials from both sides meet periodically and report their progress to foreign secretaries, who meet to review the outcome and discuss the Kashmir, peace and security issues, before, finally, the foreign ministers meet to take stock of developments and set the rules for further dialogue. The second level of engagement is back-channel diplomacy. Pakistan's National Security Secretary, Tariq Aziz, who is known to be a close aide of President Musharraf, and India's S. K. Lamba, former High Commissioner to Pakistan, are engaged in a serious dialogue. However, it has been said that only five people in Pakistan are truly in the loop on the actual state of bilateral negotiations. Therefore, no one can really assess the behind-the-curtains activities or predict the contours of solutions.

So far, at the official level, both countries have completed four rounds of a composite dialogue. This process received a dent when the Mumbai train blasts on July 11, 2006 caused a postponement in the foreign secretary-level talks. India blamed elements from Pakistan for their involvement in the blasts but no evidence was provided by the Indian government to Pakistan. This decision was in violation of the joint statement, issued on April 18, 2005, by the leaders of Pakistan and India, which states that, "Terrorist acts would not be allowed to derail the peace process." Eventually, sanity prevailed and the stalled process was resumed in November 2006. Likewise, in February, the Lahore-bound Samjhauta Express became a target of bomb blasts that killed 68 passengers, most of whom were Pakistani. Islamabad reacted with caution and did not allow the peace process to derail, despite the immense loss of its citizens' lives. The question does arise how New Delhi would have reacted had Indian citizens been the victims.

The fourth round of composite dialogue was held in Islamabad on March 13-14, 2007, with a focus on the Jammu and Kashmir dispute and peace and security. In the context of peace and security, the two sides discussed a wide range of issues relating to their conventional and nuclear military capabilities and reviewed the entire process. The Pakistani team sought India's response to President Musharraf's "ideas" on the resolution of the Kashmir issue and emphasized the need for forward movement on Jammu and Kashmir, saying it was time to move from confidence-building measures to dispute resolution.

Among related issues, Pakistan pushed for early finalization of the agreements on speedy return of inadvertent line crossers; quarterly flag meetings of the sector commanders at the LoC; and liberalization of the visa regime. Pakistan also proposed some new cross-LoC confidence building measures, including allowing sports activities and launch of helicopter and postal services between Srinagar and Muzaffarabad.

In addition, Pakistan tabled a new proposal on anti-ballistic missiles. Siachen, Sir Creek and economic cooperation were among the other issues discussed.

Following are the significant consensus points of the fourth round of foreign secretary-level talks:

- After years of reluctance, Pakistan agreed to the Indian proposal of launching a bus service between Kargil and Skardu in the Northern Areas.
- It was agreed that a truck service between Srinagar and Muzaffarabad would be launched in a few months;
- It was agreed that the Joint Committee of Retired Judges, set up to look into the prisoners issue, would begin its work soon and suggest ways to ensure the humane treatment of Indian prisoners in Pakistani jails and Pakistani prisoners in Indian jails;

- The two countries agreed to conclude an agreement on "No Development of New Posts and Defense Works" along the LoC and proposed drafts for new border control guidelines along the International Border;
- The two sides agreed to work on finalizing a liberalized visa regime, including a proposal for group tourism.

Although the meeting could not settle the problem of demilitarizing Siachen, it was able to narrow down differences on some elements. The political leadership of both countries appears optimistic about resolving this issue in the days ahead. Likewise, the formation of a Joint Counter-Terrorism Mechanism is also a significant development. India has long blamed Pakistan for any terrorist activities occurring on its territory. The Mechanism offers an opportunity for thorough investigation of incidents prior to the pronouncements of conclusions. However, it was reported in sections of the Pakistani and Indian press that Islamabad seeks to keep the armed resistance in J&K out of the ambit of the Joint Anti-Terrorism Mechanism. At a joint press conference with the Indian Foreign Secretary Shivshankar Menon, his Pakistani counterpart, Riaz Mohammad Khan, said that Jammu and Kashmir was "disputed" and should not be "mixed" with the initiatives that are between India and Pakistan only. The visible achievement of the four rounds of foreign sectaries' level dialogue is the initiation of a Srinagar-Muzaffarabad bus service and, of late, the opening of entry points along the LoC for civilian crossing. Although the 42-month dialogue process has not yielded the desired results, both the governments seem to be closer to agreements on a number of issues.

Besides, the two countries have also exchanged some proposals through the back channel on the settlement of the Jammu and Kashmir dispute. However, very few people of the two governments are fully aware of what is going on behind the scene. Concerned citizens and the general public on both sides know virtually nothing. This makes the back channel process vulnerable: nobody knows how stakeholders and the public will react when the solution is finally made public.

India's Mixed Response

Initially, the Indian leadership was quick to turn down President Musharraf's proposals on Kashmir, making it clear that sharing the sovereignty of Jammu and Kashmir with Pakistan was out of the question. However, due to the host of factors outlined above, it eventfully realized that it had to reciprocate and take the proposals into serious consideration.

The Indian Prime Minister made some reconciliatory remarks that encouraged pro-settlement forces in Kashmir and Pakistan. India resumed the negotiation process with APHC's Mirwaiz faction and also held meeting with Sajjad Ghani Lone, Chairman of the People's Conference and to the leader of Jammu & Kashmir Liberation Front (JKLF), Yasin Malk. The Indian Prime Minster held three Kashmir-related roundtables with the pro-India leadership of IHK and formed five working groups to seek recommendations on various issues.

The pro-independence leadership was also invited but it did not participate, demanding that a separate meeting be held with it instead of a joint sitting with pro-India politicians. Notably, President Musharraf personally encouraged the pro-independence APHC leadership to join talks with India and Pakistan separately, as this would be a step in the direction of trilateral talks. There is a feeling in a large section of the Indian establishment and public opinion that Pakistan has narrowed down its position and come closer to that of India's, despite its use of different jargon and nuances.

It is interesting to note that, in the last two years, Indian Prime Minister Manmohan Singh has spoken on his vision of how to settle the Kashmir issue several times. On March 24, 2006, in Amritsar, he argued for a step-by-step approach and commencement of dialogue with the people "in their areas of control" to improve the quality of governance. Regarding the future status of the LoC, he said that it might eventually become a mere line on a map, and that people might be able to visit and trade freely. He made a departure from his government's earlier stated position by acknowledging that the "the two parts of Jammu and Kashmir can, with the active encouragement of the governments of India and Pakistan, work out cooperative consultative mechanisms so as to maximize the gains of cooperation." He also offered a treaty of friendship between India and Pakistan.

Subsequently, at the Second Round Table Conference held in Srinagar in May 2006, the Indian Prime Minister indicated that he might take some institutional arrangements to bring people from both sides of the LoC closer to each other. While meeting with a APHC Conference delegation in New Delhi, he said India might create an environment in which a person could live in Srinagar or Muzaffarabad without any legal restriction. He reiterated that India was willing to move beyond its stated position, and expressed his openness to any ideas that might contribute to the ongoing thought process. Finally, speaking to a meeting of Indian businessmen in New Delhi, Prime Minister Manmohan Singh repeated his hope for a treaty of peace and friendship with Pakistan and emphasized the need for linkage among South Asian states for economic development. This was the second time he had spoken of such a treaty in the period of about a month. Just one month earlier, he had initiated his idea of a treaty of peace and friendship at a public rally in Amritsar. Echoing the same line a few days earlier, the Indian External Affairs Minster Paranab Mukarjee had said that India had to be prepared for some give and take in the border talks with China and Pakistan and should be prepared to shun rigid claims of national sovereignty if the talks were to be meaningful.

These pronouncements indicate that the Indian leadership is willing to have a phased-out formula for the resolution of the Kashmir issues. Nevertheless, it is neither relinquishing Indian sovereignty over Jammu and Kashmir, nor ready to trade off territory. At the end of the day, the people of Jammu and Kashmir may have de facto reunification of the state, which will give them psychological satisfaction. Apart from Monmohan Singh's reconciliatory remarks, a number of other key political stakeholders, such as Mufti Muhammad Sayyed's People's Democratic Party (PDP), National Conference, and APHC's Mirwaiz faction all support the Islamabad approach on Kashmir with slightly varied interpretations. In this context, the Indian government has adopted a policy of engaging both Kashmiris and Pakistan in the dialogue process, separately but simultaneously. It suggests that New Delhi has attached huge expectations to an internal agreement with the people of Kashmir, giving relatively less importance to the external factor. However, it recognises the significance of people-to-people contacts across the LoC and, therefore, agreed to initiate the Srinagar-Muzaffarabad bus service and allowed Kashmiri leaders to travel on it to Muzaffarabad in July 2005. It has also given relatively better political space to the Mirwaiz faction of APHC and frequently facilitated its travel outside the country.

On the other hand, a number of Indian officials and commentators are restlessly following the beaten track of bitterness, continuing to hurl accusations at Pakistan with no regard for the emerging environment. Officials in India's top echelons quite frequently use isolated events to accuse Pakistan of terrorism without offering any substantial evidence. At times, Islamabad's sincerity is questioned. For instance, according to Satish Chandra, former Deputy National Security Advisor to the Indian government:

Is the military in Pakistan sincere in wanting good relations with India? Pakistan's engagement in the current dialogue process is due to compulsion of external pressures and military exigencies which have tied up substantial Pakistani forces on the West.

In April 2005, when Musharraf visited New Delhi, both the gov-ernments made announcements that the peace process was irreversible and no incident would be permitted to derail it. But immediately after the Mumbai bomb blasts, New Delhi called off the dialogue process and stalled the foreign secretary-level talks for almost three months. Indeed, New Delhi left no stone unturned to prove that Pakistan was a haven for terrorists and was involved in promoting terrorist networks inside India, particularly in the occupied Jammu and Kashmir. Satish Chandra observed:

Pakistan's involvement in terrorism is well-known. It is not limited to Jammu and Kashmir, but extends to several parts of India, including the northeast. One of my major concerns was that in many parts of India, including New Delhi, we are a hair's breadth away from a major terrorist attack.

In view of such contradictions, it may be assumed that either opinion within the Indian establishment is divided on the future course of action, or New Delhi has a well-defined, official double-edged policy of conducting talks with Islamabad and, at the same time, continuing its blame game to keep the latter under pressure. It is possible that New Delhi wishes to maintain tactical ambiguity to keep both pro- and anti-peace process forces confused with mixed signals. Such an approach also allows the Indian government to drag its feet on the peace process whenever it desires. It appears that India does not care if its stance sends negative signals to the people of Pakistan, or if it reinforces the argument before them that Delhi is not responding to Musharraf's flexibility, even in diluted form. On the other hand, Musharraf has consistently applauded Vajpayee and Manmohan Singh, calling them statesmen, but the Indian leadership has never reciprocated the gesture. Musharraf has earned a lot of appreciation across the world for his efforts to solve the Kashmir problem but this too has made little impression on the Indian establishment.

Some leading Indian opinion makers believe that Pakistan had no option but to comply with Indian demands. This view has been echoed by former Indian Prime Minister Inder Kumar Gujral in the following words:

What options does he [Musharraf] have? His country faces innumerable problems. He also finds India growing taller and taller. His friends, the Americans, have told him not to rock the boat.

Thus, the process of reconciliation and the blame game are continuing simultaneously, indicating that the Indian establishment has yet to enter true reconciliation mode. Naturally, several questions arise about this complex Indian attitude. The answer primarily lies in the changed ground realities; for instance, back and forth movement across LoC has admittedly gone down, while militants are no longer a major threat to the security forces. Moreover, with the tacit approval of Islamabad, the fencing of the LoC has been completed without any real hassle. The unfaltering commitment on the part of Pakistan to respect the ceasefire along the LoC is a further encouraging factor. Inside Kashmir, the APHC stands divided into two factions and one of them, headed by Mirwaiz Omer Farooq, is in touch with Indian interlocutors, seeking a compromised settlement of the issue within the Indian Union.

New Stakeholders

Recently, Kashmiri domestic politics took a dramatic turn when the President of the pro-India National Conference, Omar Abdullah, made a striking demand. He said that no solution for Kashmir was possible without the involvement of Hizbul Mujahideen (HM) in the dialogue process. He urged India and Pakistan to hold talks with the United Jihad Council and HM's chief, Syed Salauddin. Besides Omer Abdullah, the PDP chief Mehbooba Mufti has also consistently advised New Delhi to bring HM on board. JKLF leader Yasin Malik, known as the pioneer of militancy, also sets dialogue with HM as a precondition to a peaceful resolution of the Kashmir dispute. Moreover, a number of intra-Kashmir dialogue conferences organized by the Centre for Dialogue and Reconciliation, Delhi, have persistently been arguing for a seat for militants in the ongoing process.

HM has welcomed the suggestion for the first time in its 17-year armed resistance. Its inclusion in the dialogue has become a bipartisan demand of the Kashmiri stakeholders, cutting across the political divide. However, several questions arise regarding HM's future course of action. It is a fact that HM has played an instrumental role in highlighting the Kashmir issue by rendering huge sacrifices. It commands immense respect and credibility among the masses. Its chief, Syed Salauddin, is a household name in Kashmir and is regarded as one of the most trusted leaders of the state.

CBMs: A Blank Cheque for HR Violations

Despite a number of Confidence Building Measures (CBMs), the articulation of positive statements in the top echelons of the two countries, and several rounds of high level tête-à-tête between Indian and Pakistani officials, there has not been even a slight decline in the level of human rights violation in Indian-held Kashmir. Fake encounters and disappearances are still staged. The violations are so high that even the pro-Indian mainstream, along with the "separatist parties" — as India calls them — are up in arms against the government and security forces on this issue.

In the context of the ongoing peace process, it was not a misplaced expectation that, at least to improve its democratic image, the Indian government would take special measures to ensure respect for human rights and stop indiscriminate killings of civilians in the state. It was also necessary to get public support for the ongoing dialogue process. But events show that human rights abuses have actually doubled and random killings continue as a routine matter in IHK. It is quite surprising that the world community does not let a single opportunity slip to condemn human rights violations by resistance outfits but is silent on the acts of barbarism committed by the forces.

The Indian brutalities fuel feelings of vengeance among Kashmiris and invite more violence, which helps in providing fresh blood to the dissidents. It should be borne in mind that, in the initial years, the character of the resistance movement was not violent or communalized as it later became. However, even peaceful protests were dispersed with gunfire. The Indian forces imprisoned all renowned political figures and ceased all avenues for the peaceful and non-violent components of the struggle. Eventually, not only the youth but also professionals and the political leadership were dragged into armed struggle. These views were echoed in the editorial comments of the Jammu-based *Kashmir Times* on January 5, 2005: The poor track record of Indian forces on human rights front, which includes not just physical torture but also the mental trauma and agony of being looked upon with suspicion and subjected to every day humiliation in one's own home by a man in uniform who is for all practical purposes an outsider, thus becomes a major source of spread of militancy in its fanatic form, as is evident today.

Given, Kashmiri leaders often say that the current Indian strategy is aimed at crushing the Kashmiri struggle for self-determination under the disguise of parlays with Pakistan. This is why Indian forces are vigorously pursuing their military operations in the state. Secondly, as long as the two sides remain engaged in talks, the international community and human rights organizations will not voice any concerns lest it derail the dialogue process and spoil the atmosphere. Besides, Pakistan is consciously avoiding making human rights a point in the talks, fearing that it might annoy India to the extent that it backs out of the negotiations. India is taking undue advantage of this deliberate silence. On the other hand, it has practically given India a soft opportunity to suppress all the significant voices in the state.

It is also a known fact that the Indian armed forces have developed stakes in the J&K conflict. Over a period of time, they have developed a huge infrastructure and extract immense benefits from the festering wounds of Kashmir. They are entrusted with several draconian powers and prerogatives to conduct arbitrary operations and commit custodial killings. It is a proven fact that the security forces take money from local people through intimidation and threats.

Therefore, the huge military set-up in J&K has itself become a bottleneck in the peace process. Several Kashmir watchers believe that it was the military and intelligence establishment that compelled the Congress-led government to not budge from the Indian stated position on the issue. The ruling class in Delhi today also believes that Islamabad is on the receiving end and its game plan has been exhausted. So, eventually, the Indian writ on Kashmir shall be fully reestablished.

Dissident voices

Syed Ali Gilani, Chairman of his own faction of APHC, has emerged as a leading critic of the current peace process. He believes that the process is going to bury the Kashmir issue rather than settling it according to the people's wishes. His views have a strong following of politically aware lawyers, intellectuals, youth and women inside Kashmir.

Apart from his political and religious ideology, he commands respect from all segments of Kashmiri society because of his firm stand on resolution of Kashmir according to the wishes of its people. Militant outfits, too, regard him as a source of aspiration. Hizbul Mujahideen, the largest indigenous militant outfit, has been especially under his influence since its inception. Armed groups, such as Lashkar and Jaish, have also expressed great respect for him. Because of his position within these outfits, he has emerged as one of the key influential leaders of the Valley. It is often said that he holds the key to the peaceful settlement of Kashmir.

On January 17, 2007 a strike was observed in the Valley to mark a protest against the visit of Mirwaiz Omer Farooq and his colleagues to Islamabad. Interestingly, however, public response to his recent strike call had been overwhelming, with the calling it a near to complete strike. This signifies the failure of the moderate APHC factions to take people into confidence. Mirwaiz visited Islamabad in January 19-27, 2007. He had meetings with President Pervez Musharraf twice and other government functionaries, besides sitting with a large number of political entities and Kashmiri parties.

However, he could not get in touch with Syed Salahudin, the Hizbul Mujahideen commander-in-chief, as he declined to meet him. Likewise, in Azad Kashmir, apart from the ruling Muslim Conference, no other political party or civil society group supported the current formulation of the Kashmir settlement. Evidently, within Kashmiri opinion, the current moves do not enjoy reasonable support, which makes the entire process vulnerable and weak.

INDIA-PAKISTAN PEACE: HIJACKED AGAIN

It is probably hardwired into the delicate structure of South Asian politics—which mainly revolves around the two nuclear-armed neighbors of Pakistan and India— that peace cannot last for too long. History has seen a series of failed efforts from both sides to establish cordial relations: the Nehru-Liaquat pact in 1950; the Ayub Khan-Shastri talks in the aftermath of the 1965 war; the Sharif-Vajpayee talks, culminating in the Lahore Declaration of 1999; the bilateral discussions between Indian Prime Minister Vajpayee and Pakistani President Musharraf in

2001; and most recently the meetings between Prime Ministers Narendra Modi and Nawaz Sharif.

All these attempts have either ended in futility or provided only a short-term respite. Recent efforts seem headed in the same direction, with the Pakistani high commissioner in India, Abdul Basit, revealing the suspension of dialogue between the two countries earlier this month.

Basit's statement came just after a Pakistani Joint Investigation Team (JIT) visited India to probe the January attack on the Pathankot air base. He stated that the peace process had been suspended and that there was "no meeting scheduled between foreign secretaries yet." Referring to the arrest of Kulbhushan Yadav, alleged to be an Indian spy, in Pakistan, Basit added: "We all are aware of those who seek to create unrest in Pakistan and destabilize the country."

Enjoying this article? Click here to subscribe for full access. Just $5 a month.

That the two sides understood the importance of continuing talks in the aftermath of the Pathankot attack was much appreciated by observers. However, recent calamitous developments have put the dialogue process in peril yet again. India claimed the Pathankot attack was carried out by militants coming from across the border and asked Islamabad to take immediate action against the perpetrators. To its credit, Pakistan surprisingly announced full cooperation in the investigation and assured all necessary steps in this regard. Consequently, a First Information Report (FIR) against unknown persons was lodged in the Pakistani city of Gujranwala under the Pakistan Penal Code and the Anti-Terrorism Act.

India, however, considered the FIR a "small step" and expressed disappointment that Maulana Masood Azhar, chief of Jaish-e-Muhammad (JEM), was not named. India also put forth a resolution in the United Nations to place Masood Azhar on a list of global terrorists, but this was blocked by China.

When the JIT from Pakistan traveled to India to probe the Pathankot matter alongside Indian officials, the team found it hard to come up with conclusive results because India turned down Pakistan's request to access witnesses inside the airbase. This led Pakistan to claim that India had not been cooperative enough in the investigation. Meanwhile, in late March Pakistani authorities arrested Kulbhushan Yadav, alleged to be an agent of India's intelligence agency Research and Analysis Wing (RAW), in the restive province of Balochistan. Subsequently, Pakistan released a video of Yadav confessing to carrying out belligerent activities in Pakistan to sabotage peace in the country. Together, Yadav's arrest and India's non-cooperation in the Pathankot attack investigation caused Pakistan to announce suspension of peace talks.

Since Narendra Modi was sworn in as prime minister, he has generally taken a tough tone towards Pakistan. However, in December 2015, he paid a surprise visit to Pakistan which led to optimism regarding bilateral relations. Pakistani Prime Minister Nawaz Sharif has also asserted his aspiration to build friendly yet equality-based ties with India. After the arrest of Yadav, Sharif even kept quiet over the issue, which was described by a government official as a deliberate move. Yet this silence—which also sparked huge political criticism for Sharif at home—could not prevent the suspension of talks.

Historically, any attempt to improve the India-Pakistan relationship or to come to the table for composite dialogue has been stalled due to the Kashmir issue. The more India stresses the inclusion of terrorism as an issue in bilateral talks, the more vociferous Pakistan is about Kashmir. Today Kashmir is less of the focus, but the Pathankot attack and arrest of Yadav became the new breaking point in negotiations.

Unfortunately, India-Pakistan hostilities are not tied to one particular issue. Though many believe a peaceful settlement of the Kashmir conundrum would bring about normality, there is no guarantee of durable peace. Geopolitical factors are increasingly important, including India's recent approach toward Afghanistan, Iran, and Central Asia as well as Pakistan's conviviality with China.

India is developing the Chabahar port in Iran, providing political, economic, military, and strategic support to Afghanistan, and seeking access to Central Asia. All these goals are directly or indirectly related to Pakistan. Only a helpful Islamabad could remove hurdles for India must clear to reach Afghanistan and beyond, but Islamabad continues to see the Indian presence on its western flank as an existential threat. Conversely, India has been wary of the growing Islamabad-Beijing connections, especially with the commencement of the China-Pakistan Economic Corridor (CPEC). Resolving only one issue — even the Kashmir question — will not unlock peace in South Asia. If there is the political intention to gradually resolve all pertinent issues gradually, then both Pakistan and India can compromise or bargain at some level. Therefore, the governments should not allow their dialogues to be hijacked by the Pathankot attack or the spy issue. Neither Islamabad nor New Delhi should deviate from their commitment to secure peace and regional stability.

PEACE PROCESS AND POST MUMBAI TENSION

In order to understand strange and complex Pak-India relationship, which arouses the best and the worst of emotions at different times, and thus makes the two sides obsessive about each other, one has to delve long into history. Only thus one can understand the psyche of each regarding the other. Hindu Muslim communities in South Asia claim inheritance to two great civilizations of the region- the Mauryan and the Mughal. The partition of Sub-Continent which the Congress accepted only when left with no alternative, and the bloodshed that accompanied it further exacerbated the hard feelings. Kashmir dispute ensured the continuance of the feeling of animosity between the two countries.

As both countries have not been able to resolve their disputes including Kashmir, the rift has deepened. Other issues of concern are; the water issue, Sir Creek and Siachin. As a result, Pak-India relations are laced with suspicion and mistrust, and pose a serious challenge to peace and stability in South Asia. Starting from the Simla Agreement in 1972, almost every major political party which is represented on the political horizon of Pakistan today has undertaken substantial steps for the purpose of creating stable and peaceful conditions in South Asia during its tenure in power. This was natural since it was a security imperative. The recent decade long period of CBMs was initiated in 1997 by Pakistan to resume bilateral talks with India in order to resolve peacefully all outstanding issues between the two countries including Jammu & Kashmir.

The two countries held three rounds of Foreign Secretary level talks on the agreed eight item agenda. The eight items agreed for the composite dialogue included peace and security including CBMs, Jammu & Kashmir, Siachen, Sir Creek, terrorism and drug trafficking, economic and commercial cooperation and promotion of friendly exchanges in various fields. However, little progress was achieved during this phase. During this period, a momentous development took place with far-reaching implications for regional as well as international peace and security. India conducted five nuclear tests and these were followed by six tests in the same month, May 1998 by Pakistan.

Prime Minister Atal Behari Vajpayee visited Lahore on February 21, 1999 and the Lahore Declaration signed during the visit committed the two countries to intensify efforts to resolve all outstanding bilateral issues including Kashmir. It also obliged both sides to refrain from interference in each other's internal affairs and evolve measures to reduce risk of accidental or unauthorized use of nuclear weapons, strengthen SAARC and combat terrorism in all its forms and manifestations.

The period between 1999 and 2002 witnessed a high level of tension between India and Pakistan due to a number of factors including among others, Kargil 1999, the inconclusive Agra Summit 2001, attack on the Indian parliament in December 2001, and the mobilization of a million troops on the border.

Taking over as the foreign minister in 2002, I strongly believed that normalization of relations is in the best interest of both Pakistan and India and that the people of Pakistan want peace with India provided peace is with honor.

At that time, in the wake of 9/11 India had unleashed a campaign to project itself as a longstanding victim of terrorism and to convince the world of links between Osama Bin Ladin, Taliban and the freedom struggle in Indian held Kashmir. Accordingly, very unfortunately and very unfairly the Kashmir freedom struggle was now being seen internationally in a different light. Pakistani argument and stance till then that Kashmir freedom struggle is indigenous and that Pakistan extended only political, diplomatic and moral support was not evoking acceptability from the US and EU and especially after 9/11, even Pakistan's closest friends began to advise us to think of an alternative way for achieving our objectives. It was, therefore, becoming clear amongst a large section of the influential decisions makers and the intelligentsia in Pakistan that while maintaining our position of principle on the issue of Kashmir, we have to adopt a different strategy.

Indians also learnt a lesson after the troops' mobilization (in 2002) when they realized that Pakistan did not blink or cave in because of India's show of military might. Pakistan made it clear that it would not accept Indian diktat and would counter any aggression.

Indian PM Vajpayee on April 18, 2003 offered in his own words 'a hand of friendship' to Pakistan. Prime Minister Mir Zafarullah Khan Jamali welcomed the announcement in a call facilitated by the then US Secretary of State Colin Powel. Pakistan's strategy was based on the recognition that the international community had zero tolerance for violent means for changing the status quo, no matter what the cause. The distinction between the freedom struggle and terrorism was beginning to disappear.

Some Indian parliamentarians also visited Pakistan in August 2003 interaction proved very useful at that stage. Pakistan also announced a major CBM to observe ceasefire by Pakistani forces along the LOC with effect from *Eid-al-Fitr* on November 26, 2003. Musharraf and Vajpai met on the sidelines of the SAARC summit in Islamabad in January 2004 and a joint statement was issued that included reference to the need for a resolution of the Jammu and Kashmir dispute to the satisfaction of both Pakistan and

India and that Pakistan would not allow its territory to be used for terrorism. The issue of joint statement generated optimism and contributed to the lessening of tension. It was hailed by the international community and the two leaders were given credit for their vision in breaking the impasse. During this phase of relations, Pakistan followed a three track approach, namely CBMs, Composite dialogue and back-channel on Kashmir. The four points that President Musharraf often spoke about regarding Kashmir included identification of region (Pakistan wanted to ensure that the Northern Areas are non-negotiable), demilitarization, self governance and joint mechanism.

During this period, the then government came under some criticism that Pakistan has taken a U-turn on Kashmir; President's four point proposal amounted to giving up on our principled stand, Pakistan is offering concession on all issues without any *quid pro quo; and* pro-Pakistan elements in Kashmir are being isolated. The then policy makers, however, believed that such perceptions were entirely misplaced.

In April 2005, Indian PM Manmohan Singh and Pakistani President Musharraf met in New Delhi, and declared that the Peace Process was "irreversible". As a result of the process, several high level contacts were made. People to people contact reached to an unprecedented level in 2005 when thousands of Pakistanis were visiting India monthly and an equal number were coming from India to Pakistan. The direct bilateral trade had increased from 200 million to over 2 billion dollars, the bus and rail links started between the two countries on various routes.

On terrorism, Pakistan was able to make India and the world realize that it is as much a victim of terrorism as any other country. The joint anti-terrorism mechanism is supposed to be used by the two countries to convey concerns of each other on incidents of terrorism. A lot of progress was made on the backchannel on Jammu and Kashmir. On Siachen, at the political level, the two sides were inching towards a package proposal. On Sir Creek, the two sides have already conducted a joint survey. Regarding nuclear CBMs, the two countries had concluded

Agreements on pre-notification of flight testing of ballistic missiles and on reducing the risk from accidents relating to nuclear weapons. Conventional CBMs included: re-confirmation of both sides to the commitment of upholding of the ceasefire, implementation of the 1991 agreement on air space violation, up-gradation of hotlines between the DGMOs, hotlines between Indian coastguards and Pakistan Maritime Security Agencies, across LOC travel, bus and truck service.

Pakistan was working in the hope that this process of composite dialogue, CBMs and back channel diplomacy would create the necessary environment for resolution of outstanding disputes particularly Kashmir. Pakistan continued to emphasize the need to make genuine progress on substantive issues. Coming to post Mumbai tension, it can be said that threat of military confrontation is abating. Indian forces are deployed on non-peace time formations. Pakistan has asked these forces to be reallocated to peace time positions. The cost for both countries of a conflict or a surgical strike by India will entail unforeseen risks. However, current state of tension is unlikely to pass quickly since India believes Pakistan is resisting the crackdown on militants.

India often accuses Pakistan of living in a state of denial regarding terrorism, but itself lives in a state of denial about Kashmir. Additionally, it is common knowledge that there are various types of secessionist, regional, ethnic, and ideological movements in different parts of India. I am not just referring to Muslim outrage over the demolition of Babri Mosque or the massacre of the Muslims in Gujrat; Maoists violence against upper caste Hindus is unleashed in major parts of India covering almost 1/3 of its territory. The details of Indian homegrown militancy are well documented. Even extremist elements have been identified in Indian military. India is ignoring these realities and continues to blame Pakistan.

PRE-REQUISITES OF PEACE PROCESS BETWEEN INDIA AND PAKISTAN

For any state in this universal map,cooperation and reciprocality is paramount in terms of peace process or armistice.

Peace process which can be simply defined as the process or an activity of a series and sequence of discussions or negotiations between the states in order to make efforts for finding the ways to solve the tensions, conflicts or complications within the state either at inter-regional or intra- regional bases that might be war or to any political violence. Peace process which defines the essential elements of resolving the disputes through amicable means by the mutual or joint action plan of states.

Both should climb down from their hardened positions on Kashmir and take concrete steps towards the resolution of one of the world's oldest dispute. It's a tough exercise to give concessions and to continue negotiations otherwise the past rivalries will continue. There are certain imperative prerequisites of peace process,withoutthissine qua non, peace business or peace exercise cannot be put into the water, or projected, but although certain changes could happened due to the situations existing among the states.

These are as follows,

- Readiness of political parties is crucial in order to start-off the procedure of parleying or discussions. For example, both Pakistan's and India' political parties should show readiness in order to resolve the issues relating to each other especially the oldest issue of Kashmir territory.
- Transparency in aims and goals of the leaders with great inclination in peace process. For example, in case of Nawaz Sharif and Modi, both must show transparency in their discussions with practical implications of the resolution of the disputes between each other.
- Quality and solicitation of determination and stoicism. The official leaders, the policy makers as well as the public of both Pakistan and India must concerned over their determination for the solution of issues, with the quality of stoicism both the states can remove the negative images of each other.
- Deliberation of time management. There should be proper time management in dealings and arranging negotiations with each other.

- Comfort and strength to the peace process by the political leaders support and their positive attitude towards it. In case of strengthening trade shows, economic confederations, parliamentarians dialogue process, release of prisoners, opportunities in visa policies are great signs of normalization of relations between the two actors.
- Depletion of joint suspect, obsession and intuition. For example in case of Mumbai attacks and Pathankot air base, India blamed Pakistan for such destructive attitudes in order to decrease the joint suspect, obsession and intuition, Nawaz Sharif make-up a high profile investigation team Intelligence Bureau (IB), Inter- Services Intelligence (ISI) and Military Intelligence (MI).
- Enlarging and advancing the sense, attitudes and behaviors as well as methods of understanding and interpretation. Both the countries leadersattitudes, behaviors must be positive for each other, also to interpret the disputes and resolve in peacefulways.
- Distinguishing and proper recognition of censorious issues. It is the main concern of the political leaders to have the proper recognition of hypercritical issues and have transparency in distinguishing the disputes.
- Generatingconvenient surroundings for talks. For example, on 12th April 2012, Pakistan has initiated a four day exhibition in the name of "Life style Pakistan" in New Delhi. More than 650 people were brought by Pakistan to India for the purpose of trade show. This exhibition has enabled and gives hopes to Pakistan and India that due to increase in trade would be helpful in furthering peace talks on Kashmir issue as well as on other issues.
- Focusing on fault-finding and judgmental issues rather than on less controversial matters.In 2015, Pakistan and India agreed to reopen comprehensive dialogues this was announced by the Indian External Affairs Minister SushmaSwaraj, where comprehensive dialogues are meant for the resolution of all outstanding issues to be resolved. Both Sartaj Aziz and SushmaSwaraj emphasized on talks

related to peace and security, Jammu and Kashmir, Siachen, Sir Creek, Wullar Barrage, Tulbul Navigation Project, economic and commercial cooperation, counter-terrorism, narcotics control, humanitarian issues, people to people exchanges and religious tourism.

- Struggling for accommodation, adjustment of win-win situation. For example, in case of Pakistan and India, both the governments are struggling and making efforts for fight against terrorism which has become a global issue and also in terms of the series of India-Pakistan cricket and two-twenty 20 matches were played between the two from 25 December 2012 to 6th January 2013.One day series was won by Pakistan and twenty-20 series was drawn by 1-1.However in 2007, bilateral series which was hosted by India was won by India. This was considered as the good attempt by both the states which had also increased the people to people contact and also beneficial for both the governments.
- Provide significance and boldness to the public opinion while the negotiations are going in process.For example new visa policy in 2012 was formed in order to increase cooperation between the two states. On 8th September, 2012 new visa agreement was signed by the Indian Foreign Minister S.M Krishna when he made a three day visit to Pakistan. For the very first time citizens with age above sixty-five would be given an opportunity of forty-five days single entry visa on arrival.This policy has also provide facilities to the to the tourists visas, pilgrim visas, make the things easy for the businessmen as well as for the senior citizens.
- Must have the ability to learn from the past experiences of the negotiations.For example as both the states having nuclear weapons and in case of any clash among them would result in destruction. On realistic basis, the new emerging world order focused on avoiding open confrontations. In order to think that if it is a positive policy to use force against India, it would have definitely

serious impacts for Pakistan like the Kargil war took Pakistan in economic as well as in military crisis.

- Take advantage of the services of arbitrator, when demanded. For example United Nations Secretary General Ban Ki Moon presented his services for the process of mediation between Pakistan and India on Kashmir issue.Also he emphasized talks on several strategies for promotion of education between the women of Pakistan with the leadership of the country.He played a role as a arbitrator for the dialogue process between Pakistan and India.
- Must have the knowledge of the pertinent and applicable manifestations.

There is a great need for Pakistan and India to have clear knowledge and awareness about what measures would be effectively performed in order to eliminate the negative images, actions and attitudes which have emerging nature of creating hindrance among them.

- Have the ability to captivate the role of media in such a way that represents the all-around a sound of joint-confidence and building of trust.For example, Pakistani media played a key role in terms of moulding public opinion and for developing a positive image regarding India. "AmankiAasha" is good effort by Jang group of Pakistan and Daily Times of India, where a number of seminars and conferences were arranged among Pakistan and India along with the exchange of artists in drams and movies.
- Development of good communication based on understanding and cooperation between the concerned members. For example, Pakistan Institute of Legislative Development and Transparency (PILDAT) which gave opportunity to the Parliamentarian Dialogues between Pakistan and India where in the first two rounds of talks in 2011 the delegations emphasized on the peace, security, stability. Also in 2012, the members of the Parliaments of both sides communicate in terms of trade and economic

relations.The talks were based on the understanding and cooperation for the promotion of the economic activities.

- Have authority over the bounding line rigidness.For example in terms of the territorial issues Pakistan must have an authority in the security moves over the borders connections in order to have stability and peace in the country.
- Termination of advertising of armed conflict in opposition to combatant. For example, in case of theSiachen issue a delegation was held by the defense secretaries in 2012, for the resolution of the issue. Former Pakistan's Chief of Army Staff, General PervaizKiyanicalled for the demilitarization of Siachen glacier as many soldiers were killed in it.Uptill no no proper talks were to be seen by the two states for the proper implementation and resolution of the issue.
- Emphasizing on the positive aspects and negation of the pessimistic attempts. By means of heavy military spending is a major problem and a main obstacle for the socio-economic development. Pakistan and India must focus on the capabilities regarding political potentials, economic power as well as military power which are the three gauging measures for the stable system.
- Keen observation of the environment and issues for the better outcome. For example Confidence Building Measures (CBMs) could act as a source for further improvement in Pakistan-India relations. Peace and prosperity could not reach to its highest peak unless both the states work jointly efficiency towards cooperation. As Ex-President Musharraf encouraged people to people contact between Pakistan and India which was an important step for improving relations.
- Suitable adjustment of the things or matters for the peace process.For example from the future perspective the relationship between Pakistan and India depends on the compromise which must be accepted by both the states. In order to become successful in terms of the engagements

to be alive would be mandatory by both the states for much investment in the peace process.

Mutual suspicion and distrust in the hearts of the leaders should be removed through consistency and proper implementation of peace policies and it really depends on how much each side is willing to do this.

Pakistan and India should resolve their bilateral problems and the mentality of success of one is the loss of the other should be removed and both states should come close for the betterment and welfare of their people. Both states should review the progress made on the India-Pakistan roadmap to peace which the two sides agreed again and again in their discussions and dialogues.

AN OVERVIEW OF PEACE PROCESS BETWEEN PAKISTAN AND INDIA:1997-2015

Peace process which can be simply meantas the composite dialogue process and it is taken as the process or an activity of a series and sequence of discussions or negotiations between the states in order to make efforts for finding the ways to solve the tensions, conflicts or complications within the state either at inter- regional or intra-regional bases that might be war or to any political violence. Peace process which defines the essential elements of resolving the disputes through amicable means by the mutual or joint action plan of states.

South Asiathe huge Asian continent on the world slab consists of seven states namely, Pakistan, India, Afghanistan, Bangladesh, Nepal, Sri-Lanka and Bhutan. As such the most influential place is given to Pakistan and India because of their economic developing attempts, by political contributions or due to their military-nuclear capabilities are raising their role, their performance, attitudes, actions, images, behaviors also responsive signs in the game of politics among other world powers, such as United States of America, Russia and China. The relationships between the two South Asian states arequitebitter and unfriendly since independence. Throughout their relationship has had never been even and smooth. Both the rivalries remained a debate of long discussion on international channel either from the historical perspective or due to religious conflicts, also because of the fact of three prominent wars i.e. 1948,1965 and 1971. Also the limited war in 1999 at Kargil on most antiquated issue of Kashmir. "Moreover, the arms race between the two countries has reached a point where the two adversaries, by exploding nuclear devices in 1998, have transformed the South Asian region into a plausible theatre of nuclear conflict. The peace efforts through détente between the two countries initiated since the Lahore (1999) and Agra (2001) summits have started showing positive results, as manifested in the resumption of the Delhi–Lahore bus service and growing interaction between the two countries in the domains of culture, sports, economy and trade." (Malik & Sharma, 2014:240)

Moreover, the seeds and essence of Composite Dialogue Process (CDP), initiated to be made in 1997, when the Inder Kumar Gujral who was the third Indian Prime Minister and his compeer Nawaz Sharif (Current Prime Minister of Pakistan) met at the capital city of Maldives Male, introduced the conception ofstructured dialogue which is meant for thecontinuous joint reflection on the priorities so called as the Composite Dialogue Process. Mainly on the slab of the modus vivendi, it was due to the peace process that has given the space and opportunity to both the countries to negotiate and talk on all the issues and complications inclusive Jammu and Kashmir concurrently.It was taken as a modus vivendi or accommodation in a way that as by means of India agreed upon to consider the issue of Kashmir in the scheme or plan of discussion, as India did a U-turn to encompass the issue of terrorism which are the two most provoking and troublesome in bilateral relations.On the basis of composite dialogue, this first endeavor cave in and fall down due to the effects of theKargil war in 1999.

Though on the part of the two rounds of discussions i.e. in 1998, one round of talk from 16 to 18 October and the second round of talk from 5 to 13 November, that had not appeared specifically advantageous. Even so, no discussions were likely to occur to remain alive in terms of the ensuing or future war as well as counter-accusation. At that instant,there occurred the scene of the Composite Dialogue Process at a far position when the government of Nawaz Sharif was removed forcibly from power by the General Pervez Musharraf, being the military and was the new leader of that time, who criticized and denounced the Lahore summit for permitting India, in reaction to keep away from directing the ferocity and aggression in Kashmir. By means of Kargil as well as the failure of the Agra summit, due to which the hope and anticipation for dialogues got much more ill and low in quality because of the attacks on the Indian parliament on 13 December, 2001.

Apart from this, the 9/11 incident of United States of America also come up as to organized differently in terms of the global politics on the subcontinent. Stress and tensions were rising between Pakistan and India all though season of 2002, as seemed to be the possibility of war between the two states. Although that pressure and tension come up to fade away in 2002, and subsequently within the time span of six months, the figure of Composite Dialogue was once again emphasized. Hence, in April 2003, as inaugurated by India what was highlighted as the step-by step notion heading towards Pakistan. As such July 2003 is vital due to the fact of the diplomatic ties also the direct bus connection were again re-developed and ceasefire was began in November.In June 2004, when the Composite Dialogue Process was revised and re-established, in consideration of the decision taken by ShriAtalBihari Vajpayee, former Prime Minister of India, when he visited to Pakistan.

Khurshid Mahmud Kasuri who remained the foreign minister of Pakistan during the era 2004 to 2007 under the control of government by General Pervez Musharraf. He recently wrote a book titled as, Neither a Hawknor a Dove, where he in fact emphasized that peace loving Pakistan is played out of anti-India flag- waving. It is described in his work that because of the competitive negotiations particularly on Kashmir issue at one level where both Pakistan and India were quite near to make a reliable agreement, but because of the inevitable happenings in India and Pakistan, no accordance came to the final stage."The recent visit by Kashmiri leaders from Jammu and Kashmir to Azad Jammu and Kashmir and Pakistan is the culmination of our efforts for initiation of the wide ranging consultative process to associate the true representatives of Kashmiris in the Pakistan-India peace process."

He presented the view that the Kashmir cause has a powerful legal as well as moral framework and as such the violent attempts would not assist further that cause. He is basically against the militancy, radicalization as well as extremism. MrKasuri proclaimed that in terms of his close ties with his Indian equivalents, the negotiation process among the two states has made quite reliable opportunity of progressive attitude, and that both Pakistan and India were walking far from the conflict management towards a much consequential and apt conflict resolution process. By means of the negotiation process, the significance of table talks could not be set too low."Mr. Kasuri said Pakistan was very serious and determined to carry the peace process forward a notch higher if not more." (Mahmood,2006:3) "The issue of peace in the region depends primarily on what happens in their mutual relationship. The two countries have indeed pursed a vibrant peace process since January 2004, resulting in significant Confidence Building Measures (CBMs)."(Ahmad,2015:56).In 2004, there was a composite dialogue held between Pakistan and India regarding the Kashmir issue. Similarly, in 2005 meeting was arranged by both the hostile states in order to resolve the issue of Kashmir by peaceful means. The year 2006 is highlighted in a way when General Musharraf and former Prime Minister of India Manmohan Singh negotiated in resolving the Kashmir issue by amicable means and with some purposeful and forward looking way. In 2007, the two sides leaders were agreed to go for the implementation of the Kashmir specific CBMs.

In 2005, Agreement on Advance Notification of Ballistic Missile Tests plan in force where both the countries and in advance were given opportunity to update the other 72 hours before the initiation of other ballistic missiles in terms of the 40km of the International Boundary line and the LoC.On the part of the humanitarian assistance of food, medicine and other necessities which were enlarged by India and also accepted by Pakistan, specifically after the earthquake in Pakistan Administered in Kashmir in 2005.In 2006, the transport services began from Lahore to Amritsar, Amritsar to Nankana Sahib also the railway networks between Munabao in Rajasthan and Khokhrapar in Sindh.In 2007,while crossing at the Wagah border, the first overland truck passage was initiated between the two countries.By means of air connections in 2008, there was an increase in number of flights from twelve to twenty-eight flights in a week, also the origination of triple-entry allow for cross-LoC travel as well as the prevalence of the Srinagar- Muzaffarabad bus service extend from twice monthly to weekly.On the basis of establishment of agreement by means of communication connections at the status of scholars, Institute of Defence Studies and Analysis (New Delhi) also Institute of Strategic Studies (Islamabad) was put into force in 2008.

The first Joint survey was arranged by the Pakistan and India on the issue of the Sir Creek in 2005.In 2006, both Pakistan and India negotiated on the Sir Creek dispute in Rawalpindi and decided to initiate the second round of joint survey in 2007 and as per decision the leaders of the two countries arranged a further survey from the G-pillar 46 in the water part of the creek.In 2005, both the states leaders discussed the Siachen issue for the promotion of the peaceful settlement of the dispute. As Mr. Kasuri said "the possibility of a resolution of the glacier dispute had been created but no agreement had yet been reached. Indeed, as with other issues, the glacier remains a relic of past distrust." (Mahmood,2006:10)Thus the establishment of Siachin as a peace parkland in actual is very substantial confidence building measures in eliminating the suspect between Pakistan and India ties. "If the Siachen Peace Park becomes a reality, it will save both nations the financial and human costs of conflict, improve bilateral relations, and build mutual confidence for addressing other issues in the Composite Dialogue, especially the conflict over Kashmir. A Siachen Peace Park could play a historic role in the process of peace in this war-torn region." (Kemkar,2005:56)Wullar Barrage which is named by the India as Tulbul Navigational Project, being the second project of India that is left over disputed.Even today, the issue is not resolved between the two countries and it is decided that they would make further attempts in resolution of this issue as part of the process.The economy of the country if going at a prosperous rate would give rise to the economic conditions of the states, so as the commercial links are vital for the development of the country, by all such means Pakistan and India, at the time of partitioning, were economically dependent on each other. However, later on both the actors worked out to have their potentiality on economic matters in order to eliminate the stand of interdependency. The origin of the Composite Dialogue Process was built to bring the improvements in terms of Pakistan and India's economic and commercial relations.

In 2008, Pak-India talks were arranged in Islamabad that focused on the issues of: Kashmir, Siachin, Sir Creek water dispute,Wullar barrage, terrorism and narcotics, strengthening trust, economic cooperation as well as friendly exchanges in trade.

Furthermore, since the time of independence of Pakistan in 1947, there has had been trade relations at the bilateral, regional and multilateral level. However, commercial ties between the two states get strained during the 1965 and 1974 wars. Later on trade recommenced in 1974. The status of Most Favored Nation (MFN) was given by India to Pakistan in 1995, just after the formation of the World Trade Organization and this status came into effect since 1996.Although even due to MFN status Pakistan had gone from weighty trade insufficiency with India. On the part of Pakistan did not gave the MFN image to India, although concerned about continuing a positive list regarding the importable things from India, that has been frequently in escalating process. However the list was initiated with only seven items when there was beginning of the trade once again after a long gap of nine years specifically in 1974, had stretched out somehow 800 items in 1996,when India accorded MFN to Pakistan and had moved up to 1945 items by the end of the year 2011 when the government of Pakistan stepped ahead in terms of granting India as the MFN status.

In the previous years it is being observed the great changes in terms of trade and investment ties between Pakistan and India which came up with the new phase in both the countries bilateral economic collaboration. "Since the revival of trade talks in 2011, the two neighbouring countries have come closer with a vision to enhance peace and stability in the South Asia region. There have been several initiatives taken by both these countries for strengthening bilateral relations, of which Pakistan's decision to offer the most favored nation (MFN) status to India is a remarkable one." (De &Raihan, 2013:1)As such Pakistan and India are more concerned about the expanse of barriers by several means of bilateral trade and investment. Specifically, there are three areas of cooperation originated from the previous secretarial level conference between both the actors.

1. Extending access to both the states markets by means of goods and services keeping in view the trade liberalisation inclusive to that of elimination of Non-Tariff Barriers (NTBs).
2. Shoreup the tradebenefits in order to make better physical affinity.
3. Permitting investment to make proceeds and flow in each other states.

Hence the cooperative attitude and measures in these areas could greatly come up with the major positive effect in economic and social benefits for both Pakistan and India. Weather to give MFN status to India or not, this issue was not picked up by the newly elected government of Prime Minister Nawaz Sharif in 2013 and this matter is still unresolved.

Apart from this the year 2013 is highlighted due to fact of rise of Indian Prime Minister NeranderaModi as a hurdle in Peace Process andModi was elected to lead and crown the BJP's 2014 general election movement to the lower house of the India's parliament LokSabha, whereas the masses and the proletariat was so far in place to select him prime minister.

As such, Modi then struggled and championed steely, representing himself as a realistic and practical runner with the capacity to turn around in terms of the economic matters of India. As it is said, "since becoming Prime Minister of India in May 2014, with a landslide victory and lower house majority in parliament not seen in 30 years, NarendraModi has been seen as a beacon of hope for India's prospects, both economic and otherwise".

By looking at the successful outcome, he along with his party got supremacy with prosperity in the LokSabha. The wining result came up with the notice board of squash and compressing beat towards the Indian National Congress which had contained and determine the behavior or supervise the running of politics of India for almost last sixty-years and also spread a word and piece of information that Indian citizens were at the back curtain of docket or agenda of root-and-branch change. However, some analylists perceived the Modi's intentions regarding problems of India, as "Mr. Modi seems to be taking a long-term view towards India's structural problems. He knows that he has a full five year term in which to push forward with his agenda, and more than likely two terms."(Hui,Hui, & Lewis, 2015:6)

CONCLUDING REMARKS

Normalization of relationship with India, as an objective, is not in dispute. Somebody may be called a hawk and somebody as dove, but the normalization of relationship is perhaps common between all of them. The question is that of peace with honor, justice and for resolving disputes, not deferring or sitting on them. So from that viewpoint, one has to realize that there are dynamics of power politics and idealism.

Morality is relevant but keeping in view the power equation, and the convergence and divergence of interests and finding out a more equitable sustainable equation is the real challenge. The psyche with which Indian leadership has been dealing with Pakistan; and our own mindset is not just product of current situation. It goes back to a thousand years and one cannot totally de-link from that. We have coexisted but we have never converged. We can live in peace with each other but to think of having a common civilization, culture and lifestyle is against reality. So it is a complex issue.

The issue of Kashmir is not a question of political game but an issue that deals with life, honor and liberty of 15 million people. It is not a land dispute; and India and Pakistan and for that matter any other power has no right to deny Kashmiris their right of self determination. To say that Kashmir has kept our relationship or the whole peace process a hostage is not in keeping with the human and political reality of the region. The issue of Kashmir has to be resolved and resolved with justice; and unless it is resolved with justice that satisfies the rights of the people of Kashmir, there is no future for the normalization of relationship in the region.

Water issue is also critically important. Pakistan ignored it but now we are in a situation that we can no longer ignore it. It requires a very clear vision of our own policy. Institutionalized policy making is something that we lacked. Ad-hocism needs to be done away with and medium and long term formulation of policy is required.

Another point relates to the whole business of terrorism. Terrorism which involves killing of innocent people is a crime against humanity - conducted by an individual, groups or states. But it has been seen after 9/11 that terrorism, after its denomination as war, de-linking it from the reality of its being an act of crime to be addressed to as a crime under the system of criminal justice, has changed the whole grammar of politics.

The way terrorism is being used today has become a part of new colonial hegemonic designs of the powerful. It is no longer a question of terrorism *per se* it is an instrument of policy of neo-colonialism. One has to see that who has benefited and gained from the incidents such as 9/11 in the US and 26 November 2008 in Mumbai.

It is true that Pakistanis, Muslims, in fact people all over the world, do not hate America but American policies. The policies of hegemony, exploitation, domination, occupation, support for Israel and ensuring that those who are trying to seek justice and freedom from oppression are not helped but efforts are made to exterminate them. But the agony is that beside this perception, our rulers continue to follow those very American policies in our lands. The real conflict is between the aspirations of the people and the interests of the superpower and their collaborators who are ignoring the wishes of the people and are pursuing what is aggravating the situation. Whether it is Afghanistan, Iraq, Palestine, Kashmir or FATA, these policies are failing and yet we are hands in gloves with those who are perpetrating these policies. That is the dilemma. The people have to be prepared to see it and rise; otherwise, one can not see any way out. If the people of the world want a peaceful planet and a just world order then such oppressive policies have to be checked and countered.

It can be said that even Mumbai has to be seen in this context. One should not be accused of falling back on conspiracy theories; because what is often dubbed as conspiracy may play a very important role in the making of the policy of powerful. Looking at the pre-Mumbai scenario, one sees that there was a remote possibility of some change as a result of elections in America.

Then there are the phenomenon of popular uprising during June, July and August in Kashmir, the shift from militancy or counter-militancy to a democratic uprising, the emergence of indigenous force that could have influenced the future struggle in Kashmir, elections within India and the changed situation in Pakistan. Mumbai took place in a very extraordinary context and it deserves to be examined who had benefited. Some kind of a 'reverse-engineering' is needed in political complexities of this type.

There are a number of writers within India and around the world who are pointing that there is something more fundamental behind it. While Pakistan has called for joint investigation, it is well known that people can be used by those who are playing this game of power. The Indian Prime Minister has said that what happened in Mumbai could not have taken place without state support considering the level of sophistication of planning, execution and implementation.

One can raise the question that who rules in Mumbai? Who has command of the Indian Navy? Who is responsible for Indian agencies? Was it possible that a small bunch of youth - 10 persons coming from sky or somewhere else could have held the city and the entire Indian government, agencies, system and Indian Navy as hostages? Where were the coastal guards and Navy? How the struggle was sustained for 60 hours at Taj Mahal and Oberoi hotels? How was the ammunition moved? What was the channel? Is it possible without support from within? So these are very fundamental issues.

And now the whole Kashmir issue has been sidelined and the sacrifices in the uprisings up to 2008 have been marginalized. These are very fundamental issues that are to be examined. The purpose of raising these questions is to find out what is the reality. And I have no reservation in saying that willingly or unwilling, by choice or by compulsion, if any Pakistani was involved in Mumbai attacks, he should be punished, and punished under Pakistani law, through its judicial process. It is right to say that Pakistan's cause has suffered; has not gained.

But the issue is more complicated. Who did what? Who was behind? Who was used and how this very game has been played in the past. We know that at the time of every major and historic moment particularly during the last twenty years, when something of strategic importance was going to happen, some such unfortunate event did take place. When former US president Bill Clinton was visiting India in 2000, 38 Sikhs were killed in Chattisingh Pora. Pakistan was blamed and it was later found out that local agencies were responsible for it. Clinton, while writing the foreword of the book by Madeline Albright, has very intelligently suggested that had he not visited India those 38 persons would have been saved. So the incidents like Mumbai should not be seen as simply a new phenomenon; there seems to be a pattern.

The need is to listen to each other, identify issues, continue discussion and dialogue and to help the policy makers seek these dimensions so that more informed judgments could be arrived at, and policies which are not ad-hoc and do not lack harmony are framed.

7

Process of Peace Building in Afghanistan

TALIBAN EMIRATE AND THE UNITED FRONT

The Taliban started shelling Kabul in early 1995 but were defeated by forces of the Islamic State government under Ahmad Shah Massoud. Amnesty International, referring to the Taliban offensive, wrote in a 1995 report: "This is the first time in several months that Kabul civilians have become the targets of rocket attacks and shelling aimed at residential areas in the city."

The Taliban's early victories in 1994 were followed by a series of defeats that resulted in heavy losses which led analysts to believe the Taliban movement had run its course. But Pakistan provided increased support to the Taliban. Many analysts like Amin Saikal describe the Taliban as developing into a proxy force for Pakistan's regional interests. On 26 September 1996, as the Taliban with military support by Pakistan and financial support by Saudi Arabia prepared for another major offensive, Massoud ordered a full retreat from Kabul. The Taliban seized Kabul on 27 September 1996, and established the Islamic Emirate of Afghanistan. They imposed on the parts of Afghanistan under their control their political and judicial interpretation of Islam issuing edicts especially targeting women. The Physicians for Human Rights (PHR) analyse:

"To PHR's knowledge, no other regime in the world has methodically and violently forced half of its population into virtual house arrest, prohibiting them on pain of physical punishment."

After the fall of Kabul to the Taliban on 27 September 1996, Ahmad Shah Massoud and Abdul Rashid Dostum, two former enemies, created the United Front (Northern Alliance) against the Taliban that were preparing offensives against the remaining areas under the control of Massoud and those under the control of Dostum. The United Front included beside the dominantly Tajik forces of Massoud and the Uzbek forces of Dostum, Hazara factions under the command of leaders such as Haji Mohammad Mohaqiq andPashtun forces under the leadership of commanders such as Abdul Haq or Haji Abdul Qadir. The Taliban defeated Dostum's Junbish forces militarily by seizing Mazar-i-Sharif in 1998. Dostum subsequently went into exile.

According to a 55-page report by the United Nations, the Taliban, while trying to consolidate control over northern and western Afghanistan, committed systematic massacres against civilians. UN officials stated that there had been "15 massacres" between 1996 and 2001 and that "hese have been highly systematic and they all lead back to the [Taliban] Ministry of Defense or to Mullah Omar himself." The Taliban especially targeted people of Shia religious or Hazara ethnic background. Upon taking Mazar-i-Sharif in 1998, 4,000-6,000 civilians were killed by the Taliban and many more reportedtortured. The documents also reveal the role of Arab and Pakistani support troops in these killings. Bin Laden's so-called 055 Brigade was responsible for mass-killings of Afghan civilians. The report by the UN quotes "eyewitnesses in many villages describing Arab fighters carrying long knives used for slitting throats and skinning people".

Pakistani President Pervez Musharraf – then as Chief of Army Staff – was responsible for sending thousands of Pakistanis to fight alongside the Taliban and bin Laden against the forces of Massoud. According to Pakistani Afghanistan expert Ahmed Rashid, "between 1994 and 1999, an estimated 80,000 to 100,000 Pakistanis trained and fought in Afghanistan" on the side of the Taliban. In 2001 alone, there were believed to be 28,000 Pakistani nationals, many either from theFrontier Corps or army, fighting inside Afghanistan. An estimated 8,000 Pakistani militants were recruited in madrassas filling the ranks of the estimated 25,000 regular Taliban force. A 1998 document by the U.S. State Department confirms that "20–40 % of [regular] Taliban soldiers are Pakistani." The document further stated that the parents of those Pakistani nationals "know nothing regarding their child's military involvement with the Taliban until their bodies are brought back to Pakistan."

From 1996 to 2001 the al-Qaeda terrorist network of Osama bin Laden and Ayman al-Zawahiri became a state within Afghanistan.Bin Laden sent Arab recruits to join the fight against the United Front. 3,000 fighters of the regular Taliban army were Arab and Central Asian militants. In total, of roughly 45,000 Pakistani, Taliban and al-Qaeda soldiers fighting against the forces of Massoud in mid-2001, only 14,000 were Afghans.

Ahmad Shah Massoud remained the only leader of the United Front in Afghanistan. In the areas under his control Massoud set up democratic institutions and signed the Women's Rights Declaration.

Human Rights Watch cites no human rights crimes for the forces under direct control of Massoud for the period from October 1996 until the assassination of Massoud in September 2001. As a consequence many civilians fled to the area of Ahmad Shah Massoud. In total, estimates range up to one million people fleeing the Taliban. National Geographic concluded in its documentary *"Inside the Taliban"*:

"The only thing standing in the way of future Taliban massacres is Ahmad Shah Massoud."

In early 2001 Massoud addressed the European Parliament in Brussels asking the international community to provide humanitarian help to the people of Afghanistan. He stated that the Taliban and al-Qaeda had introduced "a very wrong perception of Islam" and that without the support of Pakistan and bin Laden the Taliban would not be able to sustain their military campaign for up to a year. On this visit to Europe he also warned that his intelligence had gathered information about a large-scale attack on U.S. soil being imminent.

CURRENT CONDITIONS IN AFGHANISTAN

Twenty-three years of conflict, four consecutive years of drought, and a repressive government unconcerned with economic development or other basic communal needs combined to produce the exodus of over six million people from Afghanistan between 1980 and 2001. An estimated one million Afghans were thought to be internally displaced as well, a number that increased during the early weeks of U.S. military action in Afghanistan in the fall of 2001.

Since the final collapse of the Taliban in early 2002, over two million refugees have returned to Afghanistan. But not all have returned "home:" the majority — 60 percent — of the returnees have gone to the capital, Kabul, and the immediately surrounding areas (Kabul Province and Nangarhar Province to the east). Significant numbers of refugees are also returning to the tribal areas along the southern and south-eastern border with Pakistanm where sporadic fighting continues. A large influx of people into these insecure areas can have negative implications for the overall safety of civilians in the region.

However, over 70 percent of the total number of returnees are the relatively "new," mostly urban refugees who fled Afghanistan during the rule of the Taliban between 1994-1995 and 2001. "Long-stayer" Afghans who fled during the Soviet occupation and civil war that followed the Soviet withdrawal have been less enthusiastic about returning than those who fled the Taliban. There are various reasons for this reluctance. Many Afghan refugees have settled into lives in Pakistan during their 20 years abroad, have children who were born in Pakistan, or have seen their property and livelihoods destroyed in Afghanistan and are fearful of what would await them on return. Regardless of the reasons such refugees may be hesitant to leave, it is clear that Pakistan's government is anxious to see them go home. Public acceptance of Afghan refugees in Pakistan has deteriorated sharply in recent years, and calls by the government for the refugees to return home have become louder. Swayed by these pressures, on March 17, 2003, Afghanistan, Pakistan and the

United Nations High Commissioner for Refugees (UNHCR) signed a "historic" tripartite agreement on the return of such long-stayer populations, establishing a formal, three-year process for the "gradual and sustainable" voluntary repatriation of the estimated 1.5 million Afghan refugees remaining in Pakistan. UNHCR officials estimate that 600,000 Afghan refugees will return over the course of 2003 alone.

Returns have been difficult to "manage" because the numbers have proven to be substantially higher than anticipated. UNHCR was forced to reduce the rations given to both refugees and internally displaced persons. Though necessary in light of the fact that many international donor states had not yet lived up to their pledges, the diminished reintegration assistance may have compounded the social and economic pressures already felt both in urban centers and in villages, as well as adding to the strain of having to feed and support thousands more people in drought-stricken rural areas. The past year was been marked by cautionary statements from UNHCR, the International Organization for Migration (IOM), and international NGOs providing assistance in Afghanistan, which suggested that returns should be facilitated but not encouraged until needs assessments and regional profiles were completed to arrive at a full understanding of actual conditions in areas of return. Their reasoning was that people returning too hastily to agriculturally unstable areas lacking basic community infrastructure, agricultural inputs, and/or other means of livelihood support were likely to become displaced again once the inadequacy of local food supplies and international relief assistance became clear.

Physical security has been another profound concern in a country with a fledgling central government and judicial system. Many areas are under the control of warlords, and armed opposition to the central government continues, particularly in the south of the country. UN Secretary-General Kofi Annan, in a report to the UN Security Council on March 21, 2003, cited security as the "most serious challenge facing the peace process in Afghanistan — the re-establishment of the rule of law, elimination of human rights abuses, reconstruction and political transformation are all impeded by the uncertain security situation."

As a result of such pressures, in early spring 2003 UNHCR announced a "shift in focus" on return from one of maximizing the number of returnees to one of ensuring the sustainability of return. Additionally, more attention will be paid by UNHCR and partner NGOs to assisting returns and reintegration to rural areas in order to avoid overburdening the cities. Demobilization of combatants is another key concern. A July 2002 study conducted by the United Nations Assistance Mission in Afghanistan (UNAMA) estimated that there are 200-300,000 armed people in Afghanistan, most heavily concentrated in the north.

Demobilizing these people and decommissioning their weapons is crucial to creating a more secure post-war environment. However, the demobilization issue poses a dilemma: in a tense security environment such as Afghanistan, with several armed groups competing for power and spoils, pushing too hard for demobilization too quickly can be destabilizing. At the same time, however, a lack of demobilization is destabilizing as well.

In this light, security is as much a question of economics as of power or loyalty. Demobilization is much less destabilizing when done with a provision of economic and employment alternatives. The time nexus between demobilization and the creation of a national army, therefore, is crucial, particularly in terms of integrating former combatants, militias, etc., into the national army and thereby "solving" the twin problems of decommissioning and lack of alternatives.

AFGHANISTAN : SECURITY, DEVELOPMENT AND PERSPECTIVE

Security, an essential public good, is widely seen as a central issue for Afghanistan's reconstruction and development. Security impacts on the whole range of development issues faced by Afghanistan, ranging from state building and capacity development to revenue collection, service delivery, and encouraging private sector-led growth. For the purpose of Afghanistan's National Development Strategy (ANDS), currently under preparation, the

Government has added a Millennium Development Goal (MDG) on enhancing security to the internationally agreed list of MDGs. This demonstrates the importance assigned by the Government to security and rule of law as a critical development issue. Afghanistan's external partners (including the World Bank) have consistently highlighted the importance of security as a key enabling factor for Afghanistan's reconstruction and development And most important, the Afghan people themselves emphasize the importance of security and the protection of property rights in their daily lives and for building their livelihoods and communities. More specifically:

- Security and rule of law as public goods have been grossly underprovided in Afghanistan during the past quarter-century, with state functions in this regard usurped by factions, regional and local powerbrokers, and external actors. Remedying this situation is an urgent, high-priority task.
- Improving security is also a core component of the state-building agenda, seen by most Afghans as an essential function of an effective, accountable government.
- Moreover, an adequate level of security is a critical prerequisite for effective delivery of other public services.
- Politically, security improvements have been and will continue to be essential for the success of Afghanistan's transition toward political normalcy.
- Economically, security and law and order, along with the protection of property rights, are required for robust private sector development, which will be the only way to achieve sustained rapid economic growth over the medium term.
- Insecurity and narcotics are closely linked - insecurity is the environment in which Afghanistan's opium economy thrives, and the drug industry is a major source of instability and insecurity.
- And finally, from the individual, household, and community standpoints, security and rule of law are extremely important components and enabling factors in the quality of life, as is almost universally recognized by Afghans.

In addition to its importance as a central development issue for Afghanistan, the security sector accounts for a very high proportion of the country's total public expenditures as well as external assistance and raises major public expenditure management issues including risks to fiscal sustainability and possible crowding out of spending on other basic services. Therefore the security sector is also very important from a public finance management perspective. In view of these considerations, the Government of Afghanistan requested that the security sector be included in the World Bank's Public Finance Management (PFM) Review, and this volume is the result. There are in addition a number of specific rationales for the World Bank's engagement in analytical work on Afghanistan's security sector as part of the PFM Review and from a development perspective. First, as indicated above, security is of central importance for Afghanistan's development prospects, including in particular the state-building agenda. This means it has to be incorporated in the country's development strategy and planning (which the Government is doing), and that development partners need to be engaged in areas of their competence.

Second, given the great importance of security spending in the national budget (accounting for around 40% of total Core and External Budget expenditures), the security sector must be incorporated in the analysis of expenditure composition, budget prioritization and trade-offs, downstream expenditure implications of decisions and investments, fiscal sustainability, etc. These issues lie at the heart of the PFM Review.

Third, a weak PFM system in the security sector (and particularly if the security sector gets left behind while improvements in the PFM system are occurring elsewhere) would adversely affect the overall progress of PFM reform and institutional strengthening, distort choices made by the Government, reduce the effectiveness and efficiency of public spending, and increase vulnerability to corruption. All of these areas are of concern to the Bank. And fourth, security sector expenditures are largely donor-financed, raising important issues of aid management, aid harmonization, and aid effectiveness, as well as capacity development and effectiveness of technical assistance. These issues comprise an important part of the overall PFM agenda and hence need in the context of the security sector to be included in the PFM Review.

The main objectives of this review of security sector expenditures in the context of the PFM Review and taking a development perspective are as follows:

- To gain as complete an understanding as possible of the current level and structure of security related expenditures, recent trends, and likely future expenditure requirements based on current plans.
- To assess the extent to which coherent strategies, for the security sector and the major parts of the security sector, guide public expenditure allocations.
- To review the processes for determining funding levels, expenditure allocations, budget execution, and post-execution functions, with a view to assessing the extent to which they follow sound PFM principles.
- To describe the institutional framework for the security sector and ascertain the extent to which it embeds or is conducive to sound public financial management.
- To assess the strategic coherence and consistency and the fiscal sustainability of security sector expenditures.

This chapter sets forth the conceptual framework for analysis of security sector expenditures from a development and public finance management perspective. It first provides a working definition of the security sector. The chapter goes on to outline key linkages between security and development (based on recent international thinking on this subject). It then discusses key public finance management principles and their application to the security sector. The final section briefly summarizes the service delivery perspective and its application to the security sector.

Some background on the historical legacy from the long period of conflict in Afghanistan, and summarizes the progress made in building the security sector since 2001. It then overviews

Afghanistan's security sector at present - its legal basis, size, institutions, salient characteristics, and coordination - and at the end outlines the key security issues faced by Afghanistan from a development perspective. PFM principles and their application to the security sector, the implications for Afghanistan including gaps and constraints, and the Afghan budget process for the security sector.

The crucial issue of the fiscal sustainability of security sector decisions and investments, which is an important driver of the fiscal sustainability of Afghanistan's public finances as a whole. Building on the analysis of fiscal sustainability, At strategic prioritization and sequencing issues in the security sector and how these can be managed in particular through the national budget process. The budget execution for effective and efficient use of funds provided to the security sector.

Meaning of the Security Sector

The security "system" is defined broadly in OECD (2005b) as including the following main components: core security actors, security management and oversight bodies, justice and law enforcement institutions, and non-statutory security bodies. A broad definition of the security sector along these lines makes the most sense from a development and PFM perspective, as all different parts of the security sector have significant development implications as well as varying budgetary implications (for both expenditures and revenues).

However, some components clearly do not apply to Afghanistan (e.g. coast guards), while other institutions like Parliaments have not been functioning and hence are not relevant for analysis of recent developments and the current situation (although the role of the legislature will be important starting in the very near future). Moreover, non-statutory security bodies, although they have been major actors in Afghanistan (and mirror the breakdown of the formal security system during the protracted conflict), for the most part do not have direct budgetary implications and would require a very different mode of analysis. Therefore they are not looked at closely in this volume except in terms of their immediate budgetary implications - notably the Disarmament, Demobilization, and Reintegration (DDR) program - although their development implications and impact on the formal security sector will be kept in mind.

In sum, consistent with the overall objectives and approach of the PFM Review and in line with the increasingly recognized development implications of the security sector, this volume uses a broad definition of the security sector but focuses on those components which are of major importance from a PFM perspective. In terms of budget categories and programs, those that form part of the security sector and which are analyzed in the PFM Review include: defence, police and other internal security services, intelligence, counter-narcotics, the judiciary and penal system, mine clearance, and the DDR program.

The main security institutions in Afghanistan which will be looked at in the PFM Review include the following: (i)*government security management and oversight bodies:* National Security Council and National Security Advisor, Ministry of Defence, Ministry of Interior, Ministry of Counter Narcotics, Ministry of Border and Tribal Affairs, Ministry of Justice, Ministry of Finance, and the Auditor General's Office; (ii) *security services:* Afghan National Army (ANA), Afghan National Police (ANP), National Border Guards, Counter-Narcotics forces, National Directorate of Security (NDS - responsible for intelligence), Customs General Directorate under MoF, remnants of earlier military and police forces (the former subjected to DDR); and (iii) *justice and legal institutions:* Supreme Court, Judiciary, Attorney General's Office and prosecutorial offices *(saranwal).*

Excluded from detailed analysis in this volume are the non-statutory security bodies, including remaining unofficial militias and armed factional groups, private body-guards, and security companies. Foreign and international armed forces operating in Afghanistan also will not be analyzed in detail, except to some extent the Provincial Reconstruction Team (PRTs) which are intended to help strengthen governance and carry out reconstruction activities. However, the overall size and cost of these forces will be considered and their impact on the fiscal and

PFM aspects of the formal security system will be taken into account. The absence of a Parliament means that its oversight role with respect to security can be incorporated in terms of future options and recommendations, but not in relation to the analysis of recent developments and the current situation. Independent and civil society institutions which play a monitoring and advocacy role with respect to security, such as the Afghanistan Independent Human Rights Commission (AIHRC) are extremely important but are not analyzed in detail in this chapter.

FOREIGN INTERFERENCE AND WAR

After the fall of Najibullah's government in 1992, the Afghan political parties agreed on a peace and power-sharing agreement (the Peshawar Accords). The accords created the Islamic State of Afghanistan and appointed an interim government for a transitional period to be followed by general elections. According to Human Rights Watch: The sovereignty of Afghanistan was vested formally in the Islamic State of Afghanistan, an entity created in April 1992, after the fall of the Soviet-backed Najibullah government. With the exception of Gulbuddin Hekmatyar's Hezb-e Islami, all of the parties were ostensibly unified under this government in April 1992. Hekmatyar's Hezb-e Islami, for its part, refused to recognize the government for most of the period discussed in this report and launched attacks against government forces and Kabul generally. Shells and rockets fell everywhere.

Gulbuddin Hekmatyar received operational, financial and military support from Pakistan. Afghanistan expert Amin Saikal concludes in *Modern Afghanistan: A History of Struggle and Survival*:

Pakistan was keen to gear up for a breakthrough in Central Asia. Islamabad could not possibly expect the new Islamic government leaders to subordinate their own nationalist objectives in order to help Pakistan realize its regional ambitions. Had it not been for the ISI's logistic support and supply of a large number of rockets, Hekmatyar's forces would not have been able to target and destroy half of Kabul.

In addition, Saudi Arabia and Iran – as competitors for regional hegemony – supported Afghan militias hostile towards each other. According to Human Rights Watch, Iran was backing the Shia Hazara Hezb-i Wahdat forces of Abdul Ali Mazari to "maximize Wahdat's military power and influence". Saudi Arabia supported the Wahhabite Abdul Rasul Sayyaf and his Ittihad-i Islami faction. A publication by the George Washington University describes: utside forces saw instability in Afghanistan as an opportunity to press their own security and political agendas.

Conflict between the two militias soon escalated into a full-scale war. Due to the sudden initiation of the war, working government departments, police units or a system of justice and accountability for the newly created Islamic State of Afghanistan did not have time to form. Atrocities were committed by individuals of the different armed factions while Kabul descended into lawlessness and chaos as described in reports by Human Rights Watch and the Afghanistan Justice Project. Because of the chaos, some leaders increasingly had only nominal control over their (sub-)commanders. For civilians there was little security from murder, rape and extortion. An estimated 25,000 people died during the most intense period of bombardment by Hekmatyar's Hezb-i Islami and the Junbish-i Milli forces of Abdul Rashid Dostum, who had created an alliance with Hekmatyar in 1994. Half a million people fled Afghanistan. Human Rights Watch writes:

Rare ceasefires, usually negotiated by representatives of Ahmad Shah Massoud, Sibghatullah Mojaddedi or Burhanuddin Rabbani [the interim government], or officials from the International Committee of the Red Cross (ICRC), commonly collapsed within days.

Southern and eastern Afghanistan was under the control of local commanders such as Gul Agha Sherzai and others. In 1994, theTaliban (a movement originating from Jamiat Ulema-e-Islam-run religious schools for Afghan refugees in Pakistan) also developed in Afghanistan as a politico-religious force. When the Taliban took control of the city in 1994, they forced the surrender of dozens of local Pashtun leaders. In 1994, the Taliban took power in several provinces in southern and central Afghanistan. In late 1994, most of the militia factions (Hezb-i Islami, Junbish-i Milli and Hezb-i Wahdat) which had been fighting in the battle for control of Kabul were defeated militarily by forces of the Islamic State's Minister of Defense Ahmad Shah Massoud. Bombardment of the capital came to a halt. The Islamic State government took steps to restore law and order. Courts started to work again. Massoud tried to initiate a nationwide political process with the goal of national consolidation and democratic elections, also inviting the Taliban to join the process but they refused as they did not believe in a democratic system.

PEACEMAKING

Peacemaking refers to efforts aimed at high-level political negotiations in order to craft a political settlement. Below is an analysis of such efforts of the United Nations, the Organisation of the Islamic Countries (OIC), joint Pakistani and Saudi Arabian interventions and the Ningarhar Shura. [2] The peacemaking efforts of the UN in Afghanistan are divided into two phases; Geneva negotiations and post-Geneva peace making.

Geneva Negotiations

After six years of hectic negotiations the Geneva Accords was eventually reached in April 1988. However, the decision to withdraw from Afghanistan as Maley (1998) states was taken by the Soviet Politburo in November 1986. Whatever the reason, either the UN's efforts or the Politburo decision, withdrawal of the Soviet forces did not prevent Afghanistan from descending into further violence and destruction. Therefore, the Geneva negotiations can be analysed against a number of important factors discussed in the previous chapters and more importantly against the historical background and international and regional dimension of the protracted conflict in Afghanistan.

In the first chapter peace was defined, as *the existence of peaceful relationships, active association and planned co-operation among persons and groups*.... The talks were held in the absence of the main party (Mujahideen) to the conflict let alone promotion of peaceful relationships and active association between the contending parties. One of the principles of conflict resolution is that internal and external parties have to participate and agree to the solution. The external players, particularly supporters of Mujahideen apart from the USA with a symbolic show as guarantors together with the USSR did not actively participate in process. Instead the Geneva Accords was indirectly negotiated and signed by Pakistan and Kabul government.

The Geneva Accords failed to address the power-struggle between various groups that constitutes one of the root causes of war in Afghanistan. The negotiations were based on an incomprehensive agenda to bring about a political settlement to the crisis. "The accords said nothing about the future government of Afghanistan" in the aftermath of the Soviet withdrawal (Rubin 1995:91). Though the issue of transitional government was raised twice during the negotiations.[4]

The Geneva negotiations were mostly benefited from the political will of the Soviets and partly of the international community to prevent further East-West confrontation. But it failed to produce a comprehensive settlement for Afghanistan. In line with political will there existed a donor interest for reconstruction even on the part of the Soviets who promised to make a significant contribution through Operation Salam launched by the UN in the aftermath of the Geneva Accords. But due to incomprehensive settlement Operational Salam was never operational and donors' pledges were mostly withdrawn.

Although termination of external interference was part of the accord but external supporters as Rubin (1995) observes, continued to flood the Afghan government and the Mujahidden with weapon and means of violence and destruction soon after the Accords was signed. Only the Superpower agreed on a negative symmetry two years later.

Consideration of the operational aspects of peacebuilding that are integral part of any peace accord was totally neglected because negotiation was based on a seriously flawed agenda. Also there was no recognition of the strategic components that are necessary for sustaining the peace agreement. Regional co-operation for a permanent termination of hostilities in Afghanistan was also non-existent during the Geneva talks and with the collapse of Soviet Union the situation became worst.

In sum the Geneva negotiation produced a different outcome for each party. For Soviets it was success, for Afghans a failure and disastrous and for the UN it represents a missed opportunity because it failed to capitalise on the partial political will of the international actors for comprehensive settlement of the war in Afghanistan.

Realising the shortcomings of the Geneva Accords the UN immediately embarked on another peace making endeavour but this time with insufficient backing and co-operation of the international actors to produce a viable solution.

Post-Geneva Peacemaking

The second phase of the UN led negotiation was to address the legacy of the Geneva Accord that was to facilitate the transfer of power from Najibullah to a politically neutral body.[5] Between May 1991 and April 1992 Benon Sevan the special envoy of the UN Secretary General started an intensive negotiation among various parties.

His mission encountered severe setbacks due to the disintegration of the USSR and disengagement of the US. Both superpowers during the last round of Geneva negotiations according to Rubin (1995) had agreed to use their influence to ensure a political settlement under the auspices of the United Nations.

One of the internal factors that often works against negotiations is "the antagonists come to fear the consequences of settlement" (Stedman 1991:368). This was true in Afghanistan, the UN plan for the establishment of an impartial transition mechanism according to Rubin (1995) was suspected by the prominent Mujahideen parties as attempts to marginalize them.

The UN formula for transfer of power to an impartial body was clearly bypassing the existing armed groups who were already engaged in consolidating their power base inside Afghanistan. The second phase of the UN peacemaking efforts also suffered from absence of strategic components of peacebuilding inside the country. Wide-scale devastation of the social and economic infrastructure, the collapsed state, coupled with an atmosphere of distrust, rivalry and power-contention deserved simultaneous considerations. The UN did not establish strong a correlation between its diplomatic and humanitarian efforts so that each process enriched the other.

Collapse of the Soviet Union marked the total disappearance of political will for a negotiated settlement of the war in Afghanistan. Instead an environment of regional distrust and competition with relentless incentives for war has appeared. The mission therefore, lacked the necessary weight, leverage and support of the external actors. The foreign supporters of Mujahideen namely Pakistan, Saudi Arabia and the United States did not act with good faith either. Foreign patrons can influence the parties and shape the agenda for negotiations as in Mozambique in1991. Particularly Pakistan, Saudi Arabia and the US, instead of using their influence and leverage to unite the Mujahideen and encourage their participation in support of the process, they pressed for a pre-transition formula and resignation of Najibullah without organising a viable alternative to succeed him.

The division and internal power-struggle within the Najibullah's government was also undermined in this process. The cut-off of financial and military assistance from the USSR according to Bokhari (1995) significantly reduced the government's capacity for leverage and control of the armed forces and maintenance of unity within the government and the party. Therefore, different factions of the government allied themselves to different Mujahideen parties and the government collapsed from within (Hussain 1992 and Rashid & Ali1 992). The Peshawar based Mujahideen with the direct involvement of Pakistani prime minister and Saudi Arabian intelligence chief according Zahid (1992) were rushed to produce the Peshawar agreement on a transitional authority and distribution of government portfolios among themselves. The Peshawar Accord fell apart when Hez-b-Islami Hakmatyar did not agree to the formula and started rocket assaults against the government positions in Kabul. Later different groups became engaged in a catastrophic power-struggle that has been going on since 1992. The second phase of the UN led negotiations was based on a number of unrealistic assumptions: a) that strong unity existed within the Kabul government, b) that the Mujahideen (all together15 parties) were united and spoke with one voice; c) that the neighbouring countries were sincerely supporting a political settlement without any regard to their national interests; d) that there was a conducive social and economic environment for peace and e) that Afghanistan had a democratic culture and the democratic institution were already in place to create a conducive environment for smooth transition of power.

The third phase of the UN led negotiation started in December 1993 to broker a ceasefire and search for a viable solution. This phase of peacemaking was launched at the most difficult and less favourable circumstances inside Afghanistan as well as in the regional context. The collapse of the USSR further complicated the situation. New regional actors emerged and Afghanistan as Keating (1998) notes did not remain a focus of attention for the international community. Violence and internal fighting was widespread so was the massive destruction and extreme poverty.

In the first chapter it was argued that peacebuilding in the context of protracted conflict should be based on a multi-strategy approach through which war, its effects and its root causes have to be simultaneously addressed. The United Nations has been only focusing on one-track diplomacy trying to negotiate among internal actors whereas the direct involvement of the regional countries has not been sufficiently addressed; the economic collapse and social disintegration of the Afghan society have only been given symbolic treatment. Extreme poverty and massive destruction of the social and economic foundations of the society are among many domestic factors contributing to the conflict. Therefore, ignoring these fundamental needs is obviously not enhancing the political process.

The context of conflict is characterised by a dynamic process that so rapidly changes and often overwhelms the involved actors, peacemakers as Philipson (1999) notes, should therefore, adopt a proactive approach that requires consistency and regular analysis of the situation. Due to lack of regular follow up and inconsistent efforts of the special envoys, the UN peacemaking efforts have been unexpectedly overwhelmed by the rapid changes in Afghanistan. According to some sources, after 1992 none of the special envoys during their peace missions stayed overnight in Afghanistan. The UN peacemaking missions in Afghanistan have mostly suffered from uncooperative attitudes and irresponsible actions and decision of its member states particularly the regional countries and that of the US. The UN should have taken into account the regional dynamics of the conflict more seriously than the internal dynamics. Negotiations according to (Rubin 1995) must have taken place within a framework of regional co-operation with sufficient backing and support of major powers, as was the case in Central America.

With rhetoric the regional countries have been declaring support for the UN led negotiations but local realities suggest that the same countries are aggressively fuelling the conflict.

An opportunity for creating a social foundation for peace was missed during 11 years of unsuccessful peacemaking. The sole focus on military and political leaders diminished the possibility of the Afghan civil society to flourish and to become a civic force with appropriate capacity for promotion of peace. As argued in the first two chapters peacemaking at the political level should have been complemented with social and physical reconstruction at the grass root, but the UN treated political negotiations as an isolated activity.

In addition to the UN there has been some scattered political negotiations by the Organisation of Islamic Countries (OIC), joint Pakistan-Saudi initiative, and the Ningarhar Shura.

Organisation of Islamic Countries (OIC)

The OIC, missions were even less consistent than the UN, because most of its member states had declared their so-called support for the UN, and saw no reason to engage in a parallel effort. Second OIC is institutionally so weak that it has been unable to generate genuine interest for a political solution of the conflict among directly involved countries let alone create an additional enthusiasm in the Islamic world for resolving the ongoing wars in Afghanistan, Somalia, Sudan and in other Islamic countries. Unlike the UN the OIC does not enjoy a massive institutional and financial capacity to engage in a protracted effort of peacemaking or to address the strategic components and support implementation of the operational aspects of peacebuilding.

Similar to the UN OIC's efforts were constrained by the lack of political will on the parts of its members particularly neighbouring countries for a negotiated settlement in Afghanistan. In spite of all these institutional weaknesses, the OIC, by mobilising religious organisations of the Islamic countries (most of whom are closely associated with the warring factions) could have opened another window of opportunity for the promotion of political settlement.

This possibility was particular relevant since the warring factions have always justified their armed strife as necessary for the establishment of an Islamic government in Afghanistan.

Pakistan and Saudi Arabia

After the collapse of Najibullah government in April 1992, both Pakistan and Saudi Arabia were instrumental in brokering the Peshawar agreement on a transition mechanism between the Mujahideen parties. While both countries were strong supporters of Mujahideen and were still enjoying good relationships with all major parties they failed to produce a comprehensive agreement for the establishment of power sharing transitional mechanism and take realistic steps for confidence building among contending parties. Perhaps, the sudden collapse of Kabul government and earlier efforts of the UN and the US limited the abilities of these countries to properly negotiate a comprehensive plan. On the other hand the confrontation of strong military forces of Hekmatyar and Massoud in Kabul reduced the possibilities of a comprehensive agreement being devised. However it seems inconceivable that both countries should have had no prior knowledge of the developments in Afghanistan. The Peshawar agreement was also seriously flawed on the ground that Hezb-e-Wahdat (a coalition of 8 Shi'ite parties) was not given any role in the transition government; the role of Iran was also ignored.[6] This deliberate negligence and marginalisation of Iran by Pakistan and Saudi Arabia testifies to the regional competition and rivalries that resulted in a perpetuated human tragedy in Afghanistan.

The second joint peacemaking venture of these countries is known as Islamabad Accord reached in March 1993. This initiative was taken after a severe round of violent conflicts in the capital Kabul. This negotiation only focused on dealing with the symptoms rather than the real issues. The resultant agreement was to facilitate re-participation of Hekmatyar as prime minister in the power-sharing transition government of president Rabbani.

Even though the leaders "took an oath in Mecca to adhere to the agreement" they failed to respect it due to major shortcomings (Rubin 1995: 143). First, Ahmad Shah Massoud the then Defence ministry and a main adversary to Hekmatyar was not a signatory of the agreement. His position as defence ministry was the most controversial point. Second, the agreement lacked any provision for implementation of operational aspects. Third there was no consideration of a solid plan on how the country should be governed in post-transition and how social and economic devastation of war should be addressed. Fourth, the agreement failed to end the incentive for war by offering incentives for peace. Again the agreement was brokered without the participation of Iran and other regional countries that had been aggressively intervening in Afghanistan.

Ningarhar Shura

The Ningarhar Shura in 1993 undertook a major peace initiative by inviting all party leaders to the negotiation table in Jalalabad city.[7] This negotiation failed because the Shura did not have the backing of the foreign supporters of the warring parties as sources for leverage to influence and produce a settlement. The predominantly Pushtoon Shura of Ningarhar perhaps was not seen as impartial by some elements of Rabbani's government. Most importantly the Shura failed to follow up their peace efforts in a consistent way and to mobilise other commanders from the rest of the country in support of peace. However, the Shura in

June 1995 began a similar initiative to negotiate among warring groups but failed to bring the concerned parties to the negotiation table. The potential of the Ningarhar Shura was to engage in a continued peace advocacy at the national level.

INDIRECT CONTRIBUTION TO PEACE

In addition there are a number of local and international NGOs that are primarily involved in community-based rehabilitation and development programmes. Their approach to peacebuilding has been to use aid as leverage for resolving inter-communal conflicts and promoting community cohesion. In some cases this group of NGOs has been able to resolve a potentially violent conflict at the community level. [11] Through participatory methods this group is in a better position to minimise the negative impact of their programmes on local level conflicts. The weakness of this group of NGOs is that in most cases they are involved in short-term projects that limit their abilities to develop a local mechanism for conflict transformation or even to ensure sustainable self-help capacity within the community. Lack of meaningful co-ordination according to Strand (1998) is a major weakness of aid community in Afghanistan. Aid organisations mostly suffer from the inability to learn and benefit from each-others potentials and to ultimately promote a culture of sharing and co-operation within the community and their target beneficiaries.

There are also a large number of NGOs only concerned with delivery of aid without proper consideration of what causes the sufferings. For such organisations their very presence within the country is a contribution to peace though most of their headquarters are based in Pakistan and some of their actions and decisions are in fact contributing to conflict rather than peace. These NGOs mostly seek to work in conflict free areas. Regions and villages with even low-intensity inter communal, tribal or disputes are often ignored. Because, conflict resolution is political while NGOs are non-governmental, non-political and should not be involved in such activities. This group of NGOs are strictly bound by their mandates and procedures that do not allow any deviation. At best their conventional operations are serving as short-term relief without any prospect of future. The long term contributions of such activities to peace and their immediate impact on conflict seems to be negative because there is no indication that such programme has made a positive contribution towards capacity development, promotion of local capacities for peace or strengthening of civil society in Afghanistan.

The UN agencies led by UNDP implemented an experimental programme of community participation in the north of Afghanistan. UNDP funded programmes would be only implemented in a district if people established district Shura to priorities the rehabilitation projects and decide the location. Establishing and working through local Shura is an excellent approach for project implementation and can be a highly effective tool for peacebuilding, provided that the Shura is representative, treated as an equal partner, and actively involved in the planning, design and implementation of the programmes. But apart from this symbolic role the Shuras did not have any decision-making power on how the projects were to be implemented and monitored. With the completion of the projects the so-called Shuras also disappeared. In most cases it was district leaders, commander and rich landlord who dominated the Shuras and encircled the benefit of the programmes. In such a situation programmes are likely to increase tension within the community or strengthen the commander's position than reduce the sufferings of vulnerable families.

UNDP in 1997 embarked on a well-publicised three years programme entitled PEACE Initiative (Poverty Eradication And Community Empowerment) implemented in 32 districts and 5 urban centers. This programme with its massive budget and ambitious aim created a widespread enthusiasm and high expectations that peace was imminent in Afghanistan. Poverty alleviation, good governance, and community empowerment are the three fundamental requirements for a lasting peace and Afghanistan urgently needs such crucial programme. To achieve this aim UNPD and its implementing partners within the UN family and NGOs concentrated in the target areas (32 districts).

Integrated approach with a high degree of co-ordination and huge budget were the main features of PEACE Initiative that has undoubtedly affected a positive change in terms of improved infrastructure, increased agricultural products and economic development. However, in the social sector the programme did not make much progress, and certainly did not meet the needs for capacity development, promotion of civil society and strengthening of local capacities for peace.

There is heavy emphasis on community participation and empowerment and building of human resources throughout the programme document that prompted many people, myself included to present discussion papers to UNDP on how participatory approaches can be promoted and what are the crucial steps to be taken. Though UNDP seemed appreciative of the ideas and circulated the papers within the UN family but it practically failed to implement the suggested ideas or even to translate its stated ambitions into practice in the field. The most important aspect of the programme should have been capacity development of the implementing actors on participatory approaches and also of the communities and local structure.

Good governance is a stated objective of the programme but was very smartly interpreted as working with local NGOs and Shuras that were later narrowed down to a very symbolic role for these institutions. Local NGOs were treated as commercial contractors and local Shuras might have been consulted about the projects.

The overall aim of PEACE Initiative was set to "contribute to the restoration of peace in Afghanistan through poverty alleviation, good governance building and community empowerment..." (UNDP Afghanistan 19997-1999). With this clarity of goal one would expect that the programme to be based on a thorough analysis of the causes of bad-governance, poverty and factors that are dis-empowering people and communities and would seek to address these on a long-term basis. Unfortunately PEACE Initiative falls into the traditional UN operations of 'business as usual' where wide ranging projects were implemented without a critical assessment of how these projects would enable the achievement of the immediate objectives, poverty alleviation, empowerment and good governance let alone restoration of peace. PEACE Initiative by many accounts was not successful. Restoration of peace as discussed in the first chapter requires a multi-strategy approach with capacity development as its overarching goal to enable the communities to build and sustain their own peace.

It is appropriate to conclude with this popular saying: *When the only tool in your toolbox is a hummer - all problems start to look like a nail.* [12] It is very clear that UNDP's toolbox did certainly lack the most crucial tool (capacity development) for successful implementation of PEACE Initiative.

This assessment of peacebuilding approaches and the role of international humanitarian aid, first testifies that the 'moment is ripe' for community-based peacebuilding and there are ways and means to integrate peacebuilding into the aid programming. Second, it shows how little is happening in terms of peacebuilding while there prevails a condition of negative peace over more that 90 percent of Afghan soil. Third it enables us to further explore the *how* of peacebuilding in the context of Afghanistan and to come up with a realistic strategy in support of peace.

BUILDING POPULAR SUPPORT

Soldiers and Marines who used a population-centered approach tended to make more progress with less violence than those who focused on the enemy or the terrain. Doing so required dispersing into small outposts in or near populated areas, getting out constantly on foot, engaging and collaborating with local leaders, and implementing development projects that benefitted communities and built popular support. Units that followed this approach took on greater risk in the short term, but usually ended up safer in the long run.

The more successful units focused almost entirely on the population. Many did not bother to chase down insurgents. When the Marines cleared through Nawa in 2009, they focused on setting up outposts and beginning reconstruction. They allowed many fighters to escape, and even offered amnesty to those who agreed to lay down their arms.

On the few occasions that Afghan National Army (ANA) units led clearhold-build operations, they too focused on the population and did not give chase to fleeing insurgents. For example, in the Tagab Valley east of Kabul, Afghan Soldiers did not even shoot back when fired upon. Instead, they moved slowly up the valley, holding shuras (meetings of local leaders) in villages, setting up bases, and starting reconstruction projects. The Afghan Army managed to stabilize the valley with little fighting. Using Afghan forces to engage the population helped build relationships. Military operations that included local security forces were more effective than those that involved only coalition troops. Even more so, when US advisors were embedded with the Afghan Army—not just occasionally conducting operations with them—the effects were more positive. In many places, the local population was more willing to accept the presence of Afghan Soldiers, and they attracted fewer attacks.

Successful counterinsurgency operations involved constant interaction with local people, countless cups of tea, and sociable conversation. Relationship-building proved essential. Afghanistan, like most undeveloped rural nations, is a relationship-based society. In such places, it is necessary to build trust, which takes time, commitment, and work. It was not enough to institutionalize interactions between commanding officers and government officials. Personal rapport was essential.

Conducting foot patrols from small outposts in populated areas also proved essential. On foot, Soldiers and Marines were able to interact with people constantly—to gather useful information and understanding, and to form relationships. Small units that spread out into small outposts and patrolled every day on foot were more effective than large units that were consolidated on large bases disconnected from the local population.

Armoured vehicles and large, heavily fortified bases put barriers between local people and coalition troops. The same was true of wearing body armour and carrying weapons—especially pointing guns at civilians. In 2003, when permissive security conditions in Kandahar City allowed US troops to drive in unarmored vehicles and walk around without guns or body armour, it was much easier to engage with the people. As violence grew in later years and the coalition shifted to battle mode, coalition troops became increasingly cut off from the city's population.

Units that projected a heavier, more imposing and invasive presence often attracted more attacks. The more successful Special Forces teams operating in remote areas learned that it was important to maintain a light footprint in order to gain access to the population—otherwise, a team's actions could threaten local powerbrokers and heavily armed clans that had a penchant for taking up arms against outsiders. Providing a nonintrusive benefit won local support and therefore local protection. Leveraging Afghan leaders to mobilize the population often proved to be the best way to defeat the insurgency. The worst possible outcome for coalition troops in Afghanistan was to be seen as an army of occupation. Foot patrols and engagement with the population also saved lives. In Kandahar province, for example, Canadian Soldiers in such districts as Zharey and Panjwayi operated out of large, heavily fortified bases and moved around in armoured vehicles. These units met with intense fighting and took many casualties. In areas where the Canadians dispersed into small bases and patrolled on foot, there were fewer attacks.

The same was true for the US Marines in Nawa in 2009. They spread out into 26 small outposts, and conducted constant foot patrols out of these bases. They were out so often that the locals wondered whether the Marines ever slept. They also held shuras nearly every day near their outposts. By doing so, the Marines in Nawa were able to dominate the areas around their positions and build support among the nearby population.

In Helmand and parts of Kandahar, the insurgents used IEDs to prevent coalition troops from interacting with the people. The aim of the IEDs was to make movement so dangerous that Soldiers and Marines would no longer patrol far from their bases—ceding control over the population to the Taliban. In most cases, the best counter to the IED threat was regular foot patrols and engagement with the population. Soldiers and Marines who were able to build support among the population found that the

IED threat diminished considerably over time. On the other hand, the more troops stayed in their bases and allowed their movements to be restricted, the more intense the IED threat became.

This was the case in many places, including Sangin, the notorious town in northern Helmand where thousands of IEDs stood between British forces and the population. In many remote areas, it was the population that protected US and NATO forces—not the other way around, as is suggested by the counterinsurgency manual.

For many of the 12man Special Forces teams operating out of isolated firebases, building a base of support among the local population was essential for survival. Popular support, gained through sound counterinsurgency techniques, proved to be the best form of force protection. In some places, Special Forces teams moved safely in areas with substantial Taliban presence, because the local population supported the team's presence and pledged to protect it from attack.

The same was often true of general purpose forces stationed in remote and dangerous areas. For example, Soldiers in northern Kunar and eastern Nuristan managed to befriend village leaders who offered sanctuary to US forces passing through. These leaders also promised protection to US troops when inside the confines of their villages. Local elders sometimes accompanied US Army patrols outside their villages in order to deter attacks by local militants. These patrols were rarely, if ever, fired upon. However, not far away in the Korangal Valley, where the population was hostile and village leaders refused sanctuary to US forces, Soldiers were under constant fire everywhere and took many casualties. Where coalition troops had popular support, they faced little danger. Where they were looked upon as an occupying force, they were never secure, even in the apparently safe confines of their bases.

Using reconstruction funds

Many units learned to target their use of reconstruction funds toward specific objectives, rather than simply fund projects for their own sake. This meant using funds to gain and maintain support in key areas, draw fightingage males away from the insurgency, bring quarrelling factions to the negotiating table, and punish recalcitrant tribes and clans. It was not enough to simply execute a large number of reconstruction projects—to give people wells, roads, and other amenities in the hope of winning hearts and minds. Throwing money at problems rarely worked. Successful units used reconstruction funds to build relationships, in pursuit of clear political objectives. These relationships were often more important than the projects themselves.

Used unwisely, reconstruction funds frequently did more harm than good. For example, it was not uncommon for resentful tribes who did not receive funds to sabotage projects and attack US troops. Contractors who became wealthy and powerful as a result of their special relationship with US forces threatened local powerbrokers, leading to violence that was often mistaken for insurgent activity. The same was true of projects that employed outside labour.

Those units that were able to tie the local economy into the continued presence of coalition forces were particularly successful. They did this mainly by creating jobs and targeting certain leaders or segments of the population. The trick was to bring money into the community without upsetting the political and social balance of the locality. This worked even where the population was inclined to support the insurgency.

Reconstruction projects aimed at largescale job creation tended to be effective, especially where there were large numbers of landless laborers. For example, Canadian engineers in Dand district south of Kandahar City recognized early on that a few wealthy men owned all the land. Nearly all the people living in the district were sharecroppers and laborers who stood to gain little from roads, irrigation canals, wells, and other projects that promised to improve the productivity of the land. Such projects would merely enrich a few large landowners. The Canadians instead focused on low-tech, labour-intensive projects aimed at providing jobs to young men of fighting age. After six months, the Taliban was no longer able to recruit fighters in Dand district. When it came to getting results from job creation programs, much depended on local conditions. For example, like the Canadians in Kandahar, US Soldiers in northeast Afghanistan focused on low-tech projects aimed at providing employment. Yet, insurgent facilitators based in Pakistan offered generous salaries to wouldbe recruits—far more than the US military could provide with its limited amount of funds. Reconstruction projects in the northeast did not yield the clearcut results that Canadian Soldiers saw south of Kandahar City. In Sangin in northern Helmand, a major center for the poppy trade, well-heeled drug traffickers allied with the Taliban paid handsomely for attacks on British forces. The funds available to the drug traffickers dwarfed those available to British forces.

Successful units recognized that money is power. US Soldiers in Zabul's Shinkay Valley dispensed funds as patronage—much like a patronage-based political machine. They used their money to create a network of supporters around their firebase and in villages farther beyond. Successful units gave money directly to laborers, rather than go through local contractors or powerbrokers—unless their intention was to empower these individuals. They also spread their funds around in order to avoid the appearance of favoritism that might breed resentment. In Dand district, the Canadians hired one fightingage male from every extended family. Their intention was to spread their funds out as evenly as possible, and to tie every family in the district into the reconstruction effort.

In northeast Afghanistan, US Soldiers gave funds directly to village leaders in exchange for specific concessions—such as support for upcoming operations, actionable intelligence, or reduced attacks on convoys. In this case, the battalion's objective was to empower cooperative local leaders by giving them control over reconstruction funds, and to give the battalion leverage over these leaders. The Soldiers also pushed money into outlying areas ahead of major operations in order to buy support and soften resistance. The approach worked well and saved many lives.

In Nangarhar province in the east, US forces supported a governor who paid tribal leaders to stop growing poppy. The governor combined these incentives with threats against those who refused to comply. In just one year, Nangarhar went from being one of Afghanistan's main opium cultivators to one that was declared "poppy free."

Protecting the population

Preventing the insurgents from intimidating the population was essential to building popular support and making reconstruction work. Afghans were rarely willing to cooperate with coalition troops if they (or their families) believed they might face retaliation. Where insurgents could target individuals working with the coalition, the presence of coalition troops did more harm than good. In contested areas, where coalition forces and insurgents fought for control over the same population, the plight of civilians was the worst.

Where the insurgents managed to infiltrate back into cleared areas and operate underground, reconstruction efforts faltered or failed altogether. For example, in such places as Nawa and Musa Qala in Helmand, US and British forces managed to push the insurgents out and keep them from returning. In these places, the population cooperated with the coalition, and reconstruction efforts proved relatively successful. In other areas of Helmand, such as Marjah and Sangin, where the insurgents infiltrated back in to intimidate the population and lay IEDs and ambushes, US and British forces faced considerable difficulties at rebuilding the government and getting projects underway. In such places, the population was often less secure and less wellgoverned than under the Taliban. People played both sides in order to survive.

In many places where insurgent influence remained strong, Soldiers and Marines could not trust local government officials, especially the police. For example, in Gulistan in early 2008, a US Marine platoon was forced to work with a district governor and police chief who were actively collaborating with the Taliban. The government officials tried to lure the Marines into prelaid ambushes and reportedly engineered the killing of local police who cooperated with the platoon. Only when the Marines succeeded in pushing the Taliban out of most parts of the valley—thereby ending its campaign of intimidation—did district officials start cooperating with the Marines.

Many Afghans were skeptical about the staying power of US and NATO units. Local people had to consider their lives and those of their families five or more years down the road when the Taliban might very well return to power and retaliate against those who had collaborated with the coalition.

In some areas, it was apparent that the population did not want the protection of coalition troops or Afghan Soldiers. Permanent garrisons and checkpoints attracted insurgent attacks and led to fighting that caused harm to civilian life and property. In some of the more remote areas, Taliban influence was relatively benign; violent struggles for control between insurgents and coalition troops posed a greater threat.

Employing restraint in the use of force

Restraint on the use of force was essential to every operation detailed in this book. Killing the wrong people had farreaching consequences. In many places, illin-formed or poorly conceived combat operations reversed months—and in some cases years—worth of patient effort overnight. In other places, targeting operations had second-order effects that were not apparent until months or years later. Powerbrokers close to the US often used their special relationships with coalition forces to eliminate their enemies—by passing false information naming their rivals as Taliban. Officers repeatedly fell for these tricks, carrying out raids against individuals based on information from local interlocutors whose motives were questionable. These operations—in which US and NATO units were manipulated into killing prominent local leaders whose commitment to the insurgency was uncertain—created powerful enemies, and probably caused more harm than doing nothing at all.

For example, in the Deh Rashaan Valley north of Tarin Kowt, the Ghilzai clans in the northern part of the valley allied with the Taliban after a series of airstrikes by US and Australian forces that killed several prominent tribal leaders. Their rivals among the Popalzai and Barakzai to the south—who controlled the provincial government and had regular access to coalition forces—may have fingered certain Ghilzai leaders as Taliban, when in fact their connections to the movement were tenuous and uncertain. Rather than reach out to the Ghilzai clans and try to bring them into the government, coalition troops targeted their leaders for assassination, alienating them and pushing them into alliances with the Taliban, which deepened the divide further and led to more violence.

Killing people, even insurgents, often did more harm than good. Many insurgents were related to local people, including prominent leaders working with the government and US forces. Killing local people often fuelled demands for vengeance, even if it was obvious that these young men were involved in the insurgency. Many local people resented the killing of their loved ones no matter what their activities might have been. In many cases, it was a matter of honor to avenge their deaths. It was common for clans targeted in earlier raids to attack US and NATO forces of their own accord without establishing any connections to the insurgency.

Military units that were successful at stabilizing an area and building popular support almost never carried out raids in populated areas they sought to influence. For example, Dutch Soldiers in Uruzgan did not conduct raids in or near the areas where they intended to build popular support. The same was true of some Special Forces teams.

Raids against enemy fighters tended to yield mixed results. In many cases, they proved counterproductive—especially in remote, mountainous areas where there were few coalition forces and little accurate and uptodate information. In the mountains, the terrain was so difficult, the road infrastructure so limited, and the distances so long that insurgent leaders often had plenty of time to flee, leaving innocent people to suffer the consequences of coalition attacks. It was nearly impossible for outside forces to move through the mountains undetected. Air assault raids in particular were a problem because most of the forces carrying out these operations were based far from their targets and knew little about the areas in which they operated.

It was not uncommon for villagers to take up arms against outsiders—any outsiders, whether rival clans or US forces—who entered the confines of their villages uninvited, especially at night. In such circumstances, it was not easy for coalition troops to distinguish between insurgents trying to protect themselves and local men seeking to defend their village. Many units just assumed that anyone firing at them was an enemy fighter. Raids in which innocent people were harmed or their honor violated created enduring enmity in many areas of the country. As a result, entire families, clans, or even tribes took up arms against the coalition and allied with the Taliban. In several cases covered in this book, killcapture missions and other enemycentric combat operations caused violence to escalate significantly. For example, security conditions in Kandahar City in 2003 were so permissive that coalition troops walked around without body armour. Later units focused on raids and measured their progress by the numbers of enemy fighters killed. Kandahar City became increasingly violent and unstable, and relations between US forces and the population grew strained.

These vicious cycles strengthened the insurgency and created problems that became increasingly difficult to solve. Misplaced combat operations caused entire clans or tribes to declare war on coalition forces, prompting the shedding of more blood and demands for more vengeance. Killing more people often made the problem worse and gave strength to the insurgency.

Large-scale sweep operations in particular were ineffective and counterproductive. These operations, which involved a battalion or more of US forces pushing into a large area from different directions in order to kill or capture a substantial number of insurgents, caused significant damage to civilian life and property yet netted few enemy fighters. Most of these sweeps were slow, clumsy, and ill-in-formed. Insurgents easily escaped through porous cordons or hid their weapons and pretended to be civilians. Since holding forces were rarely left behind, the insurgents returned to business as usual when the operations were over. Afghan militia forces involved in these operations were often accused of widespread looting. These operations alienated entire valleys, causing untold damage to the over-all US effort.

Despite these pitfalls, the discriminate use of force was often an integral part of counterinsurgency in Afghanistan. The trick was to demonstrate superior strength and will—to the insurgents and the population—while doing no harm to civilian life or property. After decades of civil war in which villages have seen one armed faction after another take power, many Afghans have learned to support whichever side happens to be the strongest. For example, when the US Marines arrived in Gulistan in southwest Afghanistan in the spring of 2008, they encountered a population that was almost entirely controlled by the Taliban. Most villages initially expressed indifference or outright hostility toward the Marines. After a number of high-profile engagements where the Marines prevailed without hurting civilians or their property, entire villages began working with the Marines. In Nawa in central Helmand, the Marines defeated the Taliban in a matter of days. Once it was clear that the insurgents stood no chance—and that the Marines were there to stay—the population turned around almost immediately.

Restraint was usually the better part of valor. Diplomacy was more important than force. The insurgents exploited local grievances to build popular support and recruit fighters. Killing insurgents often aggravated these grievances, made political solutions more difficult, and expanded the pool of enemy fighters. In the words of one battalion commander in northeast Afghanistan: " We can't fight our way out of this insurgency.

The supply of fighters here is inexhaustible." Some of the vignettes in this book suggest that it may never be too late to turn the tide. It was often possible for officers to reach out to leaders whose communities had been the victims of heavy-handed operations—to offer compensation and promise that past mistakes would not be repeated. In Kunar, a US Army battalion made peace with an openly hostile village that had been the site of several botched raids during earlier years of the war. The village had since become the site of numerous attacks on US forces. Through public apologies, sustained engagement, reconstruction projects, and assurances that all future raids would cease the battalion was able to turn the village around. Attacks stopped, and insurgents were no longer able to operate there.

BUILDING INDIGENOUS CAPACITY

The quality and legitimacy of Afghan security forces, and argued that there were notable problems with the ANP. This section looks more specifically at the U.S. "light footprint" approach and the use of indigenous forces during operations. Metaphorically, counterinsurgency is about teaching people to fish, not about doing it for them. One of the most significant lessons from U.S. and coalition experiences in Afghanistan is the importance of advising, training, and assisting the host nation's ministries and security forces—and helping shift popular support from the insurgents to the host nation. For insurgent groups, popular support is an overriding strategic objective. As Mao Tse-tung argued, "The richest source of power to wage war lies in the masses of the people." Counterinsurgency operations must separate insurgents from their support base.

The United States adopted a two-pronged strategy for counterin-surgency operations in Afghanistan. The first part involved the establishment of an indigenous (rather than international) government. The public opinion polls conducted in 2003 and 2004 demonstrated that roughly 85 percent of Afghans interviewed had a "very favourable" or "somewhat favourable" view of Hamid Karzai, the first post-Taliban president of Afghanistan. The United States and its allies fostered the rapid creation of a national Afghan government that included representatives from major ethnic groups. This new government began to form even before major combat operations terminated. On December 5, 2001, Afghan delegates executed the Bonn Agreement, which established an interim administration under Hamid Karzai and called for an Emergency Loya Jirga to establish a transitional authority.

Karzai became head of state in June 2002 and president in October 2004, following the country's first national election. The establishment of an interim indigenous—rather than international—government gave the population a sense of ownership. As Zalmay Khalilzad, special envoy and former U.S. ambassador to Afghanistan, argued, "The fact that the Afghans played a key role in their own liberation gave them a sense of dignity and ownership of their destiny."

The second prong of the U.S. approach involved maintaining a light military footprint in Afghanistan. The United States did not invade Afghanistan with large numbers of forces. U.S. officials adopted a light-footprint approach for several reasons: They wanted to prevent large-scale resistance similar to what the Soviet Union encountered in the 1980s; they believed that small numbers of ground troops and air-power were sufficient to establish security; and they were deeply reluctant to become involved in nation-building. Indeed, several great powers throughout history have been defeated in Afghanistan, including the forces of Alexander the Great, Great Britain, and the Soviet Union.

U.S. GEN Tommy Franks, who put together the operational concept for Afghanistan in 2001, argued that, after major combat ended, "our footprint had to be small, for both military and geopolitical reasons. We envisioned a total of about 10,000 American soldiers, airmen, special operators, and helicopter assault crews, along with robust in-country close air support."

This strategy worked well during the overthrow of the Taliban government. But it had two drawbacks for the stability operation phase, which began after the overthrow of the Taliban regime. First, there were too few U.S. and Afghan government forces to stabilize the country. Afghan militia forces had to full the security vacuum, which, in the long run, undermined the power of the central government. The per capita level of external forces in 17 stability operations since World War II. The United States had one of the lowest per capita levels in Afghanistan among all these operations, which even included a number of UN operations in Africa and Asia. This created a challenge in targeting Taliban, Hezb-i-Islami, and al Qaeda insurgents in the early stages of the insurgency—such as 2002 and 2003—since there were virtually no trained and legitimate Afghan military and police. Nor were there sufficient forces to secure Afghanistan's borders. Insurgent forces benefited from porous borders along the Afghanistan-Pakistan frontier, as well as from assistance from sources in Pakistan and the Muslim world channeled through Pashtun tribesmen in the border region. Second, this strategy drew the wrong lesson from the Soviet experience. The key lesson from the Soviet experience was not the number of Soviet forces deployed, but rather how they were used. The Soviets fought the wrong war; they fought a conventional war against an unconventional opponent. As one of the most comprehensive studies of Soviet combat tactics in Afghanistan concluded, "The Soviet Army that marched into Afghanistan was trained to fight within the context of a theatre war against a modern enemy who would obligingly occupy defensive positions stretching across the northern European plain." The Soviets used massed artillery, tanks, and ground forces to destroy acres of defense positions, and "Soviet tactics and equipment were designed solely to operate within the context of this massive strategic operation."

The Soviets fundamentally misunderstood the nature of counterinsurgency warfare. They terrorized the population instead of working to win the people over to the government's side. The United States, Pakistan, Saudi Arabia, and other governments exploited this resentment by providing military and financial assistance to the mujahideen. This brings up an important dilemma. A lead indigenous effort is critical over the long run for successful counterinsurgency operations. Even if tactically successful, a unilateral external operation may ultimately lead to failure by unseating the very indigenous capability that the external actor is trying to build. But what if there is no competent government force in the early stages of an insurgency? In the Afghan case, there were no Afghan army forces and no trained police. While there are no ideal options in these situations, the most effective strategy may be to (a) work with those legitimate indigenous forces (especially police) that exist; (b) effectively train and mentor them as quickly as possible; and (c) temporarily back-full indigenous security forces with sufficient numbers of U.S. and other international forces to accomplish key security tasks. These tasks include patrolling streets and villages, monitoring borders, and protecting critical infrastructure. Higher per capita levels of U.S. and coalition military and police forces might have been useful in the immediate aftermath of the Taliban's overthrow.

Preparations for the war in Iraq made this increasingly difficult, because U.S. troops were needed for combat operations there.

Once counterinsurgency operations began, the United States experienced varying degrees of success in working with indigenous forces. Special forces were particularly successful at integrating ANA, ANP, and Afghan militia forces in virtually all aspects of combat and civil-military operations. Indigenous forces were involved in conducting strike operations; interdicting enemy forces along the border; participating in reconstruction efforts; and gathering intelligence. Some conventional units were also successful in working with indigenous forces.

For example, forces from the U.S. Army's 82nd Air-borne Division in the Bermel Valley involved Afghan militia forces and ANA forces in mine detection, mounted patrols, intelligence collection, vehicle checkpoints, combat operations, and search-and-seize missions. As one assessment summarized, Afghan forces "led every joint mounted patrol and most major operations," especially since they "knew the ground better and could more easily spot something that was out of place or suspicious." But others were less successful. During Operation Mountain Sweep, for example, paratroopers from the 82nd Airborne conducted operations unilaterally; their heavy-handed tactics created significant resentment among locals in Khowst Province. U.S. soldiers angered Afghan villagers on numerous occasions out of naiveté of Afghan social and cultural traditions, leading one Afghan government report to conclude,

It will be difficult for ever for the coalition forces to fully befriend the people. Instead they should try to minimize their contact with the local population and increasingly empower the Afghan forces to do the job. The more they try to be in touch with people the more they will be prone to make cultural mistakes.

PEACEBUILDING IN THE CONTEXT OF HUMANITARIAN AID

Peacebuilding in the context of humanitarian aid has gained wider recognition since the last decade. Where political will (at the national and international level) for a negotiated settlement of armed conflict is low, aid organisations are expected to fill the gap through their programming. In line with the political disinterest for resolution of conflict, humanitarian aid to Afghanistan has also become subject to political conditionalities. Particularly after the takeover of Kabul and other major cities by Taliban some donors countries started to use humanitarian aid as a weapon to pressurise Taliban authorities to change their policies towards women. This has led to further deprivation and sufferings of those whom the donors wanted to defend because concern for civilians has always been given second priority by the warring factions. But Taliban unlike former Mujahideen commanders does not have a beneficial relationship with aid organisations. Barakat and Strand (1995) argue that during the Soviet occupation much of the international assistance to Afghanistan was politically motivated. The prime beneficiaries appeared to be the military commanders more than the suffering communities. Due to perceived security risks inside Afghanistan aid organisation partnered with Mjuahideen commanders in the delivery of humanitarian aid to inside Afghanistan. This kind of direct association of humanitarian aid with commanders has served as an incentive for war rather than peace. After the Soviet withdrawal, collapse of Kabul government in 1992 and subsequent military developments the role of commanders to a large extent diminished. This provided an opportunity for aid agencies to directly interact with the focused communities. But operating with the same mentality "suffering requires urgency" projects have been implemented without proper study and social, political and relational analysis of their target beneficiaries (Anderson and Woodrow 1989). Such ignorance often led to further divisions and tensions within the communities over aid resources.

In spite of the shortcomings and unfavourable politics of the donors, a number of aid agencies have in recent years attempted to enhance the impact of aid programming on peace. These efforts will be analysed under two headings; direct peacebuilding and indirect contribution of humanitarian programmes to peace. Building on the notions of capacity development, local capacities for peace and strategic components discussed in first chapter and second chapter respectively these efforts will be analysed. Table3.2 ranks the level of activities against the criteria to determine the impact of humanitarian aid on the conflict in Afghanistan. The ranking is between 1(*) and 3 (***) to determine both the long-term contribution of these programmes to peace and their immediate impact on conflict.

Direct Peacebuilding

In terms of direct peacebuilding there are a few indigenous organisations that have mandated themselves to the promotion of peace. These organisations represent local capacities for peace in their own rights and at the same time their operations are all geared towards developing and strengthening of local capacities at the community level. The strength of these organisations comes from their knowledge and understanding of the Afghan social, political, cultural, and economic realities as well as their capacity to design and execute culturally sensitive and politically sound and economically cheap programmes.

These programmes are well targeted for example peace education programme for school children is in fact responding to the need for promotion of a culture of peace and peaceful attitudes among future generation. Similarly CPAU's district based training workshops on Working With Conflict and Do No Harm for a mixed audience of aid workers, village Mullahs, teachers and community leaders is directed at developing community's capacity for peaceful transformation of conflict and confidence building. Moreover, these activities are directly contributing to the growth of civil society in Afghanistan.

However, their impact on the overall situation due to various reasons is not so visible. It might be unrealistic to expect a dramatic impact from such relatively small initiatives on a protracted conflict with its strong national and international actors. Therefore, it is worth attempting to identify institutional and operational strengths and weakness of these organisations.

Peacebuilding, as argued in the previous chapters should be concerned with *building and strengthening social, political, and economic structures for constructive transformation of conflict and promotion of social values such as, benevolence, compassion, co-operation, and justice among persons and groups.* Given the working definition of peacebuilding and the institutional/operational strengths and weaknesses the activities of these organisations are to some extent directed towards creating and strengthening a social foundation for a lasting peace in Afghanistan. In similar circumstances aid organisations have been instrumental in preparing the ground for peace.

Therefore such operations have to be substantially improved and expanded in order to meet greater challenges of peacebuilding facing war-torn Afghanistan. Norwegian Church Aid (NCA) is the only international NGO that has taken a number of significant initiatives in this regard. Organising a workshop on "NGOs and Peacebuilding In Afghanistan" in early 1994 in Swat Pakistan NCA took the first initiative in the aid community working in Afghanistan.[8] This workshop was a significant step in many ways, it for the first time initiated a discussion in the aid community on how aid deliveries could be improved in order to make a positive impact on conflict. The workshop served as a foundation for future undertakings by NCA. In the aftermath of the workshop NCA joined the Local Capacities for Peace Project (LCPP) known as "Do No Harm" that was initiated by Mary B. Anderson. [9] One of the most significant contributions of NCA to the aid community and to Afghanistan is the promotion, advocacy and training aid personnel on the concept of do no harm. An important step was the translation and widespread distribution of the 1996, publication of LCPP "Do No Harm: Supporting Local Capacities for Peace Trough Aid" that is a direct contribution to peacebuilding and capacity development.

In 1996 NCA took another important initiative and organised a three weeks training on Working With Conflict that resulted in the creation of an Afghan network called Co-operation for Peace and Unity (CPAU) that has been supported and strengthened by NCA at the early stages. [10] NCA as a donor agency has been in the forefront of not only financially supporting peace related initiatives but also working closely with the partner in the development of the programmes.

As illustrated in table 3.2, NCA's peacebuilding initiatives combined with its relief rehabilitation and development activities are geared towards promotion of education, capacity development, promotion of local capacities for peace, strengthening of civil society in Afghanistan.

Though highly innovative and successful in implementation of the mentioned activities Norwegian Church Aid has not been able to institutionalise either do no harm or peacebuilding. NCA as a donor agency has the potential to influence its implementing partners to incorporate peacebuilding in their relief and rehabilitation programmes and to set example for others. Unfortunately, the organisation treated peacebuilding in isolation from its core programming in which business continues as usual.

NCA as an international organisation in spite of being involved in a few successful peacebuilding processes in other parts of the world has not been able to intellectually support locally initiated efforts in Afghanistan. The cross-fertilisation of ideas in this field has been totally ignored and in spite of stated policy and commitment to peacebuilding NCA has also not been able to allocate sufficient financial resources for peacebuilding. Such activities were financed as predatory projects from the emergency and rehabilitations funds allocated by Norwegian foreign ministry.

8

A Nuclear Environment in Future Battlefields War

Today, the world is in a historical period of drastic changes, the pattern of multipolar forces is taking shape, the international situation is moving toward relaxation, and peace and development have become the theme of the present world.

Therefore, we can anticipate that a new world war will not break out and nuclear warfare is avoidable. However, the world today is not trouble free, hegemony and power politics still have not withdrawn from the historical arena, the international situation is still very complicated, and the flames of war arising from local conflicts have never died out. Owing to multifarious factors, the nuclear shadow still cannot be cast away from future battlefields.

Warfare is violent action. More than 100 years ago, the capitalist strategist Clausewitz pointed out, "The use of violence knows no bounds. Therefore, a belligerent will oblige its opponent to use force as it will itself, thus producing a kind of interaction. As viewed from this conception, such interaction will inevitably lead to extreme." Warfare is the continuation of politics, and a kind of bloody politics at that. Nuclear warfare and high-tech warfare are both instruments subordinate to the purposes and requirements of wars. When countries possessing nuclear weapons and high-tech conventional weapons are involved in a war in which the conflict is intensifying, the possible use of nuclear weapons cannot be ruled out. Nuclear weapons, therefore, are still a trump card in the hands of nuclear nations.

Thomas F. Ramos, science adviser to the senior officer responsible for nuclear weapons in the U.S. Department of Defense said: "No reasonable evidence indicates that conventional weapons will be reliable shelters to cope with enemies possessing and intending to use nuclear weapons." His remarks express the consensus of some military strategists studying the Gulf War.

As estimated by some Western specialits/analysts, there are at least 12 countries which claim to have ballistic missiles and at least 25 countries that have probably developed or are developing nuclear, biological, and chemical weapons. Using this estimation, some Western publications maintain that "the world has ushered in an age of nuclear proliferation." In 1974, India carried out its first nuclear blast, which kicked off the nuclear emulation in South Asia. In 1988, India successfully developed the PRITHVI medium-range ground-to-ground missile with a range of 2,000 meters, and the capability of carrying nuclear warheads. On March 24, 1993, South African President De Klerk addressed a special session of the National Assembly, saying that South Africa worked out a limited nuclear deterrent program in 1974 and had produced six atomic bombs by the end of 1989, and that all the said nuclear weapons had been dismantled and destroyed in early 1990. It was also revealed by the South African media that if the expansion of nuclear powers shown an intimidating color, South Africa will install warheads into its missiles and will probably develop and deploy neutron weapons. Israel is one of the countries that had nuclear weapons in its possession relatively earlier. Moreover, it was prepared to use them during the fourth Middle-East war.

Other data also stated that countries like Argentina and Brazil will also be able to manufacture nuclear weapons. With the rapid development of science and technology, the technology of making nuclear weapons has almost become an open secret. The disintegration of the former Soviet Union not only resulted in a brain drain of a vast number of scientists engaged in nuclear weapon development, but also threw the supervision of nuclear materials into chaos, considerably enlarging the scope of nuclear proliferation. A terrorist organization or a maniac could, some day, claim possession of an atomic bomb and use it as a tool of intimidation and blackmail, and no one would think that this was a tale from the Arabian Nights.

What merits our attention is that in a high-tech conventional war, a nuclear environment may still emerge even if nuclear weapons are not used. The more society advances, the greater the demands for energy will be. In order to satisfy the demands for energy, nuclear power stations were built. According to the data released by the International Atomic Energy Agency in March 1994, at the end of 1993 there were 430 nuclear power plants with a total installed capacity of approximately 345 million kw operating in various places throughout the world; these accounted for more than 17 percent of the world's gross power generation.

It is predicted that by 2001, there will be 558 nuclear power generating units with a total installed capacity of approximately 460 million kw all worldwide, which will account for 24 percent of the world's gross power generation. The peaceful utilization of nuclear energy is a piece of joyous news to mankind.

Meanwhile, the extensive use of nuclear energy also constitutes a latent threat to peace and the existence of human beings. The accident at the Chernobyl Nuclear Power Plant that occurred in April 1986 inflicted air pollution on 16 Russian oblasts and victimized 250,000 people. In Ukraine, 370,000 people suffered injuries in varying degrees as land covering 40,000 square meters was polluted, and more than 2,000 residential areas were evacuated. In future high-tech warfare, if an enemy intentionally or unintentionally attacks nuclear power plants or other facilities using nuclear energy with high-tech conventional weapons, the secondary nuclear radiation produced and the nuclear environment brought about would likewise do harm.

In June 1981, Israel dispatched four aircraft to launch a sudden attack on an Iraqi nuclear reactor southeast of the capital Baghdad, dropping 16 tons of bombs in two minutes and hitting all the targets. Fortunately, the reactor was not yet operational; otherwise the attack would have resulted in very serious consequences.

NEW BATTLEFIELD FOR WARFARE

The innovation of more advanced and autonomous ICTs has engendered a new revolution in military affairs, which encompasses nations' use of ICTs in both cyberspace and the physical battlefield to wage war against their adversaries. The three most prevalent revolutions in military affairs come in the form of cyber attacks, autonomous robots and communication management.

Within the realm of cyberspace, there are two primary weapons: network-centric warfare and C4ISR, which denotes integrated Command, Control, Communications, Computers, Intelligence, Surveillance and Reconnaissance. Furthermore, cyberspace attacks initiated by one nation against another nation have an underlying goal of gaining information superiority over the attacked party, which includes disrupting or denying the victimized party's ability to gather and distribute information. A real-world occurrence that illustrated the dangerous potential of cyber attacks transpired in 2007 when a strike from Israeli forces demolished a nuclear reactor in Syria that was being constructed via a collaborative effort between Syria and North Korea. Accompanied with the strike was a cyber attack on Syria's air defenses, which left them blind to the attack on the nuclear reactor and, ultimately allowed for the attack to occur (New York Times 2014). An example of a more basic attack on a nation within cyberspace is a Distributed Denial of Service (DDOS) attack, which is utilized to hinder networks or websites until they lose their primary functionality. As implied, cyber attacks do not just affect the military party being attacked, but rather the whole population of the victimized nation. Since more aspects of daily life are being integrated into networks in cyberspace, civilian populations can potentially be negatively affected during wartime. For example, if a nation chose to attack another nation's power grid servers in a specific area to disrupt communications, civilians and businesses in that area would also have to deal with power outages, which could potentially lead to economic disruptions as well.

Moreover, physical ICTs have also been implemented into the latest revolution in military affairs by deploying new, more autonomous robots (i.e. – unmanned drones) into the battlefield to carry out duties such as patrolling borders and attacking ground targets.

Humans from remote locations pilot many of the unmanned drones, however, some of the more advanced robots, such as the Northrop Grumman X-47B, are capable of autonomous decisions. Despite piloting the drones from remote locations, a proportion of drone pilots still suffer from stress factors of more traditional warfare.

According to NPR, a study performed by the Pentagon in 2011 found that 29% of drone pilots are "burned out" and undergo high levels of stress. Furthermore, approximately 17% of the drone pilots surveyed in the study were labeled "clinically distressed" with some of those pilots also showing signs of post-traumatic stress disorder (National Public Radio 2011).

Modern ICTs have also brought advancements to communications management among military forces. Communication is a vital aspect of war for any involved party and, through the implementation of new ICTs such as data-enabled devices, military forces are now able to disseminate information faster than ever before.

For example, some militaries are now employing the use of iPhones to upload data and information gathered by drones in the same area.

Legal and Ethical Concerns

While information warfare has yielded many advances in the types of attack that a government can make, it has also raised concerns about the moral and legal ambiguities surrounding this particularly new brand of war. Traditionally, wars have been analyzed by moral scholars according to Just War Theory. However, with Information Warfare, Just War Theory fails because the theory is based on the traditional conception of war. Information Warfare has three main issues surrounding it compared to traditional warfare:

1) The risk for the party or nation initiating the cyber attack is substantially lower than the risk for a party or nation initiating a traditional attack. This makes it easier for governments, as well as potentially terrorist or criminal organizations, to make these attacks more frequently than they could with traditional war.
2) Information communication technologies are so immersed in the modern world that a very wide range of technologies are at risk of a cyber attack. Specifically, civilian technologies can be targeted for cyber attacks and attacks can even potentially be launched through civilian computers or websites. As such, it is harder to enforce control of civilian infrastructures than a physical space. Attempting to do so would also raise many ethical concerns about the right to privacy, making defending against such attacks even tougher.
3) The mass-integration of information communication technologies into our system of war makes it much harder to assess accountability for situations that may arise when using robotic and/or cyber attacks. For robotic weapons and automated systems, it's becoming increasing hard to determine who is responsible for any particular event that happens. This issue is exacerbated in the case of cyber attacks, as sometimes it is virtually impossible to trace who initiated the attack in the first place.

Recently, legal concerns have arisen centered around these issues, specifically the issue of the right to privacy in the United States of America. Lt. General Keith B. Alexander, the general who is the head of Cyber Command, noted that there was a "mismatch between our technical capabilities to conduct operations and the governing laws and policies" when writing to the Senate Armed Services Committee.

A key point of concern was the targeting of civilian institutions for cyber attacks, to which the general promised to try and maintain a mindset similar to that of traditional war, in which they will seek to limit the impact on civilians.

NUCLEAR DETERRENCE WILL BE USED IN LOCAL WARS

The local wars that broke out after World War II were mostly carried out under the conditions of nuclear deterrence if the Western powers were involved in them. During the Korean War, U.S. Commander-in-Chief MacArthur once threatened a sudden attack of atomic bombs on China's northeast and coastal strategic targets. After Eisenhower came to power, he again ordered the Pentagon to formulate a nuclear program aimed at China. During its war of aggression in Vietnam, the United States also made nuclear threats and was prepared to resolve the issue with nuclear weapons.

After the armed conflicts on Zhenbao Island between China and the Soviet Union in 1969, Brezhnev considered initiating a nuclear attack on China in an attempt to ruin China's nuclear facilities. In the Malvinas Islands War, Britain carried tactical nuclear weapons on its huge fleet and was prepared to use them if its conventional operations failed. In particular, the multinational coalition troops headed by the United States used extremely advanced high-tech weapons in the Gulf War, and although they held the trump card, they still deployed 800 to 850 tactical nuclear weapons on three sides of Iraq.

What is more, U.S. troops considered using radio flash bombs but, because of political considerations, they were not approved by U.S. President Bush. In response to Saddam's repeated threats to use chemical weapons, the British Government warned again and again that its troops would retaliate by using tactical nuclear weapons should Iraq resort to using chemical weapons. Bush also hinted that he would give field commanders freedom when necessary. These countries threatened to use nuclear weapons in conventional wars because they believed that with nuclear weapons in hand, psychologically they would be able to hold a dominant position, which would enhance troop morale and frighten the enemy on the one hand, and restrict the enemy's use of some conventional means on the other, thus changing the direction of the war. These past events should not be forgotten.

At present, nuclear deterrence is still a strategic pillar of military power. U.S. President Clinton thinks that the United States must build up military muscle that suits the new age, and this military muscle must have the capacity of nuclear deterrence. Nuclear deterrent force is an effective form of security. The 1993 defense report submitted by the U.S. Defense Department to Congress proposed that an all directional global defense system of strategic nuclear deterrence to prevent limited nuclear attacks should be set up, under which the former nuclear deterrent strategy chiefly aimed at the Soviet Union should be readjusted to an all-direction and multilevel nuclear deterrent strategy aimed at both the former Soviet Union and other regions.

On September 25, 1995, President Clinton ordered the Energy Department to maintain the three major nuclear weapon laboratories to ensure that U.S. nuclear deterrent capacity remains effective. Russia set up a defense ministry in March 1992, then founded its nuclear strategic forces and made the development of strategic nuclear weapons a top priority in the future development of eight technical weapons.

President Yeltsin said that a strategic nuclear force was the foundation of Russia's military strength. In November 1993, giving sanction to the new Russian military theory, he officially abandoned the Kremlin's 11-year-old commitment that in a conflict it would not be the first to use nuclear weapons. In its 1992 defense report, France claimed that it merely wanted to have the "most rudimentary" nuclear deterrent for as a way to cope with various kinds of unexpected events and check possible encroachments on its interests by potential enemies.

In the meantime, France announced that it is continuing to focus on the development of a submarine-launched strategic nuclear missile system to ensure the reliability of its nuclear deterrent strategy. At his first news conference after assuming office as president on June 13, 1995, Chirac declared that France would resume its nuclear tests in the South Pacific. The French Defense Minister maintained that President Chirac had made a "very serious decision."

British Prime Minister Major said, "As far as Britain is concerned, laying down the nuclear shield in whatever manner is an indiscreet move. Britain holds on to its views that as long as the CIS countries are still in possession of nuclear weapons, Britain should retain its own. The number of British nuclear weapons will not be determined by that of other countries, but by whether or not they are sufficient to make potential enemies feel incapable of sustaining their losses."

Deterrence and actual combat are complementary and closely interrelated. Generally speaking, the military strategy of all countries has a dual character of deterrence and actual combat. Before a war breaks out, a country will, by way of military deterrence, try to make the opposite side refrain from launching an attack rashly, so as to provide a powerful backing for its own political, economic, and diplomatic activities. Once military deterrence does not work, it will strive to win a victory through actual combat, so as to remove obstacles to its political, economic, and diplomatic activities.

Militarily, the immense effect of nuclear weaponry is that it can serve as a deterrent force and, at the same time, as a means of actual combat. Some countries, even those of the Third World, also consider possession of limited nuclear strength to be a significant way to contend against the deterrence of big powers or to deter one another in order to make up for the deficiency of their conventional forces. Military history after World War II has principally centered on the two superpowers that applied nuclear deterrence to each other and contended with each other for nuclear hegemony. After one of the superpowers disintegrated, a "crowd of heroes" rose up. As a result, conflicts that were in the past covered up by the Cold War surfaced with each passing day, and the collision and coalition of various political forces intensified simultaneously. Some regional powers were not weakened by the superpowers' relaxed control over them. On the contrary, they will, perhaps, go their own way even more willfully on the issues of possessing and using nuclear weapons. Both the United States and Russia believe that future nuclear threats will primarily stem from small nuclear nations in certain regions.

Hence, the world situation of nuclear deterrence will be transformed from the previous global nuclear deterrence and confrontation between the United States and the Soviet Union to multiple and regional nuclear deterrence and confrontation. In future high-tech local wars, the struggle between nuclear deterrence and counter nuclear deterrence will be even more complex.

We are materialists, so when we study an issue, we must proceed from the objective reality rather than from a subjective wish and, through investigation and study of objective reality, we derive our principles, policies, and measures. The study of issues concerning warfare can be conducted in the same way. Comrade Mao Zedong said a long time ago:

> Investigation and study are very important. When we see someone hold something in his hand, we should look into the matter. What is he holding in his hand? It is a knife. What is the use of a knife? It can kill a person. Whom will he kill with the knife? He will kill the people. After probing into these matters, we should further the investigation: The Chinese people also have hands, and they can hold knives too. They can forge one if they have none. . . .

We love peace. China's development and possession of a small number of nuclear weapons is entirely for self-defense. Since the very first day when China had nuclear weapons in 1964, it solemnly proclaimed that it would never be the first to use nuclear weapons at any time and under any circumstances. China also made the commitment that it would never use or threaten to use nuclear weapons toward nuclear-free countries or regions. At the same time, we clearly understand that only by relying on the arduous work of the people all over the world can the objective of genuinely eliminating nuclear wars and genuinely obtaining world peace be realized: "It is a universal truth since ancient times that proficiency in warfare is not tantamount to bellicosity." The stronger our national defense muscle and the more sufficient our preparations for high-tech warfare under the condition of nuclear deterrence, the smaller the possibility of the outbreak of nuclear war.

We wish that the day will come when the nuclear shadow will disappear from the blue sky and the people the world over will live under the sunshine of genuine peace. To hail the early arrival of this day, we should work with greater stamina and diligence.

NUCLEAR SHADOW OVER THE MIDDLE EAST

In the summer of 1984, *Newsweek* published the results of a Gallup poll of hundreds of top-ranking American military officers. Among the questions was this: where did they see the greatest threat of a conflict situation which might escalate to nuclear war? The majority responded clearly: the Middle East.

They might have had in mind those times that leaders of the two superpowers have threatened to use nuclear weapons in a Middle East showdown. According to former Senator Henry Jackson, Harry Truman invoked their presence in the US arsenal when he demanded that the Soviet Union withdraw from Iran after World War II. Nikita Khrushchev brandished nuclear-tipped missiles when Britain, France and Israel teamed up to invade Egypt in 1956. Lyndon Johnson and Alexei Kosygin felt compelled to use the Washington/Moscow hotline for the first time in June 1967, as Israel launched a preemptive attack that devastated Egypt, Syria and Jordan. In late October 1973, as Israel and Egypt slugged it out again in the Sinai and Richard Nixon fought off the Watergate prosecutor, Secretary of State Henry Kissinger decided that the best way to convince Moscow that American war-making capacity remained unimpaired was to call a quick DefCon 3 alert — sort of a nuclear fire drill. Then there was the scene in the middle of August 1980. In response to "clear but ambiguous" indications of a Soviet military buildup along the border north of Iran, American war planners debated the first use of tactical nuclear weapons; the Joint Chiefs told Defense Secretary Harold Brown that the US had "no other" military option to prevent the Soviets from moving south.

In 1984, when Gallup posed his questions, Congress was debating a Pentagon budget that would increase spending for Third World intervention ("power projection" is the budget rubric) by 34 percent, against 13 percent for the military as a whole. The officers quizzed by Gallup knew that some of the "power projection" weapons systems were "dual capable" — able to fire nuclear as well as conventional warheads. The big guns on the USS New Jersey that shelled Lebanon a few months earlier, for instance. The difference between "conventional" weapons and tactical nukes — the "nuclear firebreak" — was fast eroding. The newest conventional shells combined firepower and accuracy to a degree that made them as devastating as nuclear shells, while from the other end of the "conflict spectrum" nuclear warheads had been miniaturized for battlefield use.

Responding to developments such as these, the US Army had formulated a new battle doctrine — the first since World War II. Once the president approves the use of nuclear weapons, operational questions — when and how?are delegated to field commanders. AirLand Battle Operations Manual FM100-5 foresees that: "A relatively small rapidly deployable force with nuclear weapons may be assigned a contingency mission. This force might succeed as a deterrent while a larger, conventional force might deploy too late."

Oil War?

Too late for what? We've all seen the *Time* magazine cover showing an enormous bear, hammer-and-sickle medallion on his chest, reaching down across the Caucasus to menace a dozen miniature oil derricks in the Persian Gulf. Phrases like "oil jugular" trip off the tongues of news anchormen. Buried in the op-ed rejects is the fact that the Soviet Union has for a long while been the world's largest oil producer. Ten years ago, Washington "leaked" a report that showed the USSR becoming a net oil importer by the mid-1980s, with an insatiable lust for "our" oil. The figures, it turned out, had been cooked in the kitchen where William Casey is now head chef.

Suppose the CIA had been right. The Soviet Union needs to import lots of wheat, year after year. Yet the Russians have not taken over Argentina or Canada, never mind Kansas. There are branches of Bank Novostni throughout the Arab world. Moscow has plenty of experience buying or bartering for what it needs on the world market.

The Soviet Union knows very well, because the United States has made it very clear, that any effort to seize the oil of Arabia and the Gulf would lead to war. The Kremlin has demonstrated a very cautious attitude toward any steps that might lead to war with the US — much more cautious than their counterparts on the Potomac. The only situation in which the Soviet Union might move militarily against the Persian Gulf would be if a general war had already started or was truly imminent, to interdict supplies vital to the US war machine.

The national security advisors with their illuminated maps in the White House basement know this better than the rest of us. If we read their "guidance documents" closely, we see that what they fear most are political changes in the Middle East that might affect Western access to the region's resources and markets. Decisions about how much oil to produce, and the price at which it will be available, might be made in Tehran, in Baghdad and in Jeddah rather than in New York or London.

To some extent, the locus of such decision-making has shifted over the last two decades. True, the giant oil companies are still major players (six of these companies are still in the top 10 of Fortune's famous 500, and their profits account for a steady one-seventh of total profits of the 500). The world market has resiliently protected industrial societies against the aberrant behavior of people of color. This is largely because those exercising power in the oil-exporting states are people who see their future linked to the interests of the capitalist West. Shaikh Zaki Yamani, until recently oil minister of Saudi Arabia, is a case in point. The exceptions — Qaddafi in Libya, Khomeini in Iran — highlight the rule.

The enemy in the Gulf, in Alexander Haig's 1981 phrase, is "a change in the status quo." It would be met, he informed a Senate committee and the world, "with the full range of [US] power assets." This was a bit like saying the US would use its "full range of power assets" to stop the tides. Throughout the region, most regimes are tied politically to Washington. But they are not firmly grounded in their own societies. Here is a world that has undergone radical and wrenching social and economic changes in the last decades, resulting in new social forces, new internal class alliances and new links with the global market. These enormous changes in the structures of society have not received political expression. Arrangements from earlier eras have been petrified in place. It is as if the oil revenues which fueled these social changes at the same time embalmed the presiding regimes. We now have the political equivalent of geological pressures that build up beneath the surface and erupt as earthquakes. We have seen one in Iran, another in Lebanon. Tremors have struck in Egypt, Tunisia, Sudan and Morocco.

Nuclear Options

Washington's cold war perspective invests any change anywhere in the world with tremendous significance for the global contest with the Soviet Union, no matter what its local origins. The Middle East would be exceedingly important to Washington by virtue of its proximity to the Soviet Union, along its southern border, even if there were not a single drop of oil there. This global aspect of US policy engages the nuclear factor in its most dangerous dimension. For nuclear war planning is geared precisely to maintaining and extending influence in a world that can only be partially controlled, a world where Washington's weight has diminished.

Though the Soviets have not correspondingly gained, the erosion of control compels American strategists to pin responsibility for unwanted change on the USSR, and emphasize US nuclear leverage. Henry Kissinger complained after the Black September 1970 crisis in Jordan that if he could not threaten to use nuclear weapons in such cases, "We weren't getting our money's worth out of them." Kissinger, whose first book was *Nuclear Weapons and Foreign Policy*, ordered a new study of nuclear "options" in 1972 "to be sure that America's strategic forces really did cast a shadow on peripheral situations."

Today the enormous US military buildup in Saudi Arabia and the Gulf, largely accomplished under the cover of the Iran-

Iraq war, has made Southwest Asia a key strategic theater equipped with numbers and quality of aircraft, radar and nuclear blast-hardened command posts more advanced than those of NATO. And Kissinger, in more recent pronouncements, would have the rulers of the Gulf "understand that we are prepared to protect both their domestic structure and their frontiers, and they need to be given confidence in the means which we will use." In other words, Washington must wire nuclear weapons to the tottering thrones of the Gulf.

Washington's Mutt, Israel's Jeff

US policy in the Middle East, on first glance, presents a paradox. Western material interests are centered in the Persian Gulf/Arabian Peninsula. So why has Israel, the adversary state, counted for the greatest share of US military and economic aid in the region?

Through 1967, Washington did not display this favoritism. The key "intervention assets" in the region were neither Arab nor Israeli but the so-called "northern tier": Turkey, Iran, Pakistan. Arab states like Jordan played specific gendarme roles vis-à-vis the Palestinians, but Israel was kept at arms length.

The June War of 1967 marks a watershed in the balance of military and political forces in the region. Israel's smashing victory led to a new strategic calculation in Washington, expressed by the 1968 sale of state-of-the-art F-4 Phantom fighter-bombers. Set against the US predicament in Vietnam. Israel's impressive performance gave great weight to those in the White House and the Pentagon who argued that a generous military supply relationship with Israel (and Iran) represented the most cost-effective approach to advancing US interests in the region.

Nixon and Kissinger continued to describe US policy as "even-handed," but "protection racket" would be the more appropriate phrase. Yitzhak Rabin, then Israel's ambassador in Washington, boasts in his published diary of his direct access to Kissinger. "Some sources inform me," he wrote coyly on one occasion, "that our military operations are the most encouraging breath of fresh air the American administration has enjoyed recently.... There is a growing likelihood that the US would be interested in an escalation of our military activity with the aim of undermining Nasser's standing.... Thus the willingness to supply us with additional arms depends more on stepping up our military activity against Egypt than on reducing it." Nixon's esteem for Israel was not based on sentiment or electoral considerations, but on its policy of provocation and brutal reprisal against Palestinians and other Arabs. Israel was doing in the Middle East what Nixon wished he could do more freely in Indochina. "Every time I hear of you penetrating into their territory and hitting them hard, I get a feeling of satisfaction," Nixon told Rabin.

The virtues of this approach seemed to be confirmed by Israel's high-profile preparation to intervene in the September 1970 war between the Jordanian army and the Palestinian resistance. The PLO and Syria, in Washington's eyes, were significant only because they received political and material support from the Soviet Union. The new US-Israeli relationship, in the words of National Security Council staffer William Quandt, was now "seen as key to combatting Soviet influence in the Arab world and attaining stability."

This new vision quickly became operational reality. Key policy decisions in 1971 significantly restructured the military ties between the US and Israel. First, the dollar value of US weapons shipped to Israel jumped nearly ten times: from $140 million in 1968-70 to $1.2 billion in 1971-73. Second, the sophistication of weapons followed the Phantom precedent. Third, weapons sales to Israel had previously been on a cash basis; now Washington extended generous credits and grants. Finally, a little-noted agreement of November 1971 provided American technical support and licenses for Israeli manufacture of sophisticated weapons systems, laying the groundwork for Israel's own military-industrial complex and making it possible for Israel to join the ranks of the world's leading arms exporters.

It is essentially the globalist perspective of the cold war which lends Israel its significance in the formulation of US policy. Regional developments and local conflicts are important only for the impact they are assumed to have on the balance of power between the US and the USSR. This coincides with a greater centralization of policy-making within the national security apparatus. Regional experts ("Arabists") who do not ratify the prevailing geostrategic priorities and prefer to emphasize local dynamics are banished from the corridors of power.

This cold war perspective also lends a certain relativity to terms like "peace." Even people who would not accept for a minute the proposition that peace is the highest priority of the Reagan administration in Central America or Southern Africa do not blink when Reagan talks about "the peace process" in the Arab-Israeli conflict. People assume that the failure to achieve a political settlement owes to incompetence or irresolution, or to the pernicious influence of the Zionist lobby.

But the "peace process" is no more about peace than the "peacekeeping force" sent to Beirut or the "peacekeeper" label that Reagan put on the MX missile. The pattern, rather, has been to reward and encourage the most belligerent political forces in Israel. Washington lavishly endows that country's military establishment and avidly tolerates its most aggressive behavior. Then Washington can turn around and extract concessions and cooperation from the Arab states as the price for restraints on Israel. This "good cop/bad cop" routine has in fact been rather productive, if we recognize that Washington's priority has been to "expel" the Soviet Union rather than bring about a political settlement. Israel is valued precisely for its antagonistic relations with key states in a region of strategic proximity to the Soviet Union.

Armageddon's Shortest Fuse

The wars and feuds that tear the Middle East apart, with terrible consequences for tens of millions of people, chiefly grow out of local and regional struggles and dynamics. Rather than try to resolve the most outstanding political contradictions in the region, Washington has exploited them to build up its military forces in the region, directly and through arms deliveries to key allies and clients. The result is devastation for many and a pervasive insecurity for the rest, as the conflicts continue and the weapons to fight them grow in number and destructive power.

The Middle East is both a potential trigger and target for a war between the US and USSR. The US president and many of his fervent evangelical supporters have varnished the prospect of nuclear conflict in the Middle East with the biblical sanction of Armageddon. Here is where American troops and warplanes have gone into battle under Reagan, against Libya and against Lebanon. This administration tacitly supported Israel's assaults against Lebanon, Iraq and Tunisia, and tried to instigate Egypt to invade Libya. Washington's chief client in the region, Israel, evidently has developed the world's sixth largest nuclear arsenal. Another key US client, Pakistan, is on the verge of joining the nuclear club. Both politically and technologically, the Middle East has breached the "nuclear firebreak."

So far, the unfolding scandal in Washington over arms sales to Iran has been limited to the contradictions this poses for official policy in the Gulf War and the ritual rants against terrorism. The extensive media attention reflects serious conflicts within the administration and the larger establishment to the scheme itself and to the White House attempt to implement it unilaterally. The important roles of Israel and Saudi Arabia in supporting Reagan's contra war against Nicaragua over many years risk becoming footnotes to this Washington power struggle. In all of this, the real scandal has been ignored and overlooked again. This is the phony "peace process," the set of policies that has backed Israeli military solutions towards the Palestinians and towards Lebanon and prompted the hostage situation in the first place. It is the intersection of this policy with the course of superpower relations which today darkens the nuclear shadow over the Middle East.

DISTRIBUTED BATTLEFIELD MICROSCALE SENSOR NETWORKS

In modern warfare, in order to accurately reconnoiter enemy combat deployments and troop movements in a timely fashion, opposing sides have invested financial, material, and personnel strength to research, produce, deploy, and employ reconnaissance systems and apparatuses throughout the world. However, the solemn facts of the Gulf War tell us that, when hunting the highly mobile and wideranging "scud" missiles, the area covered by existing reconnaissance systems is limited. However, microscale electromechanical systems could solve the problem of crucial areas that must be kept under continuous surveillance.

One possible case would be to use unmanned aircraft or other methods to distribute a large number of low-cost, use-on-demand microscale sensor systems over a combat zone. High-altitude unmanned aircraft would employ an onboard coded laser of a modulated double-angle reflection communications system to record the position of every microscale sensor.

Then, the sensor systems begin to collect, process, and store information, until another unmanned aircraft uses an identical coded laser to send out an inquiry. Each sensor again employs modulated double-angle reflectors to transmit its data back to the unmanned aircraft.

This type of microscale electromechanical system has clear advantages in terms of deployment, endurance, and vulnerability. Compared to existing theater long-range monitoring systems, microscale sensor systems are more rapidly and conveniently deployed, and they are more complete. Existing sensor equipment, when in the open, can be seen with the naked eye within a range of 200 meters.

However, microscale electromechanical systems, which are measured in millimeters, cannot be distinguished with the naked eye when dispersed in the air and are also difficult to identify with instruments. Certain materials reveal that microscale electromechanical systems are not confined to use in the military arena. They also provide impetus for man's efforts to understand and alter his environment in the fields of information technology, the study of materials, environmental science, biology, and medical science.

In the application of specialized integrated microscale apparatuses, such apparatuses currently being developed can acquire environmental information on the local area or in remote areas and, through the specialized integrated microscale apparatuses' gene-fragment communications system, transmit the information to nearby microscale apparatuses. They can also transmit to a central processor. The uses of specialized integrated microscale apparatuses with the most vitality are the infield of space navigation. They will be able to gradually replace all sorts of subsystems on current spacecraft and carrier rockets, and then develop further into independent space systems, thus leading to the advent of microscale satellites and "nanosatellites."

Nanosatellites

"Nanosatellites" represent a revolutionary breakthrough in future satellite development. They are a type of distributed satellite structural system. Such distributed systems, in contrast to integrated systems, are able to avoid the damage that follows the malfunction of an individual satellite, and thus will increase the survivability and flexibility of future space systems. The best application of nanosatellites is their deployment in local satellite groups or in distributed constellations.

For example, if we launch nanosatellites in solar stationary orbits, with 36 nanosatellites placed evenly into each of 18 equally spaced orbits, then there would be a total of 648 nanosatellites in orbit. Thus, we could ensure that at any given time, there would be continuous coverage and surveillance of any spot on the Earth. Currently, there are already a few western countries that are researching "microscale" satellites.

DOMINANT BATTLESPACE AWARENESS AND FUTURE WARFARE

New decision aids, intelligent agents, simulation, modeling, and forecasting aided by artificial intelligence and fuzzy logic permit large volumes of data to be collected, processed, and displayed without swamping users. Data correlated becomes information. Information converted into situational awareness becomes knowledge. Knowledge used to predict the consequences of actions leads to understanding. Thus the cognitive hierarchy.

A DBK, defined not as data (the transparent battlefield) but as knowledge (a significant exploitable asymmetry) offers powerful implications for the organization of warfare. DBK provides synoptic integrative knowledge, not just data on discrete objects and events. DBK lets its possessors pierce the fog of war and thus master the unfolding progression of circumstance, decisions, and actions in the battlespace; it puts commanders in real-time command. C4I is converted from mere coordination to the orchestration of combat power focused on decisive points. Those who respond rapidly can acquire the advantages of initiators but avoid the vulnerabilities to which initiators expose themselves. Thus is altered the historic balance between offense and defense.

DBK (plus advanced communications) can alleviate classic span- of-control constraints and allow command structures to be delayered to improve rather than impede flows of critical information. Many intervening filters hitherto needed to process information and control subordinates could be replaced by automated decision- support systems that respond directly to the battle commanders. Local information (e.g., detailed health and status updates) need no longer flow up nor or detailed orders flow down.

DBK (plus precision strike) would let U.S. forces threaten enemy buildups prefatory to invasion. Excellent real-time surveillance capabilities lets us locate, track, and target enemy mobile forces and their critical logistics and C4I infrastructures. We could place their forces at risk rather than going after static (but easy-to-find) centers of gravity and chancing collateral damage.

Our response to Iraq's October 1994 feint illustrates the current practice of interposing U.S. forces in response to hostile acts. Unfortunately, as our overseas bases close and forward deployments draw down, our forces have to move farther to contingencies. Intervention costs more and takes longer and is thus less viable against repetitive or continuous threats. If we could get the same result by coupling smaller on-scene forces (so that opponents would still have to mass for attack) with devastating counter-concentration attacks staged from over the horizon, DBK would prove a powerful deterrent.

Although DBK will be implemented according to the commander's vision, it assumes a common set of capabilities and requires a core set of supporting systems (among them, wide-area sensors and fast processors). Unfortunately, DBK cannot be appreciated within the present framework of stovepipe operations and piece-part analyses. They require a shift in focus from individual elements of combat power to their integration.

Defining DBK

The synoptic vision of DBK lets commanders:

- Forge a common purpose for dispersed combat forces
- Assess the battlespace accurately by understanding its evolving dynamics and correlated patterns
- Develop their own adaptive vision of combat operations
- Project the consequences of their decisions across the space and time of combat
- Recognize periods and places of potential vulnerability as they evolve
- Create, not just find or identify, windows of opportunity that can be exploited.

By so doing, commanders can transcend the classic problems of coping with uncertainty: where to direct personal focus, how to assess prefiltered information (e.g., the directed telescope), how to avoid dependence on preplanned responses to potential contingencies, and foremost, and how to oversee and orchestrate the entire operational area despite its scale and scope. Like a counter-punching boxer, DBK lets commanders exploit the enemy's own initiatives.

One of key functions of command is to allocate resources, including time, to accommodate the progress of the operation and not give the enemy a breathing space through material shortfalls or human exhaustion. DBK allows commanders to develop an adaptive intent to unify the activities in the battlespace and let them execute a simultaneous high-tempo integrated operations against the enemy's military power and will. Quantity and tempo, in and of itself, can overload the enemy's command system and generate exploitable opportunities while minimizing casualties attendant from extended, attrition combat. DBK allows the application of force from multiple media at the right place and time. It supports both cycle-time and phase-control dominance so that agile and adaptive units can engage and defeat larger forces in rapid succession.

By conducting a seamless, continuous campaign, these tactical victories could be propagated not only throughout the extent of the opponent's tactical echelons, but they would also have a cumulative impact resulting in decisive victories. DBK is the key to achieving nonlinear combat results; even tactical units can initiate operationally decisive results, as they did at the Battle of Midway.

Operational-Level DBK: The Adaptive Campaign

If DBK is to be truly dominant, it must entail a real- time synoptic vision defined by the relationship among the strategic, operational, and tactical levels of war. Synoptic will be defined not so much by sensors but by the commander's ability to integrate widearea information and comprehend it (which depends on how good the decisions aids are) and by the planning horizon (affected by unit mobility and the reach of the weapons).

The act of acquiring DBK cannot wait for combat; assets such as submarines, mobile missiles, and mine-laying equipment are hard to find and track after units deploy. Battlespace preparation requires data (e.g., near-continuous tracking of enemy assets) to start flowing in peacetime and grow denser as crisis builds.

Such data includes enemy orders of battle, table of organization and equipment databases, and target locations. Because DBK is pointless if decoupled from the will and means to act, this suggests a more assertive posture for the United States to adopt during peace and crises to retain initiative and control, rather than react to the transition to crisis and conflict.

DBK requires that what each level sees is consistent (and proportionate to its need for situational awareness), not necessarily the same.

Scalability matters, as does avoiding information overload, a potential hazard of DBK systems. DBK must provide location and movement data on one's own forces and enemy forces, and on the complex relationships and interactions between the two.

It must allow the relative phase between the sides to be controlled through time-distance relationships.

Tactical DBK: Coherent Combat Operations

DBK can be particularly useful for tomorrow's war. Combat can be expected to be dispersed, noncontiguous, discontinuous, and nonsequential, characterized by meeting engagements (rather than planned assaults and defenses are more likely) and heir to the rapid propagation of success and failure. Hitherto, the purpose of linear deployments was to maintain a continuous front to minimize exposure and vulnerability from the flanks and salients. Nonlinear tactics try to do the same by reducing exposure times and using coordinating units to provide cover. Coherent operations provide leverage to tactical initiatives as they are exploited by a fully integrated, adaptive force capable of seizing them in real-time. A nonlinear battlespace requires different skills of both senior and subordinate commanders.

Cycle-Time Dominance: DBK improves the understanding of critical combat dynamics as they occur so that they may be translated into timing and spatial cues for tactical actions.

Many analysts have returned to the Observation-Orientation-Decision-Action (OODA) Loop (see Col John R. Boyd, USAF [Ret.], A Discourse on Winning and Losing, August 1987) to understand the potential impacts of the Information Revolution on combat operations. Unfortunately they have focussed on the decision side rather than the action side. Good communications are analogous to Boyd's key technical requirement for 3,000 psi hydraulics, to link a pilot's rapid decisions to his aircraft's performance. As with air combat, small advantages in each maneuver action ultimately result in a decisive firing solution. This is particularly attractive for repetitive action/response cycles in combat. Time becomes the critical determinant of combat advantage.

Phase Dominance: But what shorter cycle times really achieve is to let U.S. forces to select the right time to engage the enemy so as to maximize differences in relative combat capabilities. Phase-Dominance builds small advantages into decisive victories. DBK informs commanders of the natural operating cycles and rhythms of enemy forces (as well as their own) and ensures that actions can be executed exactly when needed.

Maintaining the coherence (a combination of mental and physical concentration) of combat units is never easy -- especially when they are forced to alter their state in combat (one reason why the reorientation conducted by the 20th Maine at Little Roundtop is considered a classic). Armies change their tempos and shift back and forth between road march and assault formation; between defense against air to defense against ground; or from either to offense; from one objective to another, especially in meeting engagements. Each change not only perturbs unit coherence but risks a loss in the essential phasing between the integrated joint forces that produces overall operational coherence. It requires a different mental attitude and task sets -- a resetting of the cycle. The coherence of an organization takes time to reestablish (this might be called a phase-change time-constant). In the interim, the unit cannot act in focus and is more vulnerable.

Surprise works because it comes from unexpected directions, but a larger reason is that it hits at unexpected phases in the operational cycle; it forces an unexpected and disruptive phase-change with the attendant loss of coherence while re-orientation is taking place. Thus, U.S. dive bombers caught the Japanese carriers by surprise at Midway during their extremely vulnerable refueling and rearming phase of cyclic operations.

Real-Time Learning

In the Cold War, the U.S. developed a detailed understanding of Soviet equipment, order of battle, doctrine, concepts of operations, and tactics. We observed their large-scale training, tests and experiments, and read their military texts. Thus, we could train and exercise against them (or their prot,g,s) with great realism. We also knew the battlefield. Our soldiers in Germany used to boast that they knew every rock and tree between the Inner-German Border and their positions. Similarly, submariners, as much as anyone, recognize the need for details of the operating area (such as thermal layer depths, bottom features, and even seasonally changing biota) that operational, onscene experience alone provides. With some exceptions (e.g., North Korea), we will lack these advantages against tomorrow's enemies. With today's threats so diverse, such familiarity must be acquired much faster. Real-time learning will have to be substituted for intelligence -- a new requirement that must be factored into DBK at all echelons. It also helps to know how others may respond to your moves; this helps define the size of the battlespace and focus the resources behind DBK. This creates a need to educate everyone simultaneously about enemy tactics, concepts, equipments, and system capabilities -- with profound implications for professional military education and training.

Jointness

The classic approach to jointness used discrete units from the services but ones separated in time and space through Fire Support Control lines. This reduced mutual interference and allowed each force to operate tactically by itself. This model eased problems stemming from limited real-time situational awareness and communications that complicated coordinating diverse forces. The problem was that joint capabilities were simply additive. Admiral Owens, for instance, posited two paths for jointness. The specialized path uses the best qualified force component for a given mission; the more effective path, synergism, was created by "combining forces in such a way that higher outputs (combat effectiveness) result than could be achieved by simply adding the outputs of different forces." His analysis suggested the two were fundamentally different paths rather than one dimension with different degrees of synergy and effectiveness.

Because the U.S. defense drawdown makes overwhelming force much harder to field, joint operations are required for effectiveness and efficiency. Intuitive acceptance of integrated joint forces and dependence on non-organic, non-controlled resources and capabilities are also needed. Integrating U.S. forces from different media forces opponents to counter multidimensional, multifunctional operations, but they also create opportunities for exploitation by different elements of the force at the same time they cloak vulnerabilities and disadvantages of operations conducted in single medium.

Synergy comes from focusing on a common tactical objective, employing common doctrine, synchronizing the tactical echelons, and providing mutual support. Its prerequisite is that it requires integration at lower tactical echelons and thus demands greater situational awareness, broader understanding of operational progress, and greater adaptability in procedures.

Coherent operations conduct combat as a single process with an integrated unit operating in-phase to amplify its power, exploit opportunities in real time, and get inside the opponent's cycle times. Integration cannot work without defeating the friction inherent in operations conducted by diverse forces. Phase-related differences in operating cycles among joint forces tend to explain the difficulties in managing joint operations. Subtle factors affecting when phases change and how long it takes help in understanding how to execute operations coherently. The ability to see, understand, adjust, and communicate better and faster is the foundation of integration. DBK provides these essential tools; it enables force integration and reinforcement without pausing for synchronization or mutual interference. This gives joint forces all the advantages of a single organism (e.g., cycle-time advantage) while retaining their underlying diverse capabilities (see Jeffrey R. Cooper, The Coherent Battlefield, SRS White Paper, Arlington VA, June 1993).

For that reason, complex systems operating at the edge of their performance envelope require their feedback loops to function well, which means fast, tight, and predictably. Delays can delink adaptive corrective actions and knowledge of their effects, and it is also difficult to maintain coherent processes in excessively slack systems. Both are heir to unpredictable overshoot and undershoot because of imprecise control or prediction. DBK offers unique opportunities to maintain the real-time, close-coupling required for feedback loops to assist in leading a flexible, dynamic campaign.

The key to conducting complex joint operations coherently is timely communication of the commander's intent so that the entire hierarchy shares a consistent vision and objective. DBK will provide tools to reinforce the traditional role of command exercise by promoting a shared timely image of the battle (a combination of intelligence and status indicators) even as it adapts to an evolving battlespace.

C4I Systems and Architecture Impacts

Changes in the locus and focus of decisionmaking will change the nature of the transmitted information: intelligence support, issues, data-types, and channels.

Decisive Combat: The most fundamental changes in warfare may be the return of Clausewitzian decisive victories in place of attrition warfare. The latter paradigm, exemplified by World Wars I and II, were waged by large, relatively equal, industrialized nation-states, and won largely by material and mass, not by coups de main or great battlefield victories.

DBK lets commanders exploit seams in the enemy's forces, gaps in his abilities, and openings provided by his sequential operations. Forces and fires can be rapidly reassigned between holding, breakthrough, and exploitation operations. Opponents can be kept from cohering their forces so that the United States avoids the need to take on enemy forces en bloc (as General Sullivan noted of Operation Just Cause). Mobile, lethal, and rapid operations conducted in parallel could let U.S. forces defeat units in detail at a time of our own choosing across the battlespace. The other side can act only in a pre-planned but uncoordinated manner in the face of our initiatives. The result may thus resemble the classic coup de main, except not executed as a single main-force engagement but a parallel set of tactical operations.

Throughout the Cold War, the United States worried about fighting outnumbered. Its strategy against the Warsaw Pact coupled quantitative advantages and sufficient size to dissipate the momentum of the Pact forces through tactical nuclear weapons or later Active Defense. Only with AirLand Battle (1983) did the we begin to think of decisive strokes with conventional forces.

In the brief period between the Wall's fall and the Drawdown, there remained enough overwhelming Force to wage AirLand Battle against regional opponents such as Iraq. Efficiency in deployment and sustainment of massive force rather than effectiveness in force application was the critical problem. With the Drawdown the latter is essential. DBK permits limited forces to be an effective instrument of war by allowing the conduct of decisive combat.

Altering the Command and Control Paradigm: Many suggest that high-tempo complex simultaneous operations does not let the commander control forces effectively. Command has to be automated through preplanned courses of action and rules of engagement. Yet true integration demands the reinforcement of commanders in exercising real-time command during combat. This, in turn requires reexamining the current paradigm that treats command and control as inseparable. Exploiting DBK demands decentralization of command authority and a concomitant relaxation of control at the higher levels. Existing organizational structures (themselves reactions to earlier C3I shortages) reinforce the tight linkage between command and control, as well as classic distinctions between strategic, operational, and tactical operations. The need to support seamless, continuous, parallel operations also requires modifying the C4I architectures that support the command structure.

Counterpart adaptations in commercial firms have taken so long because technologies were used to increase efficiency in performing the old tasks, rather than reengineering the entire process. Exploiting the DBK is likely to require similarly fundamental changes in military operational concepts and organization structures.

Vulnerabilities

If DBK centralizes sensor fusion and decisionmaking it can introduce new vulnerabilities. If it is built on decentralized decisionmaking and exploiting, vulnerabilities may be reduced; there will be fewer nodes that can affect the entire operation if corrupted.

DBK offers the ability to focus on key battlespace activities. But loss of critical focus may be induced by phase-change information overload, or self-induced distractions. In tomorrow's high-tempo battlespace, the opponent's C2W activities need only to distract or delay momentarily for critical focus to be lost. IW may cause loss of lock (a reason for revisiting the extensive Soviet literature on Radio-Electronic Combat). Vulnerability assessment, while warranted, must be considered as part of integral operational design, not merely overlaid as a stand-alone, counter- counter-measure plan.

Comparative Advantage

Because DBK is largely built from commercial systems, it is available to others. Whether or not the technology itself gives the United States an advantage will depend on who uses it well. Unfortunately, our intelligence community has had more success tracking system capabilities than in predicting how well others could use them -- which, for DBK, depends on complex questions of organizational cultures and adaptability difficult for outsiders to predict.

Nevertheless, because the information revolution is real, most elements of DBK are inevitable. Whether we can harvest this revolution and strengthen our national security is a matter of choice; so is the selection of focus and means of implementation, which, in turn, depends less on enhancing the individual piece-parts than on integrating all elements into a synergistic, effective organization. These issues demand the most serious consideration.

DBK WITH AUTONOMOUS WEAPONS

DBK alone is meaningless. Military relevance comes from the ability to hit what you can see. To do this it is necessary to analyze the synergy of DBK and a new class of autonomous weapons in a canonical scenario -- what might have occurred if Saddam Hussein's lunge in October 1994 had not stopped short of the Kuwait border.

Although DBK can deter, the assumption in this case is that it did not; the issue is whether DBK mated to autonomous weapons can let the United States win in a timely manner, without major deployment or without having to buy new platforms. Autonomous weapons -- sensor-fuzed weapons (SFW), brilliant anti-tank submunition (BAT) and wide-area munitions (WAM)

-- are those needing far less human guidance than earlier weapons and promising a high Pk if placed within range.

Prior Studies

Most prior studies suggest that armored thrusts can be stopped from the air alone using autonomous weapons. Examples include RAND's "The New Calculus" and "The Use of Long-Range Bombers to Counter Armored Invasions" and similar studies by Jasper Welch, Major General, USAF (Ret). A more recent study by OSD (S&R) examines the kill rate from onhand U.S. forces (plus those that can arrive over the next few weeks) in a scenario similar to Vigilant Warrior; they concluded that despite high kill ratios, most of the vehicles would reach Kuwait. A McDonnell-Douglas study showed similar results but a lower kill rate. Recent studies by JCS and the Navy suggest that more than one kill per sortie can be obtained even from today's unguided cluster munitions (v. the .01 rate in the Gulf but that mixes all sorts of sorties together).

Recent work by Dr. Raymond Macedonia suggests that sensor-fuzed weapons (SFW) can generate powerful results if wide area mines are placed in attack corridors; attackers are forced to slow down for mine-clearing (and risk being hit from the air) or take large casualties from the mines themselves. Advanced WAMs could be used to help target more mines or guide SFWs. Commanders with DBK could deploy thin lines of WAMs and use the feedback to call in more SFW or ATACM-based WAMs -- even under bad visual conditions that might frustrate DBK.

Study Parameters

The results of the study are predicated on a careful definition of DBK and a reasonable characterization of autonomous weapons.

DBK is the upper limit of what intelligence systems 10 years hence can be expected to do. It entails the precise location of enemy units and their general status, but not the status and location of each platform. The location of mobile units can be known intermittently but they do move over time. Not all this data will be known instantly by all units, nor is it equally available from difficult environments or in the face of countermeasures. There would remain a gap between DBK and actual targeting that may require additional local information, man-in-the-loop, or very intelligent weapons with terminal guidance capability.

The benefits of DBK are that it:

- Removes uncertainty as to whether an attack is underway
- Gives the location, composition, and status of the attacking units
- Ensures sufficient knowledge on friendly units.

During the Gulf War, the United States came close to achieving DBK at the outset of the air war. This knowledge, however, took a long time to acquire and degraded as soon as air actions raised uncertainties about the results. While DBK was not achieved for the ground war, JSTARS helped provide a real-time ground picture for the first time. DBK does not mean that all U.S. units would be in continuous possession of sufficient targeting information; that would require perfect C3, great mobility, and survivability. Direct-fire weapons, whether ground or air based, require more than DBK; they also need delicate and time-consuming reconnaissance, surveillance, targeting and maneuver actions, plus fast expenditure rates and therefore heavy logistics to produce sufficient kills. First-generation PGMs (e.g., laser-guided bombs) reduced the logistics requirements of combat but still required precise target information; they also put the designator and the platform at risk. Autonomous weapons, though, can be targeted with less precise information and in some cases (e.g., stand-off delivery) do not even put the launch platform at risk. DBK is needed to generate taskings, but the timing of mission scheduling is no longer so critical because moving targets can be localized again.

Autonomous Weapons

Autonomous weapons can select their own aimpoints and are available in quantity. Even though redundant kills reduce efficiency, overall kill rates can be high.

- BAT is a 20-kg, self-guided (acoustic and IR) antitank round with a large acquisition area that permits a high Pk even when launched from medium altitude or from stand-off (e.g., MLRS, ATACMS, Tomahawk, or JSOW). Now in early testing, it is expected to cost less than $100,000 per but is unlikely to appear in large numbers before 2000 absent a more relaxed procurement cycle.

SFW is a smaller, self-guided IR hit-to-kill round with a smaller acquisition range designed for counter-battery applications, MLRS and ATACMS delivery, or low- and medium- altitude air drop. It is low-rate acquisition with a $20,000 price tag.

- WAM is a 16-kg mine capable of launch an SFW to about 100 meters. It can be remotely controlled; an improved version may be networked as a sensor field. It is designed for ground, artillery, or air delivery (an anti-helicopter variant is being developed). It is projected to emerge from engineering development in 1996 and cost $25,000 per.

Order of Battle

Using the Iraqi feint as a base, the following target set is assumed:

- 4,000 armored vehicles
- 200 high altitude SAM sites
- 100 C3 sites
- 20 long-range radar sites
- 20 airfields
- 200 SCUD support sites
- 80 infrastructure nodes

U.S. forces consist of:

- 30 aircraft (F-15 and F-16) on hand because of the continued Southern Watch operations.
- An aircraft carrier with 50 attack aircraft is nearby.
- 100 long-range bombers from CONUS and Diego Garcia armed with sensor-fuzed munitions dispersed from wind-adjusted tactical munitions dispensers (WATMDs).
- 18 Apache helicopters (with Hellfire) out of Kuwait.

- 24 A-10s (with Maverick, rockets, and 30mm) out of Kuwait.
- Two reinforced brigades (to implant WAM) supported by MLRS and ATACMS (with SFW) as well as tube artillery with laser-guided projectiles (includes Allied ground forces).
- Another 100 aircraft within 5 days.

Other assumptions include:

- Air superiority is not an issue except near Iraqi air defense units; it is assumed that air attacks are launched from medium altitude to keep attrition low.
- There is enough strategic warning to permit loading up on weapons (which are otherwise too sensitive to keep in the Middle East on a permanent basis).
- No countermeasures were factored in even though anything that is a great advantage for one side will become a potential target for the other. In practice, the instruments of DBK will be attacked, dispersion will be used to frustrate autonomous weapons, and information warfare will be used to introduce delay into the sensor-to-shooter cycle.

The various weapons, operational load-out, and effective mobility kills per sortie (assuming a Pk of 50 percent). Sortie rates over the first 10 days are three a day for helicopters, two a day for fixed- wing aircraft in theater, once every 2 days for bombers out of Diego Garcia, once every 4 days for CONUS-based bombers. Launch rates for ATACMS and MLRS are 200 a day total. The figure in parenthesis is nominal kills per sortie, the difference reflecting wastage due to multiple submunitions targeted on an aimpoint. See the appendix for a more detailed discussion of the difference.

The basic results, shown in the right-most column, indicate that a modestly size air attack force, if not otherwise diverted, could kill half the targets (2618) in the first day of combat. These rates (four kills per sortie, 2,600 per day) far exceed rates from Desert Shield thanks to DBK, autonomous weapons, and the fact that armor, when it moves, is out in the open. No kills were calculated for WAM but they play a large role in slowing down the attack so that sufficient attrition can be effected before Kuwait (and thus cover) is reached.

IMPLICATIONS AND LIMITATIONS

Implications fall into five areas: DBK itself, munitions, C3/ training, geo-location, and survivability.

DBK: Even if major military formations can be located, they cannot necessarily be targeted. Environmental constraints, sensor revisit time, the complexity of processing and fusion, and simple task overloading can result in significant delays before C3 systems get their information. Many sorties will be working with out-of-date information on mobile units.

Even autonomous weapons require a degree of target localization that delays deny them. The status of targets is also hard to assess. Battle damage assessment was difficult in the Gulf War. The ability to fuze videotapes from guns, and laser-guided bombs should increase our ability to know what these weapons do, but autonomous weapons present new difficulties (no one is necessarily looking). If battle damage assessment is bad, autonomous weapons will not work as well. WAMs used to see which vehicles are moving may help BDA.

Autonomous Weapons: Although good munitions made the scenario work, the U.S. military traditionally holds off on buying high-end munitions preferring to wait until they get better or cheaper. This strategy may work for long wars but not short ones. This scenario needs between 10 and 20 thousand autonomous weapons to work. Delivery systems will cost more if they have to be stand- off (e.g., Tomahawk JSOW), but even so, they remain cheaper than new launch platforms.

C3 and Training: Sensor-to-shooter delays degrade DBK (a motivation for the other side's IW efforts). DBK is also degraded if tactical development and training do not keep up with new systems. Joint training and exercises are implied because of the global nature of DBK and the mix of forces that must be on scene to carry out this scenario. Geo-Location: The conversion of DBK to targeting requires platforms be aware of their own location, speed, and acceleration in three dimensions. Thus the vulnerability of GPS matters.

Survivability: Attack forces, DBK equipments, and their supporting C3 infrastructure all must survive enemy attack to make the scenario work. The small U.S. forces could be suppressed, attacked, or diverted (e.g., to SCUD hunts) by unexpected enemy capabilities. Often a stand-down is necessary to fix problems.

Although the number of weapons on an aircraft is subject to physical limits (weight, attach points, etc.), maximum payloads are rarely achieved because of the tradeoff of weapons for fuel, inventory limits, and the possibility of having to drop a load for tactical reasons.

The number of BAT submunitions, for example, is limited by the desire for flexibility depending, the model of aircraft, internal versus external carriage, and other factors.

A more careful analysis would consider the geometry of attack and the target set. Delivery means also matter -- e.g., whether a standoff launch can be achieved that surprises the enemy and therefore precludes the dispersion of targets. But tactics are hard to anticipate for any scenario.

The translation between nominal and effective kills per sortie must take many factors into account:

- The delivery of sensor-fuzed weapons from tactical munitions dispensers from medium altitude will probably waste most sub- munitions; they are unlikely to make contact unless targets are parked close together.
- BATs have a greater acquisition rate than SFWs, and their search behaviors can be adjusted; thus their kill rate is higher
- A night-flying B-2 can drop the same tactical munition dispenser of SFWs with many kills because its radar target mapping is accurate; with short warning time, targets are not likely to be dispersed.
- Stand off-weapons such as the SLAM (a Harpoon variant) and JSOW will provide a low wastage rate because they carry small numbers of sub-munitions and are individually

targeted from so far off that they will result in similar surprise.

- TMDs and Tomahawks carry large numbers of submunitions are inherently subject to wastage rates as high as 90 percent if the submunition has a small acquisition area (e.g., SFW). With several minutes of free fall time, they are affected by wind and are therefore inaccurate. Wind-corrected TMD can be accurate from higher up if the target location is well known at launch time. Their guidance works off GPS and would best served fixed targets and those identified by radar target mapping.
- JDAM is a GPS-guided weapon comparable in punch to the Mk-82 series of bombs. When dropped from high altitudes, it can achieve surprise, but moving targets may depart from their original location in the meantime (unless the bomb is updated in flight). Thus JDAMs are likely to be used against fixed targets (except from B-2s which can fly low at night). Both JDAM and WCTMDs can carpet bomb an area.
- MLRS and ATACMS can operate with low wastage of SFW against up-to-date locations of concentrated but surprised forces or against fixed targets. But under current conditions they would have a high wastage against moving armored columns.

JUST-IN-TIME WARFARE

Previous chapters have looked at DBK with the assumption that the U.S. Armed Forces had enough platforms and weapons available to prosecute targets, and enough time to get them all into theater. Two previous papers indicate that the equipment necessary to stop an armored column is well within expected future force levels. Another suggested that this fact would persuade enemies to eschew conventional massed attacks entirely and revert to sub rosa incursions using military assets masked as civilian ones.

This chapter presents a new philosophy of warfare, "Just-in-Time Warfare" that DBK makes possible. It examines the role of potential reconnaissance-strike-defense complexes (RSDCs). In future information wars, virtual reconnaissance, strike, and defense would be coordination in battles fought as "meeting engagements" where both sides are on the offense. With requirements to shift between offense and defense in minutes or seconds, only multipurpose systems practicing "just-in-time" warfare will survive, with military systems providing communications, multisource intelligence, early warnings of tactical and ballistic missiles, and navigation will be vital. Planners will have to coordinate reconnaissance, strike, and defense missions together, over information-and-orders data networks, linked primarily through outer space. The requirement to switch roles quickly makes time precious and coordination an even finer art. Warriors will have to synchronize schedules and orders, as well as deliver military operations to meet rapidly emerging demands. Turning inside the enemy's decision loop will determine success or failure.

To develop this capability, we must develop new procedures, equipment, and information systems, plus provide better training. Only when the U.S. military becomes learning organization -- and all that this concept implies -- would it be able to enjoy an advantage achieved by establishing a clear and favorable differentiation from the competition.

As the tempo of battle increases and militaries can engage from greater and greater stand-off distances, platforms must serve many purposes, including offense and defense. With increased battlefield awareness on both sides, future confrontations will tend to be meeting engagements, where both sides are on the offensive. It may be necessary to shift between offense and defense in minutes or seconds -- only multipurpose systems practicing just-in-time warfare will prevail.

In the business world, just-in-time means less work-in-progress (WIP), less overhead, less inventory at each stage of production, and less slack time in the system. In military terms, just-in-time uses DBK and information technology to produce real- time scheduling to cut the need for today's enormous inventories. More frequent deliveries of smaller amounts of product (i.e., destruction) allow for more flexible scheduling, quicker response, and shortened decision cycles. If the batch size of weapons and other logistics shipments into a theater can be reduced, so will the vulnerability of logistical connections.

Just-in-time suggests that forces need no longer be massed prior to attack. When mass is needed for offensive or defensive purposes, it need take place only at point of impact. Large formations of ships, planes, or armor can give way to staggered scheduling and positioning that present no discernible pattern to an adversary. Not being able to sense where the attack is coming from -- because it could come from everywhere at any time -- takes the other side's initiative away. Putting the adversary in a defensive, reactive mode simplifies our problem and complicates his. It implies synchronizing, planning, scheduling, ordering and delivering of military operations as needed to meet currently emerging demands.

Massing at the point of impact and just-in-time techniques can be applied to command, control, communications, information warfare and logistics.

Command

Just-in-time warfare requires sophisticated yet flexible command, control and information systems. It is possible to link these systems in an RSDC responsible for managing just-in-time warfare across the entire theater of operations. Such an RSDC would be a virtual vice real organization. It would draw its strengths and inputs from, and send its outputs to, other organizations via high-speed, robust data networks. RSDCs would link organizations to exploit evanescent opportunities on the information terrain. Commands would contribute whatever skills, access, and access they do best, creating a best-of-everything organization, with world-class elements unavailable to any single one. Standardized memorandums of agreement and understanding (MOA/MOU) could facilitate these lash-ups.

Operational Control/Operational Command (OPCON/OPCOM) arrangements would be less permanent, less formal, and more opportunistic. Organizations would band together to meet specific opportunities and may disband or relocate when the need evaporates or circumstances change. Virtual organizations would cause the services to rely far more on each other and require far more trust than before. They would share a greater sense of co-destiny (or if done wrong, co-dependence). Thus would traditional boundaries of the services be altered. Dense and frequent cooperation among like elements, suppliers, and customers will make it harder to determine where one organization ends and another begins.

An RSDC, to be optimized, must be viewed as a value-adding partnership (VAP) and transcend today's interservice rivalries. The services have gone about as far as they can go with regards to vertical integration -- information flows very quickly and effectively from top to bottom and back. But cross-service flow is another matter. The technologies now exist that permit communications among the services at all levels instead of just at command centers.

If the services and agencies that provide the various technologies and expertise at each point in the engagement cycle are perceived as partners rather than competitors, then each step in the process can be optimized to match with those before and after it. The services and agencies must come to the realization that they have a major stake in each others' success. Given the present and near future states of possible computer-information-communication system integration, it is possible to incorporate this value-added chain into a virtual information data bus.

Digitized information (video, visual, data, audio) will be inserted by the sensor and intelligence systems, ride the RSDC data bus, and be modified by target sequencing algorithms. Modifiers can be injected across the bus as needed (e.g., alter all report data meeting the following criteria). Users (weapons/platforms) would draw only what affected them -- a determination that could be made immeasurably more efficient by filters, artificial intelligence, and user agents. Information could be stored in a format that could go from initial report through the identification, decision, assessment, assignment and engagement/reengagement process with information itself modified only at the point of extraction.

Ultimately, the energizing of appropriate circuits, following paths of least resistance, most reliability or redundancy, or fastest route to engagement(s) could be done, to a large extent, automatically. Weapons-to-target pairings could be computer selected and ordered under a command-by-negation (CBN) doctrine where each engagement would proceed to its successful conclusion (or reengagement), unless humans intervene, or because the system recognizes that the engagement violates commander's rules of engagement, coordination, or priorities.

Control

Automating C2 functions helps free commanders to deal with the choices that systems cannot handle. Fuzing multiple-source intelligence and battle damage assessment generates information beyond the reach of any single sensor. The ability to do this in parallel would free forces from the current organic sensor-organic weapon lock (sensor and weapon hard-wired to each other on the same platform); a variety of sensors could pair with a variety of weapons on the fly.

Sensors and shooters no longer be in the same place. National, or remote, sensors may have the best picture from which to conduct an engagement. A local sensor may be paired with a theater or national weapon. An Army Ranger could, in practice, be armed with a Tomahawk cruise missile or a Stealth-delivered bomb -- the same way that the main battery of an Aegis cruiser is already not its on-board missiles but a Navy F-14, a Marine F/A-18 or an Air Force F-16.

Parallel decisions (rather than one-at-a-time, one-after- another decisions) permit much faster optempos. By inputing mission priorities, rules of coordination and engagement, and an acceptable-degree-of-difficulty, the commander can set a required confidence level that must be achieved before an engagement is executed. In a touchy face-off with a nuclear-armed peer competitor, a commander might require near certainty. Against a Third-World niche competitor where quick decisive action is required, the commander may be more willing to act on a more- likely-than-not standard, with a low degree-of-difficulty threshold.

Rules of Coordination and Engagement (ROCE) and Mission Priorities

Today, commanders provide guidance through verbal or written, rules of coordination and engagement (ROCE). These rules require a fair amount of interpretation before they can be converted into formats recognized by today's weapons and C2 systems.

Computerized ROCE's would help commanders set mission priorities between, say, strike, counter-strike, close-air-support, and defense; these weights could be fed automatically into the targeting and weapon assignment process. By using command-by-negation, automated ROCE's and mission priorities and pre-determined confidence and urgency requirements, computer-generated pairings will give the commander and their staff more time and freedom to concentrate on the problems hitherto perceived as too hard to handle, or otherwise unanswered.

Communications

Just-in-time warfare requires flattened, virtual organizations. Some of its components may actually remain and operate in the continental United Sates (CONUS), far away from any front. Using communication triggered by orders and information will ensure connectivity without requiring large bandwidth. Communications need not be passed over continually active circuits. Ships, aircraft, ground units and command centers are bogged down, today, maintaining multiple circuits that carry very little information -- most of which is static, and the rest largely unimportant -- and certainly not in an optimized format.

Other technologies can cut down on communications loading. Pre-loaded battlefield maps (on CD-ROM or silicon) would require communications only when data changes. This vastly simplifies the problem of picking out the target (thus converting a map into a super moving-target-indicator). Software agents could be used to seek out intelligence on targets -- vastly simplifying today's overwhelming correlation problems and freeing much of it from the slowness of human hands.

User Interfaces

Virtual reality's time has come. A virtual picture (supported by holographic displays and large color screens) of the battlespace may now be more accurate and usable than a real one. Presenting fused information and intelligence as 3-D images which couple weapons pairings and targets (and can be examined from all aspects) will make operations faster and more accurate. Commanders could avoid the mental gymnastics required convert read data (e.g., lat/long, bearing/range, course/speed) into a mental image. The more easily commanders can interpret the picture, the quicker they can make decisions. It is time targets looked like what they are - - not symbols that require interpretation.

Topographically replacing physical geography with infography (e.g., lines of communication) may alter the conduct of warfare. Information peaks and ridges may become the centers of gravity of future warfare. Information intersections become as important for targeting as nodes or command bunkers,both from an offensive and defensive viewpoint.

Targeting

Paradoxically, total awareness may open the door to greater reliance on dumb munitions. Before DBK, most targets were treated as fleeting. Engagements were conducted even though Pk was low and the degree of difficulty or toughness of the shot was high. With DBK, fleeting no longer means "passing quickly" but "moving quickly." DBK lets us engage threats at the right moment in terms of Pk and degree of difficulty; moving quickly matters less. Dumb ordnance may be deliverable with precision against these "new" "fleeting" targets, because they no longer disappear.

Real-time targeting, which is possible using just-in-time warfare, can be used with stand-off weapons and dumb ordnance launched from out-of-theater, and bombers and cruise missiles can be assigned en route to the theater. The success or failure of previous strikes, therefore, can be factored in real time.

While still possible, it may no longer be necessary to plan enormous raids to cover large areas to hit moving targets, because speed is no longer important when it cannot clear a target from the area. Real-time targeting allows the designation of a new type of target -- irrelevant or inconsequential, ones that are not necessary to attack unless and until they threaten something: platforms with short-range weapons (older generation tanks and aircraft), or systems that need long and easy-to-see preparation prior to use (e.g., liquid-propelled TBMs).

DBK, command-by-negation, new targeting philosophies, and existing automatic engagement systems make it possible to sharply reduce blue-on-blue engagements. Many systems, such as the Aegis Weapons System, were designed to be able to automatically engage massive Soviet raids -- last ditch features meant for engagements when no human could decide and act quickly enough. The parameters that had to be met by threats (before they were automatically engaged) were normally very exact.

This was done to make undesired engagement less likely and successful engagement more likely. With a new purpose, automatic systems can be used very effectively in an increasingly info-aware world.

They are microcosms of the RSDC, with "defense" emphasized. If we trusted these systems to make decisions when there was not time for human intervention, why can't we rely on them more when there is time? Many of these systems can and do take inputs from IFF systems. Using IFF systems and other concepts presented here might have prevented the USS VINCENNES (1988) and UH-60 shootdown (1994) incidents.

Battle Damage Assessment (BDA)

BDA is key to the operation of an RSDC and the management of ordnance. During the Gulf War, many targets had to be re-hit because BDA was not available; was indeterminable; or could not be correlated fast enough to a critical or time-sensitive target. Lack of adequate BDA was listed as a problem in the Gulf War Report to Congress for the Tomahawk, SLAM, ALCMs and others.

DBK makes it possible to use BDA more discriminately. Often, the suppression of a target is more important than its destruction. With DBK, a target's reaction to an attack would be more visible and may suffice for BDA. A retreating target is usually an inconsequential target. Reevaluating the requirements and criteria for BDA would have a direct impact on the amount of ammunition required in-theater and on the engagement process. Today, when BDA determines that a target was not killed, or when BDA is not available, a reengagement is ordered. This may no longer hold, when "fleeting" targets are redefined as "moving" targets and when only targets that satisfy the necessary criteria will be engaged.

Concept of Operations

In WWII, Korea, and Vietnam, U.S. forces took and retook real estate multiple times. This was driven by the need to "take the high ground" and to deal with the uncertainty as to when possession of the real estate was actually required. With DBK, we need only take particular physical real estate when it suits a specific mission for a specific period. The information terrain may become the real battlefield. Battles can become truly nonlinear. It will no longer be necessary to always take Hill 151 before taking 152. Holding Hill 152 might not be so necessary for our purposes, as holding hills was necessary in the past. Tough spots can be avoided, as DBK makes specific objectives (e.g., for stand-off weapons, special operations forces, or information warfare attack) singularly targetable, with the risks from nearby forces clearly quantifiable. Maps depicting troop and weapons employment might look more like measles than spaghetti. The days of the left-hook may be past.

Bibliography

Allison, Graham, *Nuclear Terrorism: The Ultimate Preventable Catastrophe*, New York: Times Books, 2004.

Amitabh Sikdar: *India and China : Strategic Energy Management and Security*, Manas, Delhi, 2009.

Atkinson, Rick: *An Army at Dawn: The War in North Africa 1942–1943*, Henry Holt, New York, 2002.

Bajpai, G.S. : *On Cyber Crime and Cyber Law*, Serials Publications, Delhi, 2011.

Basu, Prahlad K.: *Governance and Public Administration for Poverty Reduction*, Salvador, Brazil, 1997.

Bernauer, Thomas: *Genes, Trade, and Regulation: The Seeds of Conflict in Food Biotechnology*, Princeton, Princeton University. 2003.

Brenner, Susan W. : *Cybercrime : Criminal Threats from Cyberspace*, Pentagon Press, Delhi, 2012.

Buzan, Barry & Eric Herring: *The Arms Dynamic in World Politics*, London: Lynne Rienner Publishers, 1998.

Citino, Robert M: *Blitzkrieg to Desert Storm: The Evolution of Operational Art*, University Press of Kansas, Lawrence, 2004.

David Post : *The Rise of Law in Cyberspace*, 48 Stan, L. Rev. 1367, 1996.

Debray, Regis. *Revolution in the Revolution*. New York: Grove Press, Inc., 1993.

Dery, Mark. *Escape Velocity: Cyberculture at the End of the Century* . Grove Press, 1997.

Dudeja, V. D. : *Crimes in Cyber Space-Scams and Frauds: Issues and Remedies*, Commonwealth, Delhi, 2003.

Garrelick, Renee. M.I.T. Beginnings: The Legacy of Nuclear Metals. Concord, MA: Nuclear Metals, Inc., 1995.

Garstka, J J and F P Stein: *Network Centric Warfare: Developing and Leveraging Information Superiority*, CCRP Publications, Washington DC, 1999.

Gast, A. P. : *The impact of Restricting Information Access on Science and Technology* Retrieved October 1, 2008.

Ghose, S.K.: *Politics of Violence: Dawn of a Dangerous Era*, Springfield, Nataraj, 1992.

Giustozzi, Antonio: *Koran, Kalashnikov, and Laptop: The Neo-Taliban Insurgency in Afghanistan,* New York: Columbia University Press, 2008.

Habberton, William: *Anglo-Russian Relations Concerning Afghanistan 1837-1907*, Urbana, University of Illinois, 1937.

Ikram, S.M. : *Muslim Civilization in India*, Oxford, New York, 1981.

Keane J.: *Democracy and Civil Liberty in Afghanistan*, London, Verso, 1988.

Kilcullen, David: *Counterinsurgency,* Oxford University Press, 2010.

Kumar, Raj : *Weapons and Military Technology*, Sumit Enterprises, Delhi, 2009.

Nagl, John A.: *Learning to Eat Soup with a Knife: Counterinsurgency Lessons from Malaya to Vietnam,* University of Chicago Press, 2005.

Oudha, Abdul Qadir : *Criminal Law of Islam,* Kitab Bhavan, New Delhi, 1999.

Paget, J.: *Counter-insurgency Campaigning*, London: Faber & Faber, 1967.

Rhodes, Richard, *The Making of the Atomic Bomb*, New York: Simon and Schuster, 1988.

Saxena, V. K. : *Muslims and the Indian National Congress,* Discovery Publishing House, New Delhi, 1985.

Schroeer, Dietrich: *Science, Technology, and the Cyber Crimes,* Ontario: John Wiley & Sons, 1984.

Smith, W. C. : *Modern Islam in India : a Social Analysis,* Manohar Publishers, New Delhi, 1985.

Van Creveld, Martin: *The Art of War: War and Military Thought,* Smithsonian Books/Collins, Washington DC, 2005.

William Aspray: *Computer, A History of the Information Machine,* New York, Basic Books, 1996.

Zafeeruddin, M.M. : *System of Modesty and Chastity in Islam,* Idara Ishaat-e-Diniyat Pvt. Ltd, New Delhi, 1995.

Index

P

R

S

T

V

W

❑❑❑